CW01022493

MAX HORTON

AND THE WESTERN APPROACHES

THE COMMANDER-IN-CHIEF, WESTERN APPROACHES, 1943

Max Horton

AND THE WESTERN APPROACHES

A BIOGRAPHY OF

ADMIRAL SIR MAX KENNEDY HORTON

G.C.B., D.S.O.

BY

REAR-ADMIRAL W. S. CHALMERS

C.B.E., D.S.C.

HODDER AND STOUGHTON

FIRST PUBLISHED SEPTEMBER 1954
SECOND IMPRESSION OCTOBER 1954

Made and Printed in Great Britain for
Hodder & Stoughton, Limited, London,
by Hazell Watson & U...

Suppose me dead ! and then suppose
A club assembled at the Rose;
Where, from discourse of this and that,
I grow the subject of their chat.
And while they toss my name about,
With favour some and some without,
One quite indifferent to the cause
My character impartial draws.

SWIFT

CONTENTS

vii

CONTENTS

APPENDICES

ILLUSTRATIONS

ILLUSTRATIONS

PREFACE

ONE of the most jealously guarded traditions of the British Submarine Service is that a man should be judged by results. By this standard it is safe to say that Max Horton would be acclaimed the greatest authority on submarine warfare of his time.

As a young submarine commander in the First World War he earned an international reputation outshining that of any German 'ace.' In the Second World War, while he held the post of Flag Officer Submarines, his flotillas in home waters played a major part in frustrating Hitler's plans for the invasion of England, and in the Mediterranean under the direction of the Commander-in-Chief brought Rommel's army to a standstill by wrecking transports and disrupting his seaborne supplies.

As Commander-in-Chief Western Approaches, barely six months after he had hoisted his flag at Liverpool, Horton swept the U-boats from the North Atlantic. A year later, when the vast armada of transports and landing craft streamed across the Channel for the invasion of Europe, the measures he had taken for their protection in co-operation with the Royal Air Force were so effective that not a ship was lost by U-boat attack.

Horton preferred to do things rather than write about them, so it is unlikely that he would ever have written an autobiography. On the other hand he was anxious that the part he had played in the drama should be recorded, giving prominence to sea-air co-operation and also to the work of the Submarine Branch, and the officers, men and women of the Western Approaches Command. With this idea in mind, he kept carefully letters and official papers relating to events and policy. These, together with

PREFACE

other recollections and experiences, make a story of courage, tenacity and skill unsurpassed in the history of the Royal Navy.

This book is an attempt to fulfil the Admiral's wish, while at the same time tracing his uphill march to greatness and portraying impartially his complex character. The portrait is based on the first-hand knowledge of a few intimate friends, his brother, and above all naval officers who shared with him the vicissitudes of war in the depths and on the heights.

W. S. CHALMERS

ACKNOWLEDGEMENTS

I take this opportunity to thank the friends and shipmates of the late Admiral Sir Max Horton who have given me personal recollections of him, and Lady Boynton, at whose request this book was written, for providing me with letters and papers left by the Admiral.

I would also like to thank the Lords Commissioners of the Admiralty for allowing me to visit the Historical Section and Library for confirmation of facts.

I am grateful to the Admiral's brother, Mr. D'Arcy Horton, for information on early days and family antecedents, and to the undermentioned officers and friends for their criticisms, contributions and helpful interest: Captain Bernard Acworth, R.N., Vice-Admiral Lord Ashbourne, Commander F. Barley, R.N., Rear-Admiral R. M. Bellairs, Captain R. W. Blacklock, R.N., Air Chief-Marshal Sir F. W. Bowhill, Captain G. N. Brewer, R.N., Mr. A. V. Bridgland, Rear-Admiral C. G. Brodie, Rear-Admiral R. B. Darke, Admiral the Hon. Sir R. Plunkett-Ernle-Erle-Drax, Captain R. G. Duke, R.N., Rear-Admiral L. F. Durnford-Slater, The Very Reverend F. W. Dwelly, Captain M. J. Evans, R.N., Rear-Admiral G. B. H. Fawkes, Admiral James Fife, U.S.N., Engineer Rear-Admiral C. J. Gray, Captain P. W. Gretton, R.N., Captain(S) E. Haslehurst, R.N., Commander G. Herbert, R.N., Mr. C. V. Hill, Commander P. K. Kemp, R.N., Captain H. N. Lake, R.N., Commander J. H. Lhoyd-Owen, R.N., Admiral Sir L. Lyster, Captain I. A. P. Macintyre, R.N., Fr. C. C. Martindale S.J., Mr. E. F. M. Maxwell, Q.C., Fleet Admiral C. W. Nimitz, U.S.N., Vice-Admiral E. O. B. Osborne, Commander the Hon. H. Pakington, R.N., Commander R. A. B. Phillimore, R.N., Lieut.-Commander C. G. Pitcairn-Jones, R.N., Lieut.-Commander L. J. Pitcairn-Jones, R.N., Captain R. W. Ravenhill, R.N., Captain

ACKNOWLEDGEMENTS

G. H. Roberts, R.N., Vice-Admiral P. Ruck-Keene, Captain L. M. Shadwell, R.N., Rear-Admiral G. W. G. Simpson, Vice-Admiral F. A. Somerville, Commander R. St. John, R.N., Vice-Admiral Sir Gilbert Stephenson, Commander H. H. G. D. Stoker, R.N., The Hon. Mabel Strickland, Captain B. W. Taylor, R.N., Captain M. Villiers, R.N., Engineer Rear-Admiral Sir H. Wildish, Captain C. R. N. Winn, R.N.V.R.

I am also grateful to the following authors and publishers for allowing. me to quote from their works: *A Sailor's Odyssey*, Viscount Cunningham of Hyndhope, Hutchinson. *The Second World War*, Winston S. Churchill, Cassell and Houghton Mifflin Coy. of Boston, U.S.A. *His Majesty's Submarines* and *The Battle of the Atlantic*, The Controller of H.M. Stationery Office. *Submarine Jubilee*, Malcolm Baker-Smith, B.B.C. *Half Time*, Anthony Kimmins, Heinemann. *Walker's Groups in the Western Approaches*, D. E. G. Wemyss, Liverpool Echo. *The Far Distant Ships*, Joseph Schull, Canadian Dept. of National Defence.

CHAPTER ONE

1883-1916

THE BIGHT AND THE BALTIC

Forebears. Early days in submarines. Big ship time. Putting submarines on the map. 'The Riddle of the Sands.' 'Horton's Sea.' The poisoned cup. The 'Pirate.'

Lieutenant-Commander
MAX KENNEDY HORTON.

DINGLEWOOD,
COLWYN BAY,
NORTH WALES.
20th September 1914.

Dear Sir,

I should not presume to offer you my humble yet most sincere congratulations on your splendid achievement of torpedoing the *Hela* if it were not that I had in my school some eighteen or nineteen years ago a small boy of the name of Max Horton. His parents were temporarily resident in Anglesey at the time and he was a round-faced pleasant boy with a chin which promised well for his future. Under the circumstances I am sure you will excuse my writing to ask if that same small boy might possibly be the hero to whom I address this note?

Yours very truly,

STANLEY WOOD.

THE Headmaster was right. That same small boy was none other than Max Horton, the first British submarine commander to sink an enemy warship, and destined thirty years later to crush the U-boat assault on the Atlantic supply lines at the most critical moment in British history.

He was born in 1883 at Rhosneigr, a little Welsh village on the west coast of Anglesey, the second son of a family of four. His father was Robert Joseph Angel Horton, a member of the London Stock Exchange, and his mother was Esther Maud Horton the

I

daughter of William Goldsmid, also a stockbroker and cousin of Sir Julian Goldsmid, the banker. His grandfather, Captain Robert Horton of the 74th Regiment of Foot, Highland Light Infantry, married a wealthy heiress, Margaret Fanny Greenwood. His forebears, carefully recorded on the flyleaf of the family Bible, originated from the West Country. John Horton of Devizes is named in an old deed of 1577 and Max's great-great-grand-father was three times Mayor of Bath. The family home in later years was at Richmond and his grandfather Robert was often seen in Richmond Park driving a fine pair of horses. Max cherished his early recollections of the winding river and ancient palace enshrining so much of England's story. They lived in the manner of well-to-do people of the last century when world wars and social upheavals seemed to be beyond contemplation, though no doubt their fortunes varied according to the state of the markets. His father speculated freely, and money was a favourite topic of conversation at table, so, not unnaturally, Max inherited the gambling instinct. When he grew up, he seldom missed a chance to lay a wager and to play a high hand at bridge or poker.

Shortly before Max was born, his father was hard hit by a slump and possibly for reasons of economy, but more likely for fishing and shooting, bought the Maelog Lake Hotel together with the shooting rights. It was here and later at a farm nearby that Max and his elder brother D'Arcy spent most of their child-hood. They had few playmates, as the local Welsh people con-versed in their own tongue and looked upon them as foreigners. Max learnt his ABC and the three 'R's' from the village post-master. He adored his mother, and at the age of nine told her that he wanted to go into the Navy as he wished to fight for her. He attended several small schools as a boarder, and inspired by thoughts of distant seas and great adventure, worked hard. Excelling at mathematics, he passed without difficulty into H.M.S. *Britannia* (Dartmouth) where he became a cadet captain, played for the first XI at football, and won the middleweight boxing prize. It was characteristic of Max to stick to 'soccer' in a community that was wholly 'rugger'-minded. His skill at association football later proved to be a valuable link with the lower deck.

He was like a young colt, only half broken-in, wild, unruly, and liable to kick over the traces. Yet he was shrewd and stolid. The Jewish blood he had inherited from his mother, while kindling his imagination, made him cautious in his dealings with authority. He craved for independence, but quickly realised that the surest way to achieve it was to become the leader himself, even in a small community. He loved engines and gadgets, and the technical side of the Navy appealed to him strongly. So, while he was a senior midshipman, his thoughts turned with longing to the new Submarine Branch where even a Sub-Lieutenant might get a command and, in addition to the attraction of intricate machinery, there would be plenty of scope for initiative, adventure, and new ideas.

The first British submarine, a Holland[1] boat, was launched in November 1901. Later types fitted with periscopes proved their operational value in the manœuvres of 1904. In October of that year Max, to his delight, was appointed Sub-Lieutenant to H.M.S. *Thames*, the depot ship for training in submarines.

By a strange coincidence, the crest of a branch of the Horton family for many generations had been a dolphin impaled on a spear 'issuing from the waves of the sea.' When Max joined the Submarine Service he was given a signet ring engraved with this crest and the words 'In Deo Confido.' The significance of the design with its portent of things to come made a deep impression on him. Being highly superstitious, he felt that the ring would bring him luck, and vowed that it would never leave his finger. 'If it comes off,' he said to his brother, 'my luck will change.' It never came off.

Shortly after his promotion to Lieutenant, he was given command of A.1, a new submarine of 200 tons, salved after having been sunk in collision[2]. Thus, at the age of twenty-two, Max got his first command. Except for two years watchkeeping duty in the cruiser *Duke of Edinburgh* and shore appointments, he always commanded his own ship until he became a Flag Officer.

He was intensely interested in the technical side of submarines,

[1] Name of designer.

[2] A.1 was sunk on 18th March 1904, but was raised a month later, and used for experimental purposes. She was sunk again in August 1911.

3

studying closely internal combustion engines and putting forward several suggestions for improving the hull design, the fitting of periscopes, and escape helmets.

In October 1907 his commanding officer wrote this report on him:

> '*M. K. Horton.*
> '*Good* at his boat and *bad* socially.
> 'Made very good attacks in A.1. Always supposed to be very good at the engine.
> 'A boxer and footballer—desperate motor-cyclist.
> 'Troublesome in the mess—insubordinate to First Lieutenant. Bad language—but extremely intelligent.'

A contemporary says that Horton was a thorn in the side of the First Lieutenant, but canny in his defiance.

In those early days there was considerable opposition in Parliament and at the Admiralty to the development of submarines. In 1902 the Parliamentary Secretary of the Admiralty said in the House of Commons:

> 'I am glad that the Admiralty, under the advice of Lord Goschen, the First Lord, took the view that it was wise not to be found unprepared in regard to these inventions which I confess I desire shall never prosper.'

Rear-Admiral A. K. Wilson, V.C., at that time Controller of the Navy, is alleged to have stated:

> 'Underwater weapons, they call 'em. I call them underhand, unfair, and damned un-English. They'll never be any use in war and I'll tell you why: I'm going to get the First Lord to announce that we intend to treat all submarines as pirate vessels in wartime and that we'll hang all the crews.'[1]

As a result of this attitude British submarines in the first decade of their history were relegated to coast defence. Submarine officers were not discouraged. They took every opportunity in manœuvres, when targets came their way, to demonstrate how easy it was to sink a slow-moving warship by unseen torpedo attack. Drake had been branded by the Queen's enemies as a

---

[1] *Submarine Jubilee*, B.B.C., 2nd February 1951.

pirate, but he had laid the foundation of British seapower and naval discipline. His ships, no bigger than submarines, were designed to fight, and were manned by highly trained crews 'all of one company.' Being self-supporting, distance was no object. They roamed the seas in search of wealth for the Crown, and turning up where least expected, would strike a blow for God and Elizabeth, then, having taken care to exploit their gains, would disappear into the blue.

Drake had faith in the offensive power of his little ships, and it was in this tradition that the British Submarine Service grew up. Its creators had the vision to see that the true role of the submarine lay out in the deep waters where great ships ply, not tied to the coast of England.

Much development was needed, however, before a type could be produced which would demonstrate once and for all that submarines could undertake offensive operations without support in distant waters. Bacon, Hall, Addison, Little, Somerville, and other early pioneers worked as a team, pooling their experience and evolving a type which was to prove itself superior to the German U-boat.

Horton's first command, A.1, had an endurance of 500 miles. His next, C.8, although only 300 tons displacement, could cover 1,500 miles before refuelling, but the accommodation was poor. Captain Bernard Acworth, R.N., who served as Horton's First Lieutenant in C.8, gives us his impressions:

'When I joined submarines as a Sub-Lieutenant, in February 1906, Horton, as a young Lieutenant, was a prominent member of the company of submarine pioneers who were soon to make submarine history, and subsequently to hold, as Admirals, many of the highest and most responsible commands in the Navy. In those early days, the Submarine Service was, in many respects, a nest of pirates in the eyes of the old-established and austerely disciplined Navy, and there is no denying that Max K., when safely back from one of those submerged exercises which, in peacetime, cost so many submarines and lives, was the most notable pirate of all. Perhaps because life in the early submarines was exceptionally risky, and pay, for those days, extremely high (20s. 9d. a day, for the Commander of a submarine), gambling for modest stakes was popular with many of those who did not invest their 10s. 9d. extra pay in early marriage. Max K.'s reputation as a poker-player was second only to his credit for coolness and sobriety as a submarine commander, in which capacity he was at least the equal of any contemporary and subsequent submariner and the superior of most. Though gambling for amusement or personal gain is not to be regarded as a virtue, the qualities essential for first-class poker-playing have their undoubted value in the conduct of war, where successful bluff may, on occasion, be the only way to victory in the face of odds.

'In those days, which now seem so remote and relatively carefree, motor bicycles were almost as novel as submarines, and their respective engines equally unreliable. It was only to be expected, therefore, that motor bicycle races and trials were the hobbies of most submariners, and in this sport Horton excelled. It was on an old twin-Minerva, if I remember rightly, that he raced Bertie Herbert [1] down Butser into Petersfield, and to his intense surprise and disgust was beaten.

'My personal experience of him as a submarine commander was as his First Lieutenant in C.8, where I gained an insight into Horton's exceptional qualities as an executive officer, as well as a practical seaman. In the former capacity he was a perfect exponent, and perhaps to some extent a founder, of that form of discipline which, generally speaking, has characterised the Submarine Service for fifty years—a combination of ruthlessness towards any form of incompetence or slackness in the performance of duty, and a warmhearted and very real fraternity among all ranks and ratings who live in more intimate contact with one another than in any other class of ship, naval or mercantile.

'With all Horton's most manly characteristics there was always a streak of absurd boyishness, as in the case of motor bicycles which I have quoted. At sea, also, his almost childish love of "getting in first," by one means or another, was typical of him. Speed in those early days of petrol-driven submarines was then, as now, a fetish, even though ten to eleven knots was the maximum that a C class submarine could compass. After a day of exercise, south of the Isle of Wight, a race into harbour was the regular practice and the mechanical skill of her artificers, and the general efficiency of the boat were to some extent judged by the outcome of these competitions. As C.8 was a frequent winner in these races, Horton was credited with almost legendary powers with early petrol engines. But C.8's successes in these races owed something to his trick of cutting down the fields of the main electric motors to a point at which they reinforced the engines by discharging heavily as motors, instead of charging up the batteries as dynamos.

'After leaving C.8 I only met Horton occasionally and socially, but

[1] Later Commander G. Herbert, D.S.O., R.N., a distinguished submarine Commander and life-long friend of Horton.

always with the utmost pleasure, for our association in C.8 had kindled an affection and admiration which did not diminish with the passing years.'

Meanwhile their Lordships decided that submarine officers of Lieutenant's rank must spend at least two years in surface ships to gain experience in general service conditions. This ruling was welcomed by the senior submarine officers who had no wish for their branch to be regarded as a 'little navy on its own.' Furthermore it gave them a lever to remove, for a spell of cooling off, some 'tough characters' who were tending to become too 'piratical' in their outlook. Two years in a big ship, the bigger the better, would smooth down some of the rough edges and restore the necessary sense of balance required for higher rank. No one was surprised therefore to find Max, early in 1910, smartly dressed in frock coat and sword belt pacing the quarterdeck of the cruiser *Duke of Edinburgh* with a telescope under his arm—bored stiff. The gunnery officer of the ship, Lieutenant E. O. B. Osborne, R.N.,[1] quickly appreciated that Max, on account of his submarine experience, had an amazing eye for estimating the course and speed of a target. So he gave him the important duty of spotting the fall of shot, and controlling the six-inch guns in battle. 'Max was a delightful messmate,' Osborne says, 'and the best of company, a past master at snooker and poker and made quite a bit of money that way. His luck was extraordinary and he backed it.'

Horton was placed in charge of the training of junior officers, and by his courage and seamanlike qualities quickly established an influence over them. Captain (S) C. A. N. Kershaw recalls:

'He was the only one of us who would dive from the fore bridge which I think was about a fifty-foot dive. . . . He was no "paper" man, and as Captain's Clerk I had considerable difficulty in getting him to produce the few books and reports required from him. . . . He was supposed to keep a Seamanship Progress Book and a Swimming Instruction Record. Some months after commissioning when an Admiral's inspection was imminent I asked him about these books. At first he disclaimed ever having seen them. Later they were found in his cabin on the overhead shelf, of course without an entry. However,

---

[1] Later Vice-Admiral E. O. B. Osborne, C.B., D.S.O.

7

by getting various people to make entries in different inks he contrived to produce what appeared to be impeccable records of instruction. I must own to being an accessory. . . . In the *Duke of Edinburgh* he was certainly not "troublesome in the mess." He was a bit wild, but no more so than the exuberance of youth would warrant.'

He certainly had his wild moments—once, after a day's golf and a good dinner, he and his companion, the subaltern of Marines, V. C. M. Kelsey, found themselves in Leicester Square. It was very late, and they had missed the last train to Chatham. The Square was deserted except for a solitary hansom-cab, so having nothing better to do, Max challenged Kelsey to play golf round the Square for five shillings, 'holing out' under the hansom. It was a close match, and they were 'all square' just short of the cab. Kelsey 'holed out' with a perfect approach shot. It was Max's turn to play, and while addressing the ball his concentration was disturbed by a voice: 'You can't do that there 'ere.' Max, with his eye still on the ball, said: 'If I don't hit this ball, I lose my money!' 'All right,' said the policeman, 'hit that ball and it's Vine Street[1] for you.' Max lost his money. He said afterwards that the odds were too strong against him. Even if he had halved the hole, he would still have had to pay the fine for obstruction or whatever crime the constable had in mind.

His character was unusually complex, earning for him more admiration and criticism than falls to the lot of lesser men. But upon one of his characteristics there was no difference of opinion among those who had the good, and sometimes bad, fortune to serve with him. As a practical, cool-headed, and fearless seaman, whether on the surface of the sea or beneath it, he was pre-eminent. Indeed, most conversations about this much-discussed man, although prefaced with sincere tributes to his quality as a great sailor, were followed very often with a 'but.' And certainly Max Horton never earned the condemnation of being spoken well of by all men, except in his capacity as a seaman.

About a fortnight before Horton completed his 'big ship time' an incident occurred which tested this to the full. On 13th December 1911, when the squadron was at Gibraltar, a wireless

[1] Police station.

message came with the startling news that the P. & O. liner *Delhi* had gone ashore on a reef off Cape Spartel at the entrance to the Mediterranean. The Duke and Duchess of Fife (Princess Royal) and the Princesses Alexandra and Maud were known to be on board. The *Duke of Edinburgh* with Rear-Admiral Christopher Cradock rushed to the scene, and while on passage Max and Osborne threw the dice for choice of boats. Horton got the steam pinnace and Osborne took a cutter. A westerly gale was blowing with rain coming down in torrents. A steamboat from the French cruiser *Friant*, while attempting to reach the stranded vessel, turned completely over and her crew was lost. Max however managed to get his boat under the lee of the wreck, and brought back some passengers. Meanwhile Cradock decided to land the Royal party in the cutter near Cape Spartel. The boat capsized in the surf a few yards from the beach. The Duchess lost her jewel case but all got safely ashore, and after a night in the light-house went with Cradock on mule-back to Tangier.

Horton continued with the rescue operations, and, aided by boats from the battleship *London* and the French cruiser, succeeded in transferring the passengers to ships standing by. For this he was awarded the Board of Trade silver medal for heroism in saving life at sea.

On his return to submarines in January 1912, Horton was given the command of D.6. In the manœuvres of that year he penetrated the Firth of Forth and torpedoed two warships of the hostile fleet anchored above the bridge. In order to reach his target unseen Horton had to navigate the Forth for a consider-able distance at periscope depth, raising his periscope only when necessary to check his position. This successful operation not only placed him in the front rank of submarine Commanders, but also revealed the weakness of the anti-submarine defences of Rosyth.

Afterwards, while returning to Harwich, he came across the battle cruiser *Indefatigable* lying stopped at sea. Breaking surface close alongside, he announced 'I've sunk you.' He did not mention, however, that he had expended all his torpedoes in the Forth! The Captain of the battle cruiser, an ex-gunnery officer of ancient vintage, raised his megaphone and said unkind things which fell off Max like the water off his submarine. Feeling that this was too serious a matter to be decided by competitive seniority, Horton warned Captain Leveson that another submarine (D.4) was in the vicinity, and if *Indefatigable* remained stopped much longer in her present position she would be sunk again! Having delivered that broadside, Max clapped down the conning-tower hatch and dived quickly. He took care, however, to report the incident to his commanding officer, Roger Keyes. There were no repercussions.

In the grand manœuvres of the following year, Commodore Keyes asked him what he intended to do. Max replied that he would like to have freedom to act independently, as he wished 'to put submarines on the map.' It is not clear how much latitude he was given, but there is no doubt that the activities of Horton and his colleagues in these large-scale manœuvres influenced considerably the strategy to be adopted on the outbreak of war. Existing plans for blockading Germany by cruiser patrols in the central North Sea were abandoned in favour of a more distant blockade and submarines were given the honourable task of watching the German bases inside the Heligoland Bight. Submarines were 'on the map' at last.

In March 1914, Horton was selected to command E.9 of 800 tons, one of the first ocean-going submarines. She was a great advance on her predecessors, manned by a crew of thirty and armed with five torpedo tubes and a 'twelve pounder' gun. Her full speed was sixteen knots and her fuel endurance was 2,600 miles.

When the war broke out, E.9 was sent with others of her class to patrol the inshore waters of the Heligoland Bight. Horton's patrol area included Heligoland itself, so he decided to have a look inside the harbour. Having passed through the entrance, he swung his periscope round, but found nothing worthy of a torpedo. As all seemed to be quiet he thought he would rest awhile on the bottom. The crew were dismissed from their stations and the officers settled down to a game of bridge. While a hand was being played an ominous clanking and scraping was heard as a sweep wire, passing over the hull, worked along the boat in jerks. The 'jumping wire,'[1] however, kept it clear. Max, while confirming the incident, thought little of it, because, he said: 'I knew nothing would happen to us.'

Many officers have spoken of Horton's 'intuition' which some say bordered on second sight. It certainly seems that he got what he called 'hunches,' and when he did, he backed them like a true gambler. It flattered his vanity to know that when they came off—and they did with surprising frequency—his reputation for sizing up a situation correctly was enhanced. He believed that thirteen was his lucky number.

At dawn on the 13th September, Horton brought E.9 to the surface after a night's rest on the bottom six miles S.S.W. of Heligoland Harbour. It was dead calm with patches of fog. As the mist was clearing, he decided to go to periscope depth, and on his first look round sighted the German light cruiser *Hela* emerging from a patch. He closed unseen to 600 yards, fired two torpedoes, and dived. The *Hela* was hit amidships, taking a heavy list to starboard. E.9 came to periscope depth, and was shelled immediately by destroyers. She dived again, but not for long, as Horton was determined to see the effect of his attack. Although harried by small craft, he had another look. The cruiser had gone, and over the spot where she had sunk, armed trawlers were picking up survivors. E.9 was hunted for the rest of the day, and when darkness came, her batteries were dangerously low. Horton made several attempts to charge them during the night, but could not complete the operation on account of the unwelcome attentions of enemy destroyers. He managed however to work his way out of the dangerous waters, and brought E.9 safely back to Harwich.

Three weeks later he was off the mouth of the Ems looking for bigger game. The scene was familiar to him, for in the days before the War he had read with keen professional interest *The Riddle of the Sands*, a book by Erskine Childers describing a voluntary reconnaissance of the tortuous approaches to the lair of the High Seas Fleet. Max was thrilled at finding himself engaged in the same fascinating task of seeking enemy battleships

[1] A protective wire running from bow to stern, passing over the conning tower.

near their base. Childers with his yacht had unmasked their warlike preparations. Horton with his submarine hoped to be the first to curb their activities, but he was faced with a different kind of 'riddle.'

It was a vexatious patrol, with never a sign of a German heavy ship. The navigation was hazardous, and the narrow channels between the sandbanks were heavily guarded by destroyers, making it difficult for him to avoid one without getting involved with the other.

He had set the depth-keeping mechanism of his torpedoes to run deep, for he hoped to sink a deep-draught battleship. On the last day of his patrol having sighted no big ship, he decided in exasperation to square accounts with one of the destroyers which had been irritating him. After altering the setting of his torpedoes to run at shallow depth, he started to hunt the hunter. He dared not allow himself to be seen. The slightest ripple made by his periscope on the surface of the smooth waters would betray him at once. His stealthy approach to the quarry therefore was largely a matter of guesswork. When he thought he was near enough he would cautiously raise his periscope, as a sportsman would raise his head, to measure his distance and shoot to kill. Twice Max found himself in a suitable position, but just as he was about to fire, his coy victim changed her course. All this backing and filling beneath the surface had drained E.9's batteries to the limit, and as hope of a successful attack had gone, Horton decided to head for home. While taking a last look to get his bearings he saw the destroyer coming towards him. E.9 was trimmed below the surface. Horton had just time to get out of the way and into a good attacking position. He fired at close range. The torpedo hit the destroyer amidships as she dashed past. There was a terrific explosion and she sank immediately, He wrote to a friend: 'To hit a destroyer always requires maximum luck. She went up beautifully, and when I had a chance of a good look round about five minutes afterwards, all that was to be seen was about fifteen feet of bow sticking up vertically out of the water.'

Thus, in less than two months of war, Horton had played bridge under the noses of the Germans inside a strongly fortified harbour. He had sunk the light cruiser *Hela* and the destroyer

S.116, each within a few miles of their own coast. For these achievements, he had been awarded the D.S.O. and recommended for early promotion.

When E.9 returned to Harwich flying the 'Jolly Roger' she was cheered to the echo by all ships in harbour, and at this moment of triumph Max had news that further opportunities would soon be open to him.

The German battleships and battle cruisers had been spending a good deal of their time in the Baltic where they might become profitable targets for surprise attack by British submarines. The margin of superiority in numbers of the Grand Fleet over the High Seas Fleet was narrow, and since the German Fleet seemed to be unwilling to give battle, it was highly desirable to seek out their heavy ships and destroy them wherever they might be. In any case, a submarine threat to German naval forces and transports working on the flank of the advancing German army would materially assist our Russian ally. Furthermore, British submarines, with a roving commission in the Baltic, could disrupt German supplies from Sweden while the ports were free from ice. Orders were framed accordingly, and three submarines were selected for the task; E.1, Lt.-Commander N. F. Laurence; E.9, Lt.-Commander M. K. Horton; and E.11, Lt.-Commander Martin Nasmith. The Russian port of Libau was to be their base, but they were to have a look at Danzig on the way, as the High Seas Fleet was known to be operating from there. Horton felt highly honoured to be one of the chosen few, for here was an opportunity to show what submarines could do unsupported in enemy waters over a thousand miles from their home base.

On the night of 17th October 1914, E.1 passed through the Sound into the Baltic. Horton in E.9 followed twenty-four hours later. It was a hazardous passage, as he had to negotiate a minefield and was forced to dive frequently by enemy destroyers. Nasmith in E.11, having been delayed by engine trouble, did not reach the Sound until the 20th. He was sighted in shallow water by destroyers and aircraft, relentlessly hunted, and compelled to return to Harwich. Laurence went to Libau, and was followed a day later by Horton. They found that the fortifications had been abandoned and the dockyard demolished. They learnt also that they had both passed through a German mine-field recently laid at the entrance to the harbour. There was no news of E.11, and, after waiting some days in vain for her, both submarines went on to Lapvick and later to Reval, where they came under the orders of Admiral von Essen, the Russian Commander-in-Chief.

Horton quickly got to work and was able to sink a number of merchant ships carrying contraband from Sweden before the ice set in. When winter came, he took E.9 to sea on a test trip to find out how far he could go. The Russians viewed this move with jealous apprehension, as it was not their custom to go to sea after the ice had formed. An ice breaker crushed a path for him, but the submarine was soon wholly encased in ice. He was anxious to learn if the slush ice in vents and valves would make diving dangerous. Under the surface, however, he found that the salt water thawed the slush and that diving efficiency was not impaired. He followed the ice breaker for 100 miles, then set out towards the Sound and while on passage torpedoed a German destroyer. The conditions while cruising on the surface demanded the highest powers of endurance. The spray would freeze on the bridge, and men were employed continuously with hammer and chisel keeping the conning-tower hatch free of ice. The periscope could not be moved and the caps on the torpedo tubes became jammed. In order to restore her fighting value Horton would take E.9 to the bottom and rest there until she had thawed out. The British submarines had run out of rum, and the crews, unaccustomed to the intense cold, sadly missed their daily ration. Horton asked for vodka, but the Russian Navy was 'dry,' so official sanction on the highest level had to be obtained. When the Tsar heard of it he remarked: 'If they are so cold why can't they wear two shirts?'

On 31st December 1914, Horton, at the age of 31, was promoted to Commander.

The activities of the British submarines in the Baltic had upset the German plans for advancing by a series of combined opera-tions to St. Petersburg. A German prisoner, picked up after the loss of the *Blucher* in the battle of the Dogger Bank, confessed that ships of the High Seas Fleet could no longer move with

MIDSHIPMAN M. K. HORTON, 1901

THE BALTIC, 1915
E.9 returns from patrol

FORT BLOCKHOUSE ('H.M.S. DOLPHIN'), 1909

THE MEDITERRANEAN, 1935
The First Cruiser Squadron manœuvring at speed

H.M. KING GEORGE VI INSPECTS THE RESERVE FLEET, AUGUST 1939
The French Officer, (right) is Admiral Darlan

freedom in the Baltic since Max Horton had been sent there. It was not for nothing that the Germans themselves, in 1915, began to call the Baltic 'Horton's Sea.'[1]

Another German naval officer writing after the War in the 'Westfaelischer Landeszeitung' said, 'The good Max Horton was a fine fellow and knew something about Submarine Service.'

There was a price on Horton's head, and this is no legend. At a party one night he was introduced to a lovely young woman. They were mutually attracted. So when she suggested that it would be nice to have a cup of coffee together, Max happily agreed. They settled down at a table. Her English was perfect and they found that they had much in common. The waiter came with two cups of coffee. Max was about to drink, when suddenly he felt a touch on his sleeve.

'Don't drink!' she said, 'It might be poisoned!'

'How do you know?'

'They asked me to put the poison in the cup.'

'Who are "they"?'

The girl, having succumbed to her feelings for Max, gave him the names of her would-be pro-German employers, who were quickly rounded up and shot. The story goes that the Tsar, when he heard of the incident, said to Max: 'It did not surprise me—you must know there is a price on your head.' Horton refused to disclose the lady's name. They became friends, and when he left for home he gave her a gold cigarette case with his signature engraved upon it. Afterwards she escaped from Russia— travelling to England through the Scandinavian countries with the signed case as a passport. Two facts emerge from several versions of this story. The Germans had put a price on Horton's head, and his signature was honoured on the western shores of the Baltic.

In the early summer of 1915 he sank another destroyer and several merchant ships carrying Swedish iron ore. In these operations Horton observed scrupulously the conventions of International Law. Yet he seems to have had difficulty in living down his reputation for being a pirate. Some years later when the War was over, he received this letter from the Admiralty:

[1] *H.M. Submarines*, p. 57, Lt.-Commander P. Kemp, R.N.

The Secretary,
Admiralty, S.W.1.
10*th September* 1920.

Captain Max K. Horton, D.S.O., R.N.,
H.M.S. *Dolphin*,
c/o G.P.O.

With reference to the affidavits which were made by you regarding the capture and sinking of certain enemy merchant vessels by H.M. Submarine E.9 in the Baltic Sea in 1915, I am to inform you that it is desired to ascertain whether or not due warning was given to all the unarmed merchant ships which were dealt with by the vessel under your Command before any offensive action was taken against them.

By Command of their Lordships,
(Signed) V. W. Baddeley.

Horton replied:

From: Captain Max K. Horton, D.S.O., R.N.
To: Secretary of the Admiralty.
Date: 13*th September* 1920.
Submitted,

With reference to your letter of 10th September 1920, due and proper warning was given in every case in which submarine E.9 was concerned. Moreover careful search of each vessel sunk was made previous to the sinking to ensure there was none of the enemy crew remaining on board. Ample time was allowed for placing personal gear, food and water in the boats and in no case was the weather unsuitable for small boats or the distance to the nearest shore more than fifteen miles.

I was informed by Russian Intelligence Department that no casualties occurred or were reported in Sweden where enemy crews landed.

(Signed) Max Horton,
Captain.

It was difficult and often dangerous for a submarine commander to comply strictly to the letter of the law when intercepting enemy merchant ships or neutral ships carrying contraband. Only a very small party could be spared to visit a suspicious ship. The submarine carried no boat, but Horton overcame the difficulty by ordering the vessel to send one, and thus was able to answer satisfactorily their Lordships' query. In those days, however, there was no threat of hostile aircraft to disturb the leisurely procedure. We shall see later how he dealt with this aspect of the problem as Flag Officer Submarines in the Second World War.

The tedium of patrolling was relieved for E.9 by the sudden appearance in her area of a squadron of German cruisers. They were steaming at high speed with destroyers on their flanks. Horton could have chanced a long shot, but throwing caution to the winds he dived in the shallow water under the destroyers, coming to periscope depth at close range from the rear ship, the *Prince Adalbert*. He fired two torpedoes and claimed that both had hit, but only one had exploded. Four days later Max wrote to a friend:

'We really have been busy—even more so than at the beginning of the War—7,000 miles in two months: result four ships sunk and one damaged. Not so bad I think, when one considers the last was a fast three-funnelled battleship (in a whisper, I think so—just possible it was *Prince Heinrich*, a three-funnelled cruiser!) but anyway something well worth having. We hit her last Friday 2nd July—with two torpedoes —she was going pretty fast—about eighteen—with destroyers. Saw the first explosion by the foremast—fine show—debris and smoke up to the top of the masts—I was keeping a somewhat anxious eye on a destroyer, pretty close—doing its best to ram us—dirty dog! However she failed (narrowly). Day before yesterday I had a great reception in the Flagship—and in the evening, I was sent for again and the C.-in-C. (von Essen) pinned on the St. George's Cross, their highest decoration, equivalent to our V.C., as a result of a telegram from the Emperor. I feel some dog but hope I don't show it! Should have got it in any case for my show of 4th June and 11th May, I'm told. But glad it was for something bigger.

'I told you about 4th June didn't I? When we bagged a destroyer and a transport (three survivors between them) and damaged another destroyer. Too much I, I, I, in this letter and I apologise.'

Fourteen years later, Admiral Hopmann, who commanded the German squadron, gave his own account of the incident to a friend of Max's.

NAVAL AND MILITARY CLUB,

94, PICCADILLY, W.1.

9th June 1929.

Dear Captain Horton,

Last week-end I was racing a motorboat at Berlin, and met one Admiral Hopmann, who, hearing I had been a naval officer, told me certain of his war experiences. It appeared he was R.A. of a Baltic Cruiser Squadron flying his flag in the *Prince Adalbert*. The rest of the story you no doubt know—he says you fired two torpedoes at him at 1.30 p.m. 2nd July 1915—range 300 yards in foggy weather—one hit only! He asked me to write to you and express his very great appreciation of your attack and success. He also mentioned that the German Baltic Fleet feared your activities more than all the Russian Fleet!

Yours sincerely,
(Signed) GLEN KIDSTON.

Horton's torpedo put the ship out of action for four months. Just after she had been repaired Lt.-Commander Goodhart in E.8, a new arrival in the Baltic, torpedoed her in the forward magazine, and she sank in a few minutes.

The satisfactory results achieved by E.1 and E.9 in crippling the iron-ore traffic and frustrating the German plans for a coast-wise advance caused the Russians to ask for more British submarines. The British Government readily agreed, for indeed it was the only way they could assist their hard-pressed ally. So four more boats of the E class were sent to the Baltic, and by the middle of September 1915, E.8, Lt.-Commander F. H. Goodhart, E.18, Lt.-Commander R. C. Halahan, and E.19, Lt.-Commander F. N. Cromie had made the hazardous passage, and joined their colleagues at Reval.

This was no mean achievement as the Germans by now were very much on the alert. The waters at the entrance to the Baltic were heavily patrolled, navigational marks had been removed, new minefields and other traps had been laid. Moreover these submarine Commanders had had no experience of the peculiar conditions of the Baltic entrance, where the water changes density, and it is often difficult to dive below periscope depth without touching bottom.

E.13, Lt.-Commander G. Layton, as her number implies,[1] was the only unlucky one. Her compass failed in narrow waters, and she went ashore in Danish territory near Copenhagen. Two German destroyers, in defiance of Danish neutrality and with no regard for humanity, smothered the boat with shellfire at a

---

[1] Horton regarded thirteen as his own lucky number, but unlucky for other people.

range of 300 yards. Layton and some of the crew were picked up by a Danish torpedo boat. Shortly afterwards, Layton escaped and found his way home.

The arrival of reinforcements and new faces made conditions more tolerable for the two submarine crews who alone had held the fort for close on a year, among strangers in a strange land. A proper base organisation was established, and systematic patrols were arranged to provide for regular rest periods and recreation. Four more submarines of the C class which had been towed to Archangel were being sent in barges to St. Petersburg by river and canal. Hopes were high, and all worked with enthusiasm on ambitious plans for taking the command of the Baltic out of the hands of the Germans when spring came.

This happy prospect was denied to Laurence and Horton. At the end of the year the Admiralty telegraphed that both were to return to England as they were 'urgently required for service in new submarines in home waters.' On 17th December 1915, the Chief of the Russian Naval Staff asked if Horton could stay in the Baltic as Senior Naval Officer at the British base. Commenting on this request in an Admiralty docket, the Second Sea Lord wrote:

'I understand Commander Horton is something of a pirate and not at all fitted for the position of S.N.O. in the Baltic.'

Max had himself to blame, for his reputation as a pirate was of his own making. When he entered Harwich harbour after sinking the *Hela*, he flew the 'Jolly Roger' from his periscope, and after sinking S.116 he flew two of these flags. Later, when there was no longer any more room on the halyards for a flag for each victory, he adopted the system of flying one large 'pirate' flag with bars denoting the number of enemy vessels he had sunk. The sailors loved it, and so did the Press. Indeed, most submariners took a delight in flaunting the idea, for they knew very well that senior officers of the 'old' Navy had spoken of them as 'pirates.'

Yet at heart Horton was orthodox. In dealing with subordinates who failed to come up to his standard he would be strict in his application of the Naval Discipline Act. And, as we have seen, he was careful to observe the conventions of International Law.

Sir George Buchanan, the British Ambassador at St. Petersburg, disagreed not only with the Admiralty decision but also with their Lordships' estimate of the character of Max Horton. On 31st December 1915, His Excellency telegraphed:

'I learn that Commander Laurence and Commander Horton are under orders for England. The latter gets on particularly well with the Russians which requires special qualifications, and his experience in the Baltic is also valuable. Would it not be possible to allow him to remain?'

The Admiralty refused to give way. Laurence and Horton came home and Commander Cromie took command.

For his services to Russia, Commander Max Horton was awarded the Order of St. Vladimir with swords, the Order of St. Ann with swords and diamonds (a unique honour for a junior officer), and the Order of St. George. In addition the French Government made him a Chevalier of the Legion of Honour for gallantry in attacking enemy warships. And in 1917 he was awarded a bar to his D.S.O. 'for long and arduous services in command of overseas submarines.'

Fate had been kind to Max. With the coming of the Soviet regime one of the first to fall was the gallant von Essen, the Russian Commander-in-Chief, for whom all British officers in the Baltic had a high regard. The British submarines were blown up to avoid capture, and in April 1917 the crews returned to England. Commander Cromie remained behind to work for the Allied cause, but met his death at St. Petersburg on the steps of the British Embassy trying to resist the entry of a bloodthirsty mob.

CHAPTER TWO

1916-35

BETWEEN THE WARS

The Baltic again. Promotion to Captain. 'The strong man apart.'
Running a battleship. Monte Carlo. Flag rank.

MAX came home from Russia in plain clothes on a faked passport, travelling by rail through Sweden and Norway, thence by sea to Newcastle. He was met by his brother who had difficulty in recognising him, wrapped as he was from head to toe in an immense coat of Russian sable which, needless to say, had been given to him. D'Arcy Horton says that in the train going south Max smoked Russian cigarettes continuously, and the mixture of odours from these and the coat was more than their fellow-travellers could endure, so the two brothers had the compartment to themselves all the way to London.

On 25th January 1916 Max was appointed to command a new submarine J.6 of over 1,200 tons. After supervising her building at Devonport, he spent the next eighteen months patrolling in the North Sea, a monotonous and exacting task with few opportunities for spectacular achievement. It was the policy of both sides to fill the Heligoland Bight with mines and it was the business of British submarines to patrol the edge of the minefields, keeping a watch on all enemy activities. Accurate navigation was essential, which was not easy in waters where fog and mist prevail and the currents are strong and variable. The enemy coast was too far away for British aircraft to maintain reconnaissance patrols, so the Commander-in-Chief of the Grand Fleet had to rely on submarines for news of a sortie by the German Fleet beyond the minefields. The submarines had to be constantly on the alert, and the tedium of many weary months of patrolling with never a sight of an enemy ship must have been a strain on a man of Horton's temperament. However, it does not seem to have depressed him. In a letter from J.6 at Blyth on 17th June 1917, he wrote:

'Here things are speeding up fast. Longer at sea and half the time in harbour—so it is necessary in order to preserve the proportions to speed up oneself during the short hours of liberty. With that object in view, I and another are the proud possessers of an automobile—not as you might suppose a Rolls Royce—for it only cost £53! Still it takes us to Newcastle as fast as may be, and when, after an excellent dinner, one starts her up and leans back on the cushions smoking a large Cabbagio, one wouldn't change places with any swollen plutocrat for anything.'

He seems to have had no difficulty in getting petrol.

At the end of the year, Horton was selected to command and supervise the building of the experimental submarine, M.1, the first of a type which, like its immediate predecessor the K class, was a notable departure from existing design. The ' K's ' were virtually submersible destroyers, but M.1 was the first step towards the submersible battleship. In addition to her torpedo armament she carried a twelve-inch gun mounted in a turret. Although her trials were successful and she was used operationally, she was never fully tested in war. In her successor, M.2, the gun turret was replaced by a seaplane hangar, but experience showed that neither of these functions could be usefully embodied in a sub-marine, so the design was abandoned. It will be noted, however, that when new construction and new ideas were coming forward Horton was among the first to be selected by his peers to try them out. He was in fact their chief 'test pilot.'

The end of the war brought no peace to the Navy. Early in 1919 British light naval forces were sent to the Baltic to assist the small States against Bolshevik aggression. This call upon the Fleet came at a time when the 'short-service' men were thinking about demobilisation, and the Navy, like the other fighting services, was war-weary and looking forward to enjoying the fruits of victory.

Although he had not yet reached Captain's rank, Horton was appointed to the *Maidstone* and sent again to the Baltic, this time in command of a submarine flotilla.

The *Maidstone* was a seagoing submarine depot ship, and it must have been thrilling for Max to view the scene of his early adventures from her spacious bridge as he led his flotilla through the Sound into the Baltic. He wrote from Copenhagen:

'Am going through my bad spot in the Narrows of October 1914[1] this afternoon on the way out of the Sound. I shall be very interested to see it by daylight on the surface.'

On arrival at Reval in September 1919 he found himself in one of those difficult positions, not unusual for naval officers, where he had to take responsibility for decisions made on the spot without political guidance·from the Government. A false step on his part might cause international complications and might even involve the country in another war.

It was difficult also to keep up the spirits of the men who had reason to wonder why they were in the Baltic at all.

On 30th September 1919 he wrote:

'This Bolshie business seems very infectious. . . .

'Things are calming down a little now, having got into the swing a bit. . . .

'. . . All the Baltic States delegates with the Finns as well are meeting today to discuss whether they are going to make a combined peace with the Bolshies or not. . . . I expect it will come off, for everyone seems tired of scrapping and the conditions are certainly damnable.

'One has to be so careful not to appear to be either pro-Russian or pro-Estonian, for they both hate each other like poison and since in many ways I have to judge between them, one has to be extra careful. In consequence I don't go anywhere except to our own Missions, political and military.'

In the spring of 1920 the British naval forces came home. Horton was awarded a second bar to his D.S.O. for distinguished service in command of the Baltic submarine flotilla and as Senior Naval Officer, Reval. In June of that year he was promoted to Captain at the age of thirty-seven, and a month later became Chief Staff Officer to the Rear-Admiral Submarines, Douglas Dent.

It was about this time that people noticed a change in Max Horton. To his officers he was no longer the devil-may-care good companion. He seemed suddenly to have lost his boyishness.

[1] Q.v., page 13.

Although no one could say that he was pompous, he seemed to have drawn a curtain between himself and his naval companions. A friend and contemporary[1] writes:

'Before the First War the Navy was not so free with Christian names, and I doubt if anyone called him "Max." I remember calling him "M.K.," as did others, but surnames were more usual between us. After the war, hundreds spoke of him as "Max," if very few to him, it became so familiar that it was hard to think of him without the "Max." I thought I knew Horton better than my own soldier brother, yet it did not strike me as odd that I never knew of any relative until in 1925 when his brother came into my cabin. Only now do I realise how reticent he was.'

An officer who had been a golfing companion, but was no longer his equal in rank, hailed him as 'Max' one day while passing on the links. Afterwards Horton sent for him and reproved him officially for undue familiarity. On another occasion while playing with the children of a friend they called him 'Smacks.' He told the parents that they should be 'spoken to' about it.

This unexpected attitude annoyed many who had been through the mill with him, and who respected him for his professional ability and high qualities as a leader in war. Inside a submarine where the crew, so to speak, were all of one family he was on good terms with everyone and would wear any old clothes, but he was always conscious of his dignity, which to him was a personal thing and nothing to do with rank. He had an inherent dislike of familiarity. The use of the Christian name, except in the case of life-long friends, denoted a familiarity he did not feel, therefore he discouraged it. He loathed the habit prevalent in the ' old school tie' fraternity of calling each other 'old boy' and 'old chap.'

Horton was devoted to the Service and had a passion for efficiency. Influenced possibly by what he had seen in Russia and what had happened in the German Fleet, he feared that industrial unrest might spread to the Navy. He agreed with his chief that, since the incentive of war had vanished, the officers and men must be 'kept on their toes' and strict discipline enforced.

He loved power and used it mercilessly, albeit with the highest motives, taking upon himself the mantle of the strong man apart.

[1] Rear-Admiral C. G. Brodie.

24

He was not of the type who could reprimand an officer on the quarterdeck and afterwards enjoy a glass of gin with him in the wardroom. Probably he was afraid to give the impression that by resuming social contact he had condoned the offence. In any case all must be treated alike. His standard of efficiency was so high that he knew that some of his old friends and shipmates might fail to attain it. Having achieved rapid promotion himself, he may have been embarrassed by the thought that it was his painful duty to suggest the names of some close to him in age who would have to be retired under the Geddes scheme for retrenchment. He framed his policy on the survival of the fittest and was sparing with his praise.

There were moreover other sides to his nature which remained for long unguessed and may astonish Service readers. As early as 1919 he is found reading St. Augustine's 'City of God' and saying that he 'loved it'; also 'St. John of the Cross'[1] of whom he said 'I could not fully fathom him, but caught a glimpse of his meaning.' Speaking of these things he said in a private letter: 'At night I often sit in my cabin and think and think and think.' Facts such as these already explain some part of his withdrawal from Service social life—more will be said about them later. Inside the Navy, however, the legend ran something like this : 'A new "Jacky Fisher," efficient and ruthless. A leader and a driver. A master handler of a boat and a ball. One whose motto is "All's fair in love and war" and wins accordingly. As hard as nails and close as a clam.'

In 1922 he was appointed to the cruiser *Conquest* for command of a flotilla of fast submarines of the K class attached to the Atlantic Fleet. Horton announced his arrival to his commanding officers, all seasoned veterans, with characteristic pugnacity. He told them that they needed shaking up, and that they could look out for squalls. All of them had known Max when he and they were Lieutenants. They had liked him as a messmate, and rejoiced at his triumphs and his early promotion, but they did not regard him as the greatest submarine hero of the war. Nasmith[2] and

[1] The famous Spanish mystic.
[2] Later Admiral Sir Martin Dunbar Nasmith, V.C., K.C.B.

Talbot[1] were recognised as equally outstanding in skill and determination, but it must be said that Horton did not regard himself in this light. Whilst holding a high opinion of Talbot, he admired Nasmith and had a lasting affection for him. Talbot, whom Horton had relieved, had pulled the flotilla out of a bad patch, and they were a loyal and happy team. Indignation ran high, so the senior submarine officer (Brodie) felt it to be his duty to voice a protest: 'Horton listened in grim silence. I got little change out of him, and could only hope that my chief argument, that he had damned us before he'd seen us, had made more impression than was apparent.' Neither Brodie nor his colleagues could then discern the future Flag Officer Submarines, whose name was to be such a tonic to all submariners in the Second World War. Still less could they foresee in him the great Commander-in-Chief Western Approaches, whose smallest word of praise was to mean so much to the thousands engaged in the mortal struggle against the U-boats in the Battle of the Atlantic in 1943-45.

The K class submarines were steam-driven, their submerged displacement was 2,400 tons and they carried a crew of fifty-five officers and men. They were clumsy and dangerous, and had already taken a heavy toll of highly trained personnel. The pressure hulls were known to be weak and, owing to their great length, care had to be taken not to dive at too steep an angle. A high degree of skill was required therefore when diving these ungainly craft under a screen of destroyers to attack battleships moving at high speed. Horton, always war minded, had no sympathy with the idea that risks which must be taken in war were not justified in peace exercises. He took every opportunity to practise his flotilla in this form of attack, and the submarine commanders soon learnt that sheer efficiency was the true safeguard against accidents, and the key to success. It was exacting service for them. Yet they knew that Horton would never expect them to do what he would not do himself. He boarded their submarines frequently for routine exercises and always for experimental diving which might lead to better performance of the K class. His technical knowledge surprised even the engineer

[1] Later Admiral Sir C. P. Talbot, K.B.E., C.B., D.S.O.

officers, helping them to overcome their difficulties; nothing pleased him more than to put his fingers on some material defect not evident to others—it was one of his vanities. The crews must be trained to the highest peak of efficiency. 'In submarines,' he would say, 'there is no margin for mistakes, you are either alive or dead.'

One day in a full-dress battle exercise, six K class submarines, guided by Horton in the *Conquest* to a perfect position ahead of the advancing battle fleet, dived to the attack. They fired twenty torpedoes and secured sixteen hits; probably a record in submarine history. Glowing commendation came from the Commander-in-Chief, but the only encouragement the submarine commanders got from Horton was 'Attack satisfactory.'

The number of officers in the submarine branch itself was above peace-time requirements, and Horton had to submit a list of those whom he considered should be transferred to general service. Before making his final selection he left no stone unturned to make sure that only the best submariners should be retained. He drove them hard, and during exercises would take the *Conquest* close to the target so that he could spot the officers who used their periscopes too freely. Being anxious that those recommended for transfer should suffer no stigma, he took care to point out that they would probably do well in general service. And many of them did.

Although Horton discouraged familiarity with his own officers and seldom went ashore with them, he visited the wardroom daily, usually before dinner, when he would play a few hands of 'whisky poker.' Gone were the days of gambling with his messmates until the dawn. His shipmates were spared that. Probably he would have denounced the practice in the interest of discipline had he known it occurred. He was ably supported by Engineer Commander L. Turner, who was not only a remarkable personality but also a brilliant engineer. Being Horton's match in technical knowledge, he was always ready to stand up to him on behalf of the submarine officers. He had a flair for inspiring others with his own loyalties and thoroughly understood that the Captain's object was to attain the highest standard of efficiency. As the commission drew to a close, Horton's motives became clear to all on board and they responded accordingly.

MAX HORTON AND THE WESTERN APPROACHES

On leaving the *Conquest* Max received this letter from the Chief of Staff, Atlantic Fleet :

H.M.S. *Queen Elizabeth.*
25th May 1924.

My dear Horton,

I came back from leave only yesterday and that is my partial explanation of not having written you a line when you left your Atlantic Fleet command.

But however late I cannot let you go without saying how intensely we shall miss you—you yourself personally—and what you represent, which to my mind is Discipline, Devotion to Duty and enthusiasm for your work which is so infectious that everyone near you feels it.

All that you undertake is bound to prosper, and I hope we may have some sort of liaison in the years to come for it is such a great pleasure to work with you.

Yours ever,
(Signed) W. W. FISHER.[1]

In 1925 while commanding the large submarine depot at Fort Blockhouse, Portsmouth, Horton continued to apply his rigorous methods, especially to the dress and bearing of the ship's company. The weekly inspection on Sunday usually lasted about two hours, whilst each of several hundred officers and men endured his searching scrutiny. The young officers were asked pertinent and penetrating questions about man after man. Knowing what to expect they could usually give the correct answers; no mean feat in a drafting establishment where the personnel is ever changing. Horton would pause and stare at a new face before passing on, for he wanted every man to know him and he liked them to think that he knew them. Without being fussy, he was able to detect any fault which might affect the discipline and well-being of the establishment. But his inspection took a long time, and the men going on shore leave were lucky if they reached their homes less than an hour after those in other Portsmouth depots.

Although there was a certain undercurrent of discontent at this and other rigorous treatment, the sailors were aware of his stature and took pride in being under the sway of such a character.

Horton's chief recreation was golf and his handicap was over-assessed at eight. Those who had suffered on this account

---
[1] Later Admiral Sir W. W. Fisher, G.C.B.

unkindly called it a 'financial eight,' but he preferred to take it out of friends ashore rather than shipmates whom he knew could ill afford it. Although careful about money, he was always a generous host and kept a good table. At a dinner party one night, an Admiral's wife congratulated him on the high quality of everything and the excellence of the cooking. 'But,' she added, 'it is all very extravagant and you ought to have a wife to look after you.' 'Not at all,' said Max, 'I have a wonderful housekeeper; she pays for everything in cash and I give her the money at the end of the week. It seldom amounts to much and saves a lot of bother.' One day the paragon vanished, leaving behind many unpaid bills. For once, Max had been bluffed, but he bore her no grudge. She was efficient, so he allowed her to get away with it.

After four years of shore service at the Admiralty, and as Chief of Staff to Admiral Roger Keyes at Portsmouth, Horton was given command of the battleship *Resolution* destined for the Mediterranean. The ship was in Devonport dockyard where she had undergone a long refit. On the day he joined, he sent for his Second in Command, Commander R. G. Duke, and in course of conversation told him quite candidly that the only time he had served in a battleship was as a midshipman some thirty years ago. The Commander replied in all modesty that as he had spent the last eighteen years doing navigating duties and most of it far away from the big Fleets, he felt he had a great deal to learn too. Horton replied 'Well, m'lad, you're the youngest and I'll expect you to learn quickest.'

It was a friendly conversation. They had previously met, socially only, but it was abundantly clear to the Commander that he would be ill advised to take that statement too lightheartedly; he'd better take his coat off and get down to it, or else. . . .

'By way of a start,' said Horton, 'this ship has been in dockyard hands for months, and she probably leaks like a sieve. As a submariner, I have a horror of water coming into a ship, and there have been too many cases lately of ships making a lot of water just because they meet a bit of bad weather on passage from the dockyard. So I want every gunport, hatch, and skylight properly tested by water and put right before we sail.'

The Commander, having many other things to do, admits 'he

got sick to death of testing hatches' but the number of small defects, hitherto unrevealed, surprised him. Horton's thoroughness was rewarded, for the ship arrived on her station bone dry, despite several days of exercises on passage in the Atlantic.

Horton was more than a match for the dockyard officials when it came to a conflict of interests. From the dockyard point of view it was very often convenient to defer certain items and keep to the final date of completion by a glorious burst with hundreds of workmen in the last few days. This would usually result in very little time being left to clean and paint the ship before sailing. Horton, who had no intention of taking the *Resolution* to sea covered in patches of red lead, would have none of that. As the refit went on he was at considerable pains to collect promises in writing or by signal of dates of completion of many items. When some of these began to lag behind, he armed himself with the necessary evidence and stated his case, chapter and verse, personally to the Admiral Superintendent. Within an hour or two of his call, representatives of the dockyard management appeared on board, with the result that the *Resolution* was given high priority for labour, and finally left the yard seaworthy and decent in appearance.

Shortly before the ship sailed to join the Mediterranean Fleet, Horton received a letter from his Admiral, W. W. Fisher, suggesting that the *Resolution* should be his flagship. Fisher wrote that he realised that this would mean considerable inconvenience and might be a heavy burden for a newly commissioned ship. He asked Horton to say quite honestly if it would be too much of a strain, and added that other Captains in the squadron had already given various reasons against accommodating their Admiral.

Horton replied that he would be delighted, and in a letter to a friend said:

'W.W. wants me to take his flag—and of course I am thrilled at the prospect—it means hard work for all of us, to reach the standard, in a newly commissioned ship as we are—not only flagship standard, but W.W.'s standard—but he has given me a chance to show what we can do and I trust I shan't fail him. . . . We are 'new boys' in some ways—but my Commander [Duke] is a good lad and I can trust him. . . .'

After the Admiral came to the *Resolution* he followed the old custom of addressing the Captain by the name of his ship. Although he may have extended the practice to the rest of his squadron, he used the name in Horton's case perhaps more often because it suited him so well. Max disliked nicknames, but he could not fail to appreciate the significance of 'My dear Resolution' in a letter received after Fisher had hauled down his flag.

Duke says:

'In those first months of the *Resolution's* commission Horton was in some respects feeling his way. He admitted that his knowledge of big ship organisation and life in the big Fleets was very small. Now, for the first time, he found himself dependent on the advice of others on many matters, small perhaps in themselves and not vital to the fighting efficiency of the ship, but which did have considerable bearing on the making of a successful commission in the Battle Fleet. What he could do, however—and did—was to see that it was through no lack of encouragement or backing from him that any of us should fail to give him the best they were capable of. As a result, I, who as his Second in Command was one of those chiefly concerned, found that contrary to all my preconceived notions of Max Horton, he was above all "approachable." There was nothing I couldn't discuss freely with him, and it was sometimes hard to believe that the man who every evening after rounds would discuss the day's happenings with complete candour and a very impish sense of humour was indeed the same man who usually presented such a sphinx-like exterior to the world in general. If his previous experience of some of the problems brought to him was small, his judgment and his knowledge of human nature and of the different sorts and conditions of men it takes to make up the world of the Royal Navy were vast. No one was quicker at putting his finger on the weak spot in any scheme or plan, and no one was more ruthless to inefficiency. A mistake could be made once, but never twice, without swift retribution falling on the culprit's head. Woe betide the officer or man who tried to bluff him; he was much too old and skilful a hand at poker not to bowl out very quickly any effort to do so.

'Not that he ever had any late card parties in those days; he was devoting all his energy to the efficiency of his ship. He gave and attended such official and semi-official parties as custom required, but beyond that, an occasional rubber of bridge and early to bed was the rule. The ship had been in commission for well over a year and was more than holding her own in most of the Fleet's activities, before he took a few nights ashore. We were a private ship[1] by this time, and

[1] Not a flagship.

an old friend of his early submarine days (Bertie Herbert) came to stay on board for a few days. Monte Carlo was only a short distance away, which was an opportunity not to be missed. Much to my surprise the Captain arrived back on board the evening before he was expected. I went to his cabin to find out what had brought him back twenty-four hours early, only to be met with "It's all right, Commander, I'm off again at once, I'm only collecting more money." And in ten minutes off he went full of optimism and determination.

'A bathe from a boat, or from the ship, and a game of golf when a course was handy were his relaxations; to the latter he brought the same great powers of concentration as he did to everything he under-took, as I discovered to my repeated discomfiture. He would nearly always beat an opponent of his own handicap, and this I think gave rise to an idea that his handicap was a "commercial" one. It wasn't, but his attention never wandered from the game till it was over. Many a man has found to his cost that being in the happy position of "two up and three to play" on Max Horton was no justification for letting attention wander to the sunset or the scenery.

'I suppose he was a hard man and a hard taskmaster, but he was a mighty efficient one, and underneath a rather firm and forbidding appearance there was a very human and understanding nature. As far as his Second in Command was concerned he was ideal. No Com-mander could have asked for a better Captain. A lot of it, in the begin-ning, was due to the fact that he was in some respects walking on strange ground. Fate and their Lordships had put me in the position of being his best bet for the job, so to speak, and he always backed a bet well when he made up his mind to it.'

'I admit that when I was promoted, after eighteen months of "W.W." and Max Horton, I had to wipe a bead or two of perspiration from the forehead. I'd had to live on my toes all the time, which you, I'm sure, will admit was quite contrary to our old conception of a navigator's existence.

'But he was a grand man to serve, and those days were the start of a friendship between us that lasted till he died.'

Horton sought perfection, but since this ideal is beyond human attainment, a certain feeling of frustration permeated some of those he commanded between the wars.

All respected him for his knowledge, his judgment and the intuition which prompted his decisions. There was the time when the divers of the Fleet had been searching fruitlessly all day for a lost anchor. Towards evening, Horton suddenly directed a diving boat to go to a totally different spot as he was sure that the anchor lay there. They found the anchor. Pure luck?—possibly—but more likely the instinct of a seaman. Then there was the time when an aeroplane came down in the sea, the visibility was poor, and its whereabouts was nebulous. The *Resolution* was ordered to the rescue; Horton told the navigator to steer a certain course. After a while the aircraft's wing was sighted sticking out of the water about a mile ahead. They were just in time. Coincidence?—perhaps! But consider yet another instance vouched for by Duke: the *Resolution* was embarking ammunition. Half an hour after the start, Horton told Duke that the young Lieutenants supervising the hoisting of heavy projectiles were to be replaced by Lieutenant-Commanders. Duke was surprised at the order, for he felt that junior officers should be given the responsibility. However, he had no choice but to comply. Shortly afterwards a whip broke, and down came a 'fifteen-inch' projectile. Fortunately, only one man was hurt. Later, in the Captain's cabin, Duke asked him about his 'hunches' and Horton said 'Yes, I do get them. I knew some accident was going to happen, but had no idea what it was going to be. I ordered the Lieutenant-Commanders to take over in case of trouble.'

In September 1932 the King of Greece made Captain Horton a Commander of the Order of the Redeemer for rescue work carried out by the men of the *Resolution* after a serious earthquake in the Chalcidice Peninsula. For his services on this occasion he was also awarded a medal and two diplomas by the Hellenic Red Cross Society.

What with his life-saving medals, his war medals, D.S.O. and two bars, French and Russian Orders, he must have been for his age and seniority the most decorated naval officer of his time. As the sailors say 'he had a proper fruit salad on his chest,' but most of them knew that every single ribbon had been gained by outstanding skill, courage and devotion to duty.

On 17th October 1932, after two years in the *Resolution*, Horton was promoted to Rear-Admiral and flew his flag in the battleship *Barham* as Rear-Admiral, 2nd Battle Squadron, second in command of the Home Fleet.

In this, his first flag appointment, he was inclined at times to interfere with the handling of the ship and her internal affairs. With characteristic thoroughness he directed that the eyes of all

33

on board should be tested to discover the group from which the best night look-outs could be chosen. The results were unexpected and useful. In all tactical and technical matters he was eminently realistic and practical, never leaving a problem until he had probed to the bottom of it.

If some error had been made, he would send for the officer concerned and go on questioning him until there was an admission of fault. After a time they learnt that, on such occasions, it was always best to say at once 'This is where I went wrong.'

He never addressed the men unless it was absolutely necessary. However, they appreciated any commendation from him the more; when he left the ship, he said: 'I have been happy in this ship, because she is efficient, and I could never be happy in an inefficient ship.'

Horton's duties in the peace-time Home Fleet were largely administrative, affording few opportunities for him to display those characteristics of tenacity, courage and leadership which immediately came to the fore in the test of war.

After eighteen months in this appointment he was selected to command the First Cruiser Squadron in the Mediterranean, a powerful force of fast, heavily armed cruisers.

CHAPTER THREE

1935-37

MARE NOSTRUM

*Mediterranean Crisis. The bluff that was never called. Cold
War in the Mediterranean—Hot War in Spain.*

HORTON was certain that war with Germany would come
again and he had a presentiment that it would find him
where he was most wanted. So, putting two and two together, he
believed that Mussolini's designs on Abyssinia would set the world
alight and that he and his cruiser squadron would be in the
'front line.'

The League of Nations was proving to be a broken reed, and
France showed no inclination to support Great Britain against
Italian aggression. Failure to implement full sanctions on Italy
would be a clear indication to Hitler that collective security had
broken down, and with this encouragement he would undoubtedly
accelerate his preparations for the war that was to come.

On 10th September 1935, Max wrote to a friend:

'I pray that our Government's policy will not result in tragedy for
an infinitely greater number of people than the comparatively few they
are trying to save. I have real misgivings on this matter which no
specious arguments of our officials or Press can alleviate. "Those whom
the gods are about to destroy they first make mad," and that applies
as much to us as to Italy, I fear.

'To the devil with this depressing talk! I expect it is largely because
I am cooped up on board and only my own kind to talk to—one day
we shall laugh at it all, and see how much more we appreciate things
because of the trials and tribulations we have been through.'

While the politicians were vacillating, it was perfectly clear to
the Commander-in-Chief, Admiral Sir W. W. Fisher, that the

only sure way of calling Mussolini's bluff would be to close the Suez Canal and to stop oil supplies to Italy. If force had to be used, the only instrument available would be the British Mediterranean Fleet which in the early stages of the crisis was sadly short of cruisers, destroyers and submarines. Reinforcements however were being rushed to the Mediterranean from all over the world. As soon as these arrived, Horton shared the view of his Commander-in-Chief that the Fleet could overcome the Italian Navy and thus cut off their army in Abyssinia.

Malta had no air defences and was only sixty miles from the Sicilian airfields, so partly as a precaution and partly for reasons of strategy the whole Fleet was concentrated in August 1935 at Alexandria. From here ships, squadrons, and flotillas were exercised constantly at sea by day and night, bringing them to a peak of fighting efficiency probably higher than any other fleet in the world. Horton's squadron consisted of the cruisers *London* (flagship), *Shropshire, Sussex, Devonshire*, and *Ajax* later reinforced by the *Exeter* from South America, the *Berwick* from China, and the *Australia* and *Sydney* from Australia. It was a powerful force, all except *Ajax* and *Sydney* being armed with eight-inch guns, and all having a speed of over thirty knots.

On the day he arrived at Alexandria, Max was deeply grieved to learn of the death of his mother. She had been an inspiration to him all his life, and he had often sought her wise counsel. Only a few days previously, he had written 'All my love, darling, do please not be rash going out in bad weather and do change shoes and stockings after damp pavements.' To a friend he wrote: 'It was a frightful shock, but I've tried to argue it out that grief, when an old darling such as she goes the inevitable way at the age of eighty-three, is more being sorry for ourselves than anything else. All this crisis has helped to assuage things, but I have been very miserable . . . it is a dreadful blank.'

Horton set about the training of his squadron with characteristic thoroughness. Having decided that his principal task would be to destroy the Italian 'eight-inch' cruisers,[1] he designed a series of tactical exercises and laid down certain principles for the guidance of his Captains. Addressing them beforehand, he said:

[1] Large cruisers carrying eight-in. guns.

36

'A number of different situations *may* arise, but the most urgent for our consideration are those involving battle between the two forces of eight-in. cruisers.

'The general principles governing the tactics of our battle fleet now apply equally well to our eight-in. cruisers.

'It is to provide an opportunity to put these principles into practice that a series of tactical exercises will be carried out in the 1st Cruiser Squadron.

'A theoretical knowledge of the principles can and should be acquired by all officers. The confidence necessary for their successful application in the stress of battle and in the preliminaries to battle can only be attained after much practice in the comparative calm of peace-time exercises.

'In these, as in all fleet exercises at sea, tactical mistakes are made which would seem incredible to their makers if they were examining the same problem on paper in a quiet study.'

Horton then went on with the details of the tactics he intended to employ, stressing the need for simplicity which he said could only be achieved when the principles were understood by all Captains.

At a 'post mortem' following the exercises, Horton addressed his officers thus:

'I have often thought that every naval commander at the conclusion of a battle, real or simulated, must realise afterwards on analysis where he might have done better. No one but God Almighty could tactically fight a perfect battle at sea. Even Nelson, I am sure, would not have denied this fact after his great victories.

'Such being the case with the greatest and most experienced commanders, none of us should hesitate a moment or feel any loss of face in most frankly admitting, after a simulated battle, where we could have done better. Inexperienced as all of us are, to a greater or less degree, in the novel situation that confronts us, the mistakes made in these exercises were obvious—afterwards—sometimes immediately after they had been made.

'Most of the great sea and land battles have been won by doing the obvious right thing (as seen afterwards) and lost by making very obvious mistakes (as seen afterwards). It has been well said that battles are won by the side which makes the fewest mistakes.

'One knows so well from experience in the last war what a big factor that state of mind arising from tension in contact with the enemy is —how it affects every individual to a greater or less degree and in different ways. In some it leads to quickening up of action and thought,

37

in others to a corresponding slowing down. The former is not necessarily the better since it often leads to over-hasty action and mentally falling over oneself—*I tell you quite frankly that that is one of my worst failings, but I know it, and that's something*. There is always hope for one who realises his limitations and mistakes; it is a step to improvement—that is why I only worry people who will not cheerfully admit their mistakes. . . .

'Tension, produced by contact with the enemy as well as other factors, makes it imperative to simplify to the greatest possible degree all the operations for bringing the enemy to grips, and to practise these operations so that the tactics to be pursued become part of ourselves . . . in battle you cannot rely on signals. A team that knows what the leader requires from them without signals is truly fortunate.'

Horton lost no time in making his personality known to the officers and men of his squadron. He visited every ship and spoke to them from his heart. Although they knew he was a driver and a hard taskmaster, his natural manner and lack of pomposity appealed to them.

On the quarterdeck of the *Shropshire* he said to her ship's company:

'I am determined never to ask you to perform an unnecessary task. At the same time I ask you to take it on trust, in case the purpose is not clear at the time. Everything you are asked to do is solely to gain the object I am sure we have in common—fighting efficiency, raised to such a pitch that we can have real confidence when we meet an enemy that we can sink him before he sinks us—by day and by night. . . .

'. . . I therefore ask you for the utmost candour in regard to any mistakes or hitches . . . I expect you personally to investigate every hitch, material or otherwise, that occurs in your ship, whether it is specialist or otherwise. If not, I recommend you to do so. I always do, being insatiably curious. I have a knack of going to see myself if it is at all possible.

'These ships have to rely on two main features—first our eight-in. guns, secondly our speed. Our lack of other protection puts added responsibility on the engine room to work up to and maintain our trial speed when occasion demands. The other principal factor is "look-out." It is essential to see the enemy before he sees you. At night, the one who first sights is three parts of the way to winning the battle. I want you to develop "look-out"—for your lives and much else depend upon it. . . .'

The ship's companies responded with a will. Captain R. Malleson, R.N., who commanded a division of destroyers, says that in fleet exercises he always had the greatest difficulty in getting within striking distance of Horton's squadron on account of the efficiency of its look-out system.

Horton was genuinely interested in the machinery of his ships, and his technical knowledge surprised many engineer officers.

The propelling machinery of each cruiser was designed so that sections of it could continue to function if other sections had been damaged. When enemy action was expected the boilers and machinery would be connected up as four independent self-contained units, isolated from each other. In event of damage to one unit, the ship could continue to steam on the other three with only a proportionate loss of speed. In peace conditions the 'unit system' was seldom used, so practice was necessary to change over quickly from the normal cruising arrangement into 'units.'

The first time that Horton took his squadron to sea he ordered them to work up to half power with all boilers alight. Then without previous warning he made the signal 'Go into units and work up to full power.' The result was chaotic. Within a quarter of an hour several ships came to a dead stop, and most of them were blowing off steam. Max viewed the scene with relish, for he knew that it would not happen again.

Horton's ruthlessness and blunt manner alienated him from some senior officers who said he was intolerant and obstinate, and that equally good results could have been obtained by less rigorous methods. Nevertheless, by the end of the year he had brought his squadron to the standard of efficiency expected by the Commander-in-Chief. On Christmas Day 1935, Fisher wrote:

My dear Max Horton,
. . . The 1st Cruiser Squadron will inevitably be the decisive factor. I know with what pains you have been training them and with you to lead them I have no fear that if the call comes there *will* be a "fulfilment of all my hopes for the New Year."
                                        Yours ever,
                                        (Signed) W. W. FISHER.

In the light of experience in the Second World War, we can say with certainty that if the British Government had appreciated the moral strength and material efficiency of the Mediterranean

Fleet and had used it in support of decisive sanctions, Fisher's hopes would have been fulfilled. A British naval victory at that time of political testing in international affairs would probably have ensured peace for many generations to come. But the lessons of the Nile and Trafalgar had been forgotten in Whitehall, and the powerful instrument, so close at hand in Aboukir Bay, was kept in a state of suspended animation for many months.

The pale sanctions imposed on Italy when Mussolini invaded Abyssinia made it clear to the world in general and to Hitler in particular that the League of Nations was not prepared to force the issue to the point of war. In the words of Mr. Churchill:

'Mussolini's bluff succeeded and an important spectator drew far-reaching conclusions from the fact. Hitler had long resolved on war for German aggrandisement.'[1]

By midsummer the tension had relaxed, but there was to be no respite for the First Cruiser Squadron. On 21st July 1936 Horton's flagship, the *London*, was on her way from Alexandria to Malta, and all on board were looking forward to a quiet spell with friends and families whom they had not seen for ten months. At noon, when the ship was within sight of the longed-for haven, a signal came ordering her to go immediately to Barcelona to embark refugees from the Spanish Civil War.

The ship's company, dismissing from their minds all thoughts of the delights of Malta, set about transforming the flagship into a reception centre for over a thousand distressed people. Within twenty-four hours the organisation was completed. Officers and men were turned out of their quarters and every available space was prepared to meet all contingencies from childbirth to death.

On arrival, Horton was told that the Captain of the Port had been killed, but berthing arrangements would be made by the pilots, who would take their orders from 'anybody with a gun.' Without further parley, a pilot was engaged and the ship berthed at the Customs House Jetty. The *London* was the first foreign ship to arrive, and the only one to stay inside the harbour. This was a wise move, as the large bulk of the British cruiser so near the town had a sobering effect on trigger-happy Italian warships

[1] *The Second World War*, Vol. I, page 138.

who might wish to take reprisals for the murder of their nationals. She remained at the jetty for four weeks acting as a clearing centre for refugees who, after being sorted out and identified, were transferred to destroyers for passage to Marseilles. Some found their quarters so comfortable it was difficult to persuade them to leave.

Among the first to reach the ship was a party of British Communists of both sexes wearing red ties and mounted on bicycles. They were followed by a troupe of dancing girls. A photographer, looking for 'hot news,' arranged a group with the girls wearing the sailors' caps and the men embracing them lightly round the shoulders. When the photograph was published in the English Press, the sailors had some difficulty in explaining it away to anxious sweethearts and wives who believed them to be doing the work of good samaritans in the midst of unspeakable horrors.

In the first three days 900 people were assigned sleeping and eating quarters according to age, sex, and state of health. Young children were fed during the day and tucked up at night by domestic-minded sailors, who pooled their scanty pay to buy comforts and toilet requisites from the canteen.

Some of the crew turned out at 3 a.m. to help the refugees over the gangways to the destroyer ferry service. The stewards and cooks worked for nineteen hours each day, preparing food for new arrivals in addition to the people on board. The conditions in Barcelona are described in a letter from Max to a friend:

H.M.S. *London*,

BARCELONA.

23rd July 1936.

The papers will have told you we are here. Heavy work and rather thrilling. I have started the evacuation of British residents and expect to have to compete with 1,500 or so.

The town is in a complete mess-up. The Army marched against the Left Constitutional Government last Sunday, but the Government were ready and armed the workers at short notice. The Army came into the main square and were shot down in hundreds from the windows all round. A big massacre of officers took place, and the Army was completely wiped out—at least all those who didn't come over to the other side.

Now the workers (syndicalists, anarchists and all sorts including the inhabitants of the jails who have been let out) are riding about the town in commandeered cars, rifles sticking out in all directions, wild with excitement. The Government are quite unable to exercise proper control over them, and it is feared the workers may try to take over, as the Bolsheviks did in the early days in Russia. The chief danger is a shortage of food. The roads leading to the town are barricaded. I have not seen anything like the streets, real revolutionary.

I went to call on the President yesterday in a police car with two guards, rifles at the ready to shoot, sticking out of the windows. I had two motor-cyclists hooting like in American movies and all driving like hell. The President was very pleasant, but his entourage and guard—my God! They looked just like the French Revolutionaries "sans culottes." Beautiful rooms in his palace with lovely decorated ceilings and furniture—a big desk and his private guard of four of the most frightful ragamuffins I have ever seen, *sitting* around the desk with rifles and cigarettes. The President came and saw me off at the entrance to the palace; an enormous crowd cheered, somebody thrust a huge bouquet of flowers in my arms, and off went my cavalcade (back-firing, hooting, and making every conceivable noise known to the American movies) to the ship.

We are moored with stern to wharf, and the officers on the quarter-deck said my arrival was a most spectacular event. It sounded to them like an attack on the ship, but when the car doors opened and I stepped out with my huge bouquet, they thought I had got married on the quiet!

Have been to the Consulate again this morning arranging about the evacuations. The centre of the town is in good control at present, but the outskirts are in much worse plight and looting and sniping is going on all the time. Unfortunately most of the English live on the outskirts.

Am sending this letter in the first destroyer to take refugees to Marseilles.

Now something very important. I have had a letter from the Naval Secretary to say I shall be promoted to Vice-Admiral on 19th August, and also that he had heard it would suit me to be relieved early. I am replying asking to be relieved end of October or first week in November—the point I didn't explain to you in my last letter but one was the promotion. It makes a lot of difference to be promoted at sea because to fly one's flag as a Vice-Admiral makes one eligible for a full Admiral's pension, and without having done so, one is not eligible to be promoted to a full Admiral.

A fortnight later he wrote again:

MARE NOSTRUM

H.M.S. *London*,

BARCELONA.

7th August 1936.

We stay here till 22nd or 23rd and then get relieved by another cruiser and another Admiral. After that, Malta. By then we shall have done five and a half weeks without setting foot ashore. A bit grim but the sailors are really wonderful, for they realise the real good they are doing for so many unfortunate people. We have had between 50 and 180 men, women, children and babies on board continually up till now—changing them every day, of course, as the destroyers take them away to Marseilles next morning.

As to the next job, I have no idea whatever and probably shan't have when I have been to the Admiralty. The only possible jobs I can see are Controller (and it's quite likely Henderson may keep it another year, he will have done three years in April), the other one is Reserve Fleet going in July next—there are no others—but *I don't care*. I have about ? saved, and with half pay can live reasonably for a couple of years—the end of the world may have come before then—and if it hasn't they'll probably be in a jam and *will send for me whatever has been arranged previously*. Anyway, I want a rest and a change from ship life.

C.in-C. [Admiral Sir Dudley Pound][1] in *Queen Elizabeth* was here for twenty-four hours and left yesterday for Gib. He has been very good in giving me a completely free hand.

Situation at present regarding British in Spain is that practically all have been evacuated who want to go. A nucleus remain behind—200 here, 200 in Madrid, 80 in Valencia, 20 in Alicante, who have either big business interests or have lived in Spain so long that they prefer to stay, rather than be sent home with no money and be on the dole a week after arrival.

I had a destroyer in last night when the Government's expedition arrived on the coast. Have only had wireless messages yet. Our one destroyer (*Douglas*) had just taken off some fifteen refugees from San Antonio and was going round to Iriza to pick up any others when they made this expedition. Two Flotilla leaders and a transport (all Spanish); the Spaniards sent a boat ashore with white flag which was fired on from the beach (rebels) then the Flotilla leaders opened fire with their guns. *Douglas* says she asked them to postpone the bombardment after a few minutes in order to allow her to take off refugees. This proposal was agreed to—"Bombardment postponed for five hours"—haven't heard any more yet—but this move to reduce Iriza should, I hope, lead to willingness on the part of foreign nationals to leave.

[1] Admiral Pound had recently relieved Admiral Fisher as Commander-in-Chief Mediterranean.

43

So far evacuations have gone without a hitch, but those that will not stir are living on a volcano—it makes me so mad. We get our papers from home in two days and the terrible stories in them about Spain are not much exaggerated.

Where's Ward Price? Surely he ought to be somewhere about in this trouble. The *Daily Mail* man here has sent a very alarmist report to *Daily Mail* today, saying Italians and Germans intend to bombard or take drastic steps here next Monday or Tuesday—but I don't believe it. Certainly some Germans and Italians have been killed, but any drastic interference might well result disastrously to all the other foreign nationals that remain. Mussolini has ordered every single Italian to leave and he is being obeyed of course. Germans are leaving too, but they won't all be cleared for some days yet.

Bar the lack of exercise which affects us all, it has been a most interesting experience and things have gone pretty well.

On 19th August 1936 Horton was promoted to Vice-Admiral, and three days later the *London* was relieved at Barcelona by a sister ship, the *Shropshire*. The flagship spent three weeks at Malta, where Horton and the ship's company after ten months of continuous strain enjoyed a well-earned rest. During his stay there, he was perturbed by false reports in the English Press alleging that he had prevented the Italian Admiral from bombarding Barcelona. The *London* returned to Barcelona for another spell of duty and shortly before leaving Malta, Max wrote:

H.M.S. *London,*
MALTA.
13*th September* 1936.

We are off for Barcelona tomorrow but it is only six weeks now until we get home, thank God!

What nonsense that Spaniard talked about our sympathies and reactions at Barcelona. Just to show you how absurd his statements were—the six Italians have been killed *since* I left Barcelona. So any bombardment by the Italian Admiral when I was in Barcelona could obviously have no reference to these Italians who have been killed *since.*

Secondly, to say we only looked after our own nationals is equally ridiculous. We evacuated over 4,000 refugees from the east coast of Spain alone, of whom less than half were British. The last trip of our hospital ship *Maine* took thirty-nine different nationalities. We took all those nationals whose Governments had not made any arrangements themselves, and our boast was that not one single refugee had ever been turned away from the ship whatever his or her nationality was.

44

Thirdly, imagine bombarding Barcelona at all! It contains precisely 1,000,000 inhabitants, of whom about 200,000 at most are really "Red." Since shooting into a town must always be more or less blind —imagine any responsible person destroying a town and 1,000,000 men, women, and children indiscriminately! As the Spaniard was in the town himself at the time, he would have been killed too.

We also took all those Spanish refugees who couldn't get a visa and pass the Government barrier—we also did many other things too to help, but that I cannot write about. He must be a nice sort of chap to take refuge in England, and then hand out such vile and false charges against us.

One other point about bombardment. At that time living in Barcelona were 600 British, 4,000 German, 3,000 Italian, 10,000 French and about 5,000 to 6,000 other foreigners. The first shot from a warship would have been the signal for a massacre of all foreigners, especially the Italians and Germans who are particularly detested (very naturally) by the "Reds" as being Fascists or Nazi. So you see how impossible and utterly untrue the whole story was and is. The Italian Admiral and I were always in complete accord, and I hope to remain so with him.

I played tennis with the *Enchantress*'s party yesterday. They have sailed this morning for England going all the way back by sea (such a little ship too). I liked the new First Lord[1] very much, and had an interesting talk with him at dinner one night, also with H.M. King Edward VIII. My lunch party for him was a success I think. My cook surpassed himself and they all talked about the food afterwards.

H.M.'s visit to Constantinople was a huge success, I hear from one of the destroyer Captains escorting him. Mustapha Kemal went with the King for a drive in an open carriage through the crowded streets, driving slowly, and this impressed the crowd more than anything else, for Mustapha has never once done so before in all the years he has been dictator. (He always goes in an armoured car with armed outriders.) The Turkish people were most demonstrative, and it is thought that the visit will have excellent reactions. The whole of the Dardanelles for miles was manned by cheering troops and everything possible was done to convey their enthusiasm for him. A good show. We want some allies in the Eastern Mediterranean.

International tension did not disturb the excellent relations which existed between the British and foreign warships in Spanish waters. The Captain of the *London* (the late Captain F. H. Goolden) wrote in his official report:

[1] Sir Samuel Hoare, First Lord, was visiting the Mediterranean Fleet in H.M.S. *Enchantress*, the Admiralty Yacht.

'It has been interesting to note that whereas all the foreign navies have been on most friendly terms with our own, they are not equally so with each other. Ill-concealed coolness on at least one occasion was evident between German and Italian officers in the wardroom. The former quite openly asked how the British could be so friendly with the Italians "after Alexandria." In this connection, when Italian officers first met the British off the Spanish coast it was painfully obvious that they were extremely nervous as to the type of reception they would be accorded, and their gratification on perceiving that the British were fully prepared to be friendly was evident.'

And at the end of the year Max received this letter from the German Admiral Carls:

COMMANDER-IN-CHIEF'S OFFICE,
KIEL.
30th December 1936.

Very esteemed Admiral,

I cannot allow the New Year to go by without expressing my good wishes to you. It has always been a joy and honour to meet Your Excellency when occasion offered during our common sojourn in Spanish waters. Not less have I welcomed how warm feelings of comradely collaboration brought the officers of our respective fleets into ever closer amity.

That this may also be the case in coming and later years is a wish that I shall continue to cherish in my present position.

In the hope that the path may unite for us again in coming and later years, I am, with sincere greetings,

Yours Excellency's
Very devoted,
(Signed) CARLS.
Rear-Admiral.

Shoals of letters from refugees and public bodies of many nationalities were received by Horton and his officers. The following letter to the *Daily Telegraph* from Major-General Lord Ruthven gives a good idea of the deep feelings of gratitude and admiration shared by all who enjoyed the hospitality of the Royal Navy:

Sir,

I wonder if the public realise the wonderful work that the British Navy has been doing during the last few weeks on the coasts of Spain.

Most of us have read of the rescue of British subjects by H.M. Ships, but few, I believe, realise what these rescues really imply.

An extract from a letter I have just received from my daughter who, with her husband, was resident in Barcelona, and who, in the course of the recent troubles, was forced to take refuge on board H.M.S. *London*, may give some idea of the whole-hearted way in which the British Navy goes about its work. My daughter's gratitude to the officers and crew of H.M.S. *London*, and afterwards of H.M.S. *Douglas* to which they were transferred, is evident from her letter, but I should like to add the heartfelt thanks of myself and my wife for all their kindness to those in distress. She writes:

> You never knew such kindness and hospitality as we received. I don't think anyone belonging to the ship had anywhere to sleep, eat or sit and we had everything.

> There were sixty-two of us on board, including a twelve days' old baby, which was looked after by a sailor. I do think publicity should be given to the amazing care, kindness, and unselfishness of the Navy in the way they treated us. From the Admiral down to the sailors who carried our bags on board and the stewards who cooked coffee and made sandwiches all night, everybody slaved for us all, and we must have made an infinity of work and trouble for them all.

> I have never in my life received more kind hospitality with thought and organisation behind it. I would so very much like them to get a little public appreciation from at least one unspeakably grateful recipient of everything they gave, which was not only the physical safety and care but the amazing thought and kindness behind it all. I can't put it into words, and I don't think I will ever forget it.

> It was so surprising, somehow, I had expected great efficiency in getting us off, but I thought there might be a certain amount of red tape; but they were all like very old and very welcoming friends from the moment we set foot on board. And how typical it was that the British ships were tied up alongside with the mob on the quay, the Italian cruiser had to lie outside, quite far away for fear of incidents.

Yours faithfully,

BEMBRIDGE,   · RUTHVEN.
ISLE OF WIGHT.
5th *August* 1936.

On 14th October 1936 the *London* left Barcelona for home and a few days later Horton received this letter from his Commander-in-Chief.

MAX HORTON AND THE WESTERN APPROACHES

COMMANDER-IN-CHIEF,
MEDITERRANEAN STATION.

27th October 1936.

My dear Horton,

I hate your disappearing without an opportunity of seeing you and thanking you for all you have done, but with this Spanish business it was inevitable.

Anyway you will go home after having commanded the finest Cruiser Squadron that any British Flag Officer has commanded and you brought them to the highest pitch of fighting efficiency.

I wish this Spanish business would come to an end as our ships have had quite long enough on the coast of Spain, and what with winter weather in the Gulf of Lyons and having to continually shift about to evade bombardment, service on the coast of Spain must be getting monotonous as even the excitement of refugees has almost ceased to exist. . . .

I hope you will find that the Admiralty have another job ready for you.

The best of good luck and my deep gratitude for your most loyal co-operation.

Yours ever,

(Signed) DUDLEY POUND.

Shortly before arrival at Portsmouth, Horton inspected the ship's company of the flagship and afterwards sent them a message notable for its simplicity and appeal to self-respect:

'I was very pleased with the result of my walk round this morning. The steadiness of all ranks was particularly noticeable and the general smartness excellent. There were one or two details of dress which require adjustment before we enter Portsmouth. All cap ribbons and cap badges should be practically new for that great day, similarly with ties. The upper deck was very good. I did not fail to notice the many details which mark the difference between ordinary cleanliness and true class.'

Horton was succeeded in command of the First Cruiser Squadron by Rear-Admiral Kennedy Purvis on 1st November 1936, and after foreign service leave spent about six months on half pay, visiting the capitals of Europe and Mussolini's African Empire. He was keenly interested in foreign affairs and characteristically sought the company of diplomats, politicians and military authorities to acquaint himself with their attitude towards Axis aggression and the quality of their armed forces.

48

He travelled by car, wherever he could, along the North African coast, noting the details of harbours and roads. He went to Pantellaria and to Sicily not only for the wonders of Agrigento and Segesta, but mainly to have a look at beaches where troops might be landed. While investigating one of these from a motor boat he narrowly escaped arrest by the Italian Army who were engaged in manœuvres under the eye of Mussolini himself.

Italy held for him another, perhaps at first sight incompatible, interest. He had long been fascinated by the history and ideals of St. Francis of Assisi; he read all he could about him; followed his footsteps from Assisi to Alverna; stayed in Franciscan friaries for weeks at a time—and often when visiting Venice, preferred to live in a little friary on a lagoon, San Francesco Del Deserto, than to stay in an hotel. He went, too (more than once), to Lourdes, and to Lisieux, where St. Thérèse—a young Carmelite—had her convent (1858–1885), not to be confused with the great St. Teresa of Avila (1515–1582). He developed a great affection for this young saint, which may help to explain several lighthearted allusions to her in his letters; 'having a word with St. Thérèse before whose statue I lit a candle.' On his first pilgrimage to Lisieux he was given a crystal plaque of St. Thérèse which he kept with him till he died. The discipline and colour of the Roman Catholic church appealed to him, but he never joined it. Those who may be surprised at what has been written about Horton's private religious life will not be surprised that he *did* keep it private.

He was not selected for the post of Controller,[1] which on account of his technical knowledge and 'drive' he would have filled admirably, especially at a time when the Navy was expanding to meet the German threat. He was in no way disappointed, however, when at midsummer 1937 he was given command of the Reserve Fleet. He was quite certain that war would come soon. Even if the appointment were to be his 'swan song,' the responsibility of bringing this heterogeneous collection of big and little ships to a state of readiness for war appealed to him strongly. To his mind it was a task of the highest importance and he was determined to leave no stone unturned in completing it. His

[1] The Third Sea Lord and Controller of the Navy is responsible for the development and efficiency of material, including research and new weapons.

secretary, Edgar Haslehurst,[1] says: 'People were apt to regard the Reserve Fleet as a "dump" for "passed overs" and it was considered to be a backwater. It was the first appointment I had ever had that looked like a "quiet number"—no such luck; I got Sir Max, two mobilisations, and a war!'

[1] Later Captain (S) E. Haslehurst, C.B.E., R.N., of whom Horton had the highest opinion.

CHAPTER FOUR

1937-39

WIDE SEAS AND THIN AIR

The Reserve Fleet goes to war. The Northern Patrol.

THE Reserve Fleet consisted of about 140 ships of all shapes and sizes laid up in the Royal Dockyards and ports around the coast. They were manned by nucleus crews and maintenance parties, according to their age and degree of readiness. Horton was not satisfied with the general state of efficiency and, ever mindful of the submarine danger, made proposals for the destroyers in particular to be brought forward to a seagoing condition. Haslehurst says:

'Sir Max certainly put a new spirit into the Reserve Fleet by making people feel that they were doing a worth-while job which was likely to come to fruition very soon. He insisted that everything should be looked at from the point of view of "What would happen to this on mobilisation?"

'One of his earlier measures was to carry out a mobilisation exercise on paper, but the facilities for victualling, kitting up and drafting the men, and the transport and labour for delivering the stores had to be actually there. This exercise proved to be most useful in showing up deficiencies in organisation, many of which were corrected before the Munich mobilisation in 1938. In addition to the measures taken within the Reserve Fleet, Sir Max kept up a constant pressure on the Admiralty to try to get made in advance those arrangements which he foresaw would be required.'

The Munich crisis of 1938 provided the necessary spur, and by midsummer 1939 the whole fleet with a few exceptions was ready to sail as soon as the ship's companies could be brought to full strength.

51

A few weeks after Munich, Horton was puzzled by a letter from the Naval Secretary at the Admiralty offering him the post of First Naval Member of the Australian Navy Board. The appointment was to take effect in October 1939, and there was a dark hint that 'the First Sea Lord does not see any other suitable appointment for you after being relieved as Vice-Admiral commanding the Reserve Fleet.'

In his reply dated 14th November 1938, Horton asks for more information about rates of pay and pension in event of his retirement, then goes on:

I hope that answers to my questions will not trouble you too much. Personal decisions of the nature you require are doubly difficult at the present time, for all forecasts of what is likely to happen during the next three years lead me to suppose that the probability of war in Europe, in which this country would be involved, is not much better than an even chance.

It is only natural that in the event of such a war I should hope to be more usefully employed than in an office so remote from the struggle as Australia. My unusually wide experience in important appointments of the main fleets over the last eight years would have little chance of being actively useful in such circumstances.

Apart from these considerations I would have no objection to going to Australia. I like and admire many of the Australians I have met, and experience of the Royal Australian Navy in the 1st Cruiser Squadron at Alexandria, when *Australia* and *Sydney* were under my command, was definitely happy.

Yours very sincerely,

MAX HORTON.

He was awarded the K.C.B. in the New Year Honours, and was even more perplexed when he received this letter dated 3rd January 1939 from the First Sea Lord:

Dear Max Horton,

I feel I should write you a line to congratulate you on your K.C.B., which I know very well you have thoroughly earned and never more than in your present appointment in the Reserve Fleet.

Come and see me some time when you are in London and we will have a talk about things.

My best wishes for 1939.

Yours ever,

(Signed) ROGER BACKHOUSE.

It would appear that their Lordships, while appreciating the work that Horton had done for the Reserve Fleet, had not foreseen how valuable his services were likely to be in the vital area of Home Waters if war came. Apart from his knowledge of the Mediterranean, it seems that they had also overlooked his great experience of submarine warfare. Much as he admired the high state of efficiency of the Royal Australian Navy, and would have liked to control it, he was certain that war would come. So, knowing where he would be 'most wanted,' he backed his hunch in a letter to the Admiralty dated 22nd January 1939:

'After further reflection I do not wish to be considered for the Australian appointment for the reasons given in my original letter to you.
'The general situation now developing confirms the views expressed therein.'

Horton was most anxious that the arrangements he had made for bringing the ships to a state of readiness for war should be put to the test. He urged that they should be manned, exercised and sent to their stations before the fateful day. He was encouraged and highly delighted therefore when the Admiralty announced that H.M. King George VI would inspect the Reserve Fleet at Weymouth on 9th August 1939. Over 12,000 reservists were called up, and in the course of a week battleships, cruisers, destroyers and submarines, 133 ships in all, were fully commissioned, stored and assembled in Weymouth Bay. Max wrote: 'Three weeks' normal work done in a week and everyone cheerful.' Fifty-four of these ships, including the battleship *Iron Duke* and the destroyer *Warwick* of Zeebrugge fame, were over twenty years old; many of the officers and men were veterans of the First World War.

By the King's wish, his visit was to be more in the nature of an inspection than a review. Accordingly the ceremonial drill of lining the rails was dispensed with: instead the crews were massed informally and cheered spontaneously. Before leaving for Balmoral His Majesty signalled to Admiral Horton:

'Please convey to all ranks and ratings what a great pleasure it has been to me to inspect the Reserve Fleet under your command.

'The bringing forward for sea service of so many ships in a few days proves how smoothly the organisation works.

'The efficiency and smartness obtained in such a short time after commissioning can only have been achieved by the enthusiasm and wholehearted co-operation of all hands, and it leaves no doubt in my mind that the Fleet will quickly reach a high standard of fighting efficiency.

'I realise what sacrifices are being made by many of the retired officers, pensioners and reservists in leaving their work and their homes to make possible this quick and important addition to our naval strength.

'To all in the Reserve Fleet I send my hearty congratulations and good wishes.'

The Vice-Admiral replied:

'Vice-Admiral Commanding the Reserve Fleet with humble duty has the honour to thank your Majesty on behalf of all under his command for your Majesty's gracious message.

'All officers and men are deeply sensible of the honour which your Majesty has done them by journeying especially from Scotland to inspect the Reserve Fleet, and your Majesty's visit will encourage them to give of their best to the task of bringing their ships to a high state of fighting efficiency.'

Afterwards Horton, flying his flag in the cruiser *Effingham*, led the fleet to sea for exercises, and by the end of the month when the ships had reached a reasonable standard of efficiency they were dispersed to their war stations. A remarkable achievement; considering that the official war plan required the ships of the Reserve Fleet to be ready on Z+30 days.

On 27th August 1939 Max wrote from Scapa Flow to a friend:

'I saw Charles Forbes [the Commander-in-Chief Home Fleet] on arrival, as cheerful and pleasant as ever. Thank goodness we have such a cool and level-headed fellow in charge. We, like you, await the result of Neville Henderson's[1] visit to Hitler. Have just listened to the 6 p.m. news. I have practically given up any idea of the possibility of peace and merely await the signal for war.

'This foggy weather is very advantageous for the other side—gives them such excellent opportunities to get any raiders or warships out of the North Sea. It will take some time to round them up—I am sure they won't let themselves be tied up in the North Sea this time.

'One cannot deny that the Russian Alliance—for that I think it actually is with Germany, is a tremendous coup for Hitler for the moment. I expect the offer made to Russia was three parts of Poland

[1] Sir Neville Henderson, British Ambassador.

(what they had before the last war) and possibly the Baltic States. I cannot believe that such an unholy alliance can last, or that we can make any impression on it in a year or more whilst they are solid. . . .

'What bothers me is that our blockade will not be so effective with Russia supplying all Germany's raw material requirements.'

At the start of the war Horton became Vice-Admiral Northern Patrol, entrusted with the task of intercepting merchant ships of all descriptions between Iceland and Scotland, thus enforcing a distant blockade of Germany. Pending the arrival of armed merchant cruisers and armed trawlers, hastily fitting out for war service, he had available only eight old light cruisers to cover a patrol area 435 miles long.

These speedy and well-armed little ships had been designed for fleet work in the narrow waters of the North Sea in the First World War. They were quite unsuited for continuous patrol in the gale-swept seas of the Denmark Strait, Iceland and the Faeroes. Their fuel endurance was short, and having very low freeboard they suffered much damage from heavy seas when moving at speed. However, they held their patrol lines manfully, and would sometimes return to refuel looking more like wrecks than ships.

On 4th September 1939 Max wrote from the *Effingham* at Kirkwall:

'I went to see a couple of my ships today just in. They looked very weather-worn. We have all been at sea for some ten days or so before the war started, and not a let-up for a lick and clean.'

Bone fide neutral ships, when intercepted by a cruiser, could usually be diverted to Kirkwall or Lerwick for examination. But those suspected of carrying contraband had to be either escorted there or boarded in mid-ocean. All enemy merchant ships had to be boarded to prevent scuttling, and an armed guard or prize crew placed on board to take the ship to a British port. Horton goes on in his letter:

'The first booty of my party came in today with a very young Sub. absolutely overwhelmed with joy and pride at having got her safely in. After all, it was a big responsibility for him to take charge of a big ship with over 10,000 tons of oil and a foreign crew, and command them to do this and that with his armed guard, and then leave her safely anchored where ordered!'

And two days later he wrote this prophetic letter from the *Effingham* at sea:

'Although without sight of an enemy these days, the earlier ones were full of incidents—everything has gone quite well and I feel very well too. Isn't this war, only three days old, taking an odd course? My first reactions are that Hitler is merely stalling against us and the French, waiting until he has overrun Poland to offer terms of peace, *or* the full force of his mailed fist as an alternative.

'Of course he will probably offer peace for twenty-five years and disarmament and Lord knows what besides. I wonder if this surmise is the thought of others too? In reality it would only mean an armed peace, and so there doesn't seem any use to accept such an offer. Nevertheless, I feel if we both go all out, there will be little Western civilisation left at the end of it.

'I have the medal of St. Thérèse from Lisieux in my pocket now and she never leaves me.'

Horton soon found that it was impracticable for him to co-ordinate the work of his widely spread cruisers from his flagship at sea. In addition to the reasons given in the following letter he wished to be in close touch with the Admiralty (for information) and with Coastal Command of the Royal Air Force (for co-operation). At midnight on 8th September he wrote from an hotel at Kirkwall in the Orkneys where he had established headquarters :

'I have decided to move out of the flagship to this my shore base as soon as possible, since all the ships are being continually ordered in every direction (my flagship included) and it is impossible to do my proper duty in a ship at sea, with wireless silence naturally always imposed.

'Well, it has been a hectic day. It took three drifter loads to land the staff and all the material—a full day's work, for the pier is eight miles sea trip from my ship. I didn't start till 9.45 p.m. to come ashore myself and have only just arrived, soaked to the skin. We lost our way in the Flow—pitch dark, no lights, and my B.F. of a coxswain had forgotten the chart; pouring with rain too, the compass went in circles. However, I have just had a hot bath and a large whisky and soda and am sitting down in my office.

'I feel miserable at leaving the ship. They all came out in the pouring wet to cheer me away—but to come ashore when they are just off on another long patrol isn't very nice. Of course, I am no use aboard a single ship working on its own, but still—!

'All the fun has gone out of war anyway. I don't feel anyone is keen on it. Of course, everyone will do their damnedest as cheerfully as may be, but somehow this doesn't feel like a war.

'My business is the dullest of the lot—blockade, the sure weapon after ages and ages, but stopping neutrals and arguing about contraband is not the sort of job I like, although I have only had a few days of it.

'Am off to bed now. Last night, staring into the night for an enemy that is never there. Tonight in a house that cannot be torpedoed anyway, whatever the other dangers are. The fun and romance has gone out of war, but perhaps that's because I am twenty-five years older.'

On the following day he wrote again, giving himself a pat on the back for having the Reserve Fleet destroyers ready in time. He needed them badly himself, but for obvious reasons they had all gone elsewhere. He was to need them much more three years later when the great test came in the Western Approaches:

'I have settled in quite comfortably here and my radio is playing soft music behind me. I feel a scoundrel being so comfortable, and sending my ships to sea in a treadmill job, which, although all-important, is just about as dull and tedious an affair as can be imagined. They work very much alone and away from all little craft that could come and help them if they cop one—so at the back of their minds is a bit of a dread of the submarines. Nobody minds sudden death particularly, but an *Athenia*[1] affair with nobody to help is unpleasant.

'I shall do whatever is possible to make things better in the way of assistance, but everybody is yelling for something, especially destroyers, of course, despite the forty the Reserve Fleet produced *ready* before "the day". . . .

'Of course every job has its anxieties, and not being the most patient of people I don't find waiting for information and waiting to get messages through and waiting for the weather to clear conducive to evenness of temper.

'I get about a bit in my barge which gives me plenty of fresh air, and it's terribly interesting in some respects—but it isn't like the last war when one had a job to do in enemy waters and one was the "attacker," always so much pleasanter a job—and then one returned to harbour where there was a chance of seeing one's friends.'

---

[1] The liner *Athenia* was torpedoed and sunk by a U-boat without warning on 3rd September 1939.

The Home Fleet came into Scapa Flow, and Horton's depression was dispelled when the Commander-in-Chief asked him to meet Mr. Churchill at dinner in the *Nelson*:

17th September 1939.

'I had a very pleasant evening last night, dined with Charles Forbes and Winston Churchill who was up here for a short while.

'The latter impressed me very much and was most approachable and charming—we all had a devil of a cag [argument] about things and Winston was most interesting, of course. Now this morning comes the news (officially) that Russia is attacking Poland—what a blow for poor Poland. It may be, of course, that the Russians are merely making sure of their share before the Germans overrun the whole country—what will happen when the Huns and Ruskies meet? I am sure that Russia is simply out for world Communism and is making friends with Germany temporarily to down us, who are the cornerstone of democracy and the most real and important obstacle to world-wide Communism.'

He foretells the future course of the war with considerable accuracy:

'As ever, with all our wars, we are going to have a hell of a stiff time to face and overcome. This is indeed the supreme and greatest task this country has been faced with for 134 years; I am sure of that. Is it indeed wisest to fight it all out now, or give time for Russia and Germany to fall out over the spoils in Poland and perhaps Rumania, before gathering all our forces for the real war that must be fought eventually to a finish? Unless the Hitler regime dies another way.

'The kaleidoscope is ever changing and one never knows what will happen, but I reckon I am here unless big changes occur and things get a good deal worse than they are at present; I do not think the time has come for that yet. . . .

'Am really very busy, signals and movements every moment of the day it seems—however, I had an hour's walk this afternoon up on the golf course, with one club and a few balls. I don't manage to get out oftener than once every few days. However, things are quite comfortable, and if one only lives for the day and does not let one's imagination look forward, relatively pleasant.'

And again:

23rd September 1939.

'I suppose everyone must be asking themselves why the course of the war is taking so curious a shape. I quite understand why we remain more or less fixed to our lines in France, but if both sides remain on the defensive on land and we gradually throttle the Hun on the sea, then the active war must almost inevitably become a bombing affair with consequences I hate to contemplate to both sides.

'Almost anything seems preferable to that, as Russia would quite likely be the only real winner.'

And in another letter:

25th September 1939.
'If it comes to a fight to the last gasp, I honestly fear that Russia will be the only winner. What clever tactics Stalin has pursued—his object is to let Germany and ourselves exhaust each other then we shall all go Communist or anarchist and maybe Stalin has ground to think so.'

The pressure exerted by the Northern Patrol supported by the Home Fleet was having its effect on the enemy.

'The young Sub-Lieutenant I wrote about walked in again yesterday, having brought in another ship with 14,000 tons of good petroleum which I expect we shall use and not the Hun.'

German shipping had been brought to a standstill and the Prime Minister announced that 'by the end of September 300,000 tons of goods destined for Germany had been seized in prize against a loss to ourselves of 140,000 tons by enemy action at sea. . . . German ships totalling nearly 750,000 tons were immobilised in foreign ports.'

'You will have read what the Prime Minister said about the capture of German ships—we were rather pleased at the Northern Patrol's successes. The Germans have orders to scuttle themselves if caught, and it is a race to try and prevent it. The best deterrent is very bad weather, as you can imagine.'

About a dozen armed merchant cruisers had now reinforced the hard-worked cruisers on the Northern Patrol. They were large liners armed with six-inch guns. They had a good turn of speed and could keep the sea in any weather. Many of them were ill-equipped for war and some of the officers and men were rather bewildered at finding themselves part of a naval squadron. Horton boarded each ship on arrival, taking with him a team of experts (Gunnery, Engineering, Supply, etc.) who helped the ship's officers to understand the strange ways of the Royal Navy.

In the last war the armed merchant cruisers had proved themselves in ship-to-ship combat more than a match for German raiders of similar type, but they could not stand up to a cruiser and were particularly vulnerable to submarine and air attack. Horton was anxious about them, and had asked repeatedly for more long-distance reconnaissance aircraft to supplement his tenuous patrol lines. He was also concerned about the frequent visits of enemy aircraft to Kirkwall and their immunity from interference. On 22nd November he signalled to the Commander-in-Chief and the Admiralty:

'This morning, 22nd November, an enemy aircraft circled the anchorage at about 3,000 feet for some time, disregarding a few shots from the Bofors gun at Hatston airfield. The absence of any air activity on our part with an air station in full view of the anchorage must counteract our propaganda as to the numbers of British fighters. If importance is attached to neutral opinion, or to information reaching Germany, it is unfortunate that this state of affairs should exist at a base where a large number of neutral observers is always present. In view of increasing recklessness of German action against neutral ships the masters of those compulsorily concentrated in this unprotected harbour are somewhat apprehensive. The lack of any indication that protection would be afforded in event of air attack must adversely affect any intention to call voluntarily on subsequent voyage.

'It is also natural that some misgivings should be felt by local inhabitants. Anonymous letter received this evening addressed to Admiral in Charge, Kirkwall, runs as follows: "PLEASE, PLEASE give us some protection. If not we will have to appeal to the heads of the Government. We want to be proud of our little island. At present it is, thanks to you, a disgrace. It will be interesting to know what Mr. Churchill would say. Do you hold the lives of hundreds of people in your hands and never lift a finger to protect them? Where are our fighter aircraft? From a defenceless citizen." '

On the next day the armed merchant cruiser *Rawalpindi*, Captain E. C. Kennedy, R.N., on patrol between Iceland and the Faeroes sighted the German battle cruiser *Scharnhorst* closing rapidly. Kennedy, having informed the Commander-in-Chief and all authorities concerned, accepted battle. His ship was unprotected, and she had only four six-inch guns which she could bring to bear against her heavily armed antagonist. The result was therefore a foregone conclusion. Nevertheless the *Rawalpindi* fought on until all her gun crews had been killed and their guns put out of action. Ablaze fore and aft, she sank after dark with the loss of her Captain and 270 of the crew.

On receiving the *Rawalpindi's* report of the enemy, Admiral Forbes took the Home Fleet to sea but the *Scharnhorst*, knowing that her position had been disclosed, retired at full speed to Germany in company with the *Gneisenau*. An adequate disposition of Coastal Command aircraft, had they been available, might have located the enemy in time to save the *Rawalpindi* and also would have assisted the Commander-in-Chief to bring the German ships to action. On 24th November, Max wrote:

'There is absence of news for many hours, but it doesn't decrease my anxiety for a big one of mine who met a bigger one of the enemy yesterday evening.

'I have lots of people looking and searching, of course, but it's blowing a northerly gale and it took place hundreds of miles from here. I fear there is not much chance for them. The enemy is having most of the luck it seems for the time being.'

Two days later he wrote:

'. . . then of course that very unfortunate loss of *Rawalpindi*, one of my very best armed merchant cruisers.

'Kennedy, the Captain, the proper old-type naval officer—aged about 61 but fit and hardy and full of ginger. He got a German merchant ship first time out and did a battle practice at it, after removing the crew, and then he got another! I saw him at Glasgow just before he started on this last trip.

'There are other reactions to *Rawalpindi* [air reconnaissance] which I cannot talk about yet. I don't expect to be able to leave this place for some weeks, although one never knows, and something might happen any minute.'

The work of the Northern Patrol went on relentlessly, causing a steady stream of neutral merchant ships to come to Lerwick and Kirkwall for examination.

One day in late November, while a captured German merchant ship was being brought in by Lt.-Commander Maloney with a British prize crew, a U-boat appeared on the surface. Maloney hoisted the British flag over the German ensign and tried to ram, but missed her narrowly. The infuriated Germans in the U-boat immediately opened fire on their own ship, killing four of their fellow countrymen and setting her alight. As darkness fell the blaze attracted Horton's armed trawlers to the scene. The U-boat made off, leaving the German survivors and the prize crew to be picked up by the British ships. Horton wrote:

'I had the Lt.-Commander in charge of the prize crew to dinner with Ward Price as he had such a good story to tell, but despite my champagne, or because of it, the young officer failed to make anything of a rather wonderful yarn. . . .

'. . . One of my trawlers did a fine bit of rescue work on Saturday in the middle of the gale far out at sea, taking off eight Swedes from a torpedoed empty Swedish oiler that had been sunk without warning in the dark. The Swede *Gustav Reuter* hadn't come from England and was on her way to America.

'I cannot understand why the Huns are doing such brutal and senseless things against neutrals, except to terrify them.

'I am sure it isn't generally realised what our Northern Patrol forces have to stick—they bear up and *say* that they are happy and cheerful, but it wants a bit of saying and a damned fine spirit throughout.

'. . . St. Thérèse sits over my looking glass and looks benignant... I'll never forget those few moments in the Cathedral, never, never, never.'

[When the Reserve Fleet was at Portland, Max, believing war to be imminent, hastened to London for a few hours to settle his affairs. He knelt in prayer for a little while at Westminster Cathedral before returning to his ship.]

Although the time spent at sea by the small cruisers between refuelling was comparatively short, the hardships endured by their crews in the winter gales were as great as in the old days of close blockade. The wooden walls of Nelson and Cornwallis could keep reasonably dry inboard in conditions where Horton's cruisers with their low freeboards would be washed down by green seas. In spite of the care and attention that Horton had paid to watertightness when he commanded the Reserve Fleet, the material could not be expected to stand up to the strain of twenty-five years' service and two world wars. Consequently, in bad weather it was often impossible for the men to dry their clothes or get a hot meal.

Although the spirit of the men was willing, the strain on the material was causing anxiety. In an official letter to the Commander-in-Chief dated 5th December 1939, forwarding reports

from commanding officers on their experiences in heavy gales'
Horton said:

'These reports speak for themselves. . . .

'The morale of the officers and men remains excellent and the Engine
Room efficiency of all ships is still very high, but it is quite evident that
the damage which they are sustaining to their hulls and equipment is
assuming serious proportions. In effect they cannot now be considered
to be fully efficient fighting units, and they would be at a serious dis-
advantage against ships of their own class.

'The D class cruisers have definitely proved themselves to be better
seaboats than the C class, and I am of the opinion that after a refit
of, say, fourteen days the D class should be able to render useful
service on the Northern Patrol provided that they are not driven too
hard in heavy weather and are given reasonable time in harbour to
make good defects—chiefly upper deck defects affecting fighting
efficiency—resulting from being continually washed down.

'The C class, on the other hand, are no longer suitable for this
arduous work. If they are taken in hand for repair now they will only
suffer similar damage next time they meet heavy weather, and the
money and time spent on their refits will be largely wasted. Even in
their present state they can continue for a short time to do Contraband Control work, but it must be recognised that their fighting
efficiency is only about 50% of normal—as a maximum.'

The D class (*Diomede, Delhi, Dragon* and *Dunedin*) were
slightly larger and more seaworthy than the C class (*Colombo,
Cardiff, Ceres, Calypso* and *Caledon*) so while proposing to retain
the 'D's' Horton suggested that the 'C's' could be more usefully
employed in waters where weather conditions would be less severe.
The following extracts from individual reports give some idea of
what these ships had to endure in their battle with the elements:

From *Diomede*, 15th November 1939:

'It was impossible to control the ship at a speed of less than eight knots
on the engines, and I steamed into the wind's eye. Nevertheless,
considerable bumping was experienced, seas were coming green over
my high bow, two 'Carley floats were lost, guard rail stanchions bent
and the depth charges worked in their chutes and securings, one being
lost overboard.'

From *Dunedin*, 15th November, 1939:

'The ship was immediately brought round to 040° and speed reduced
to seven knots, but it was too late, and the motor boat and crutches,

the accommodation ladder and the cutter's griping spar were all smashed. The tail of the spare port paravane was also snapped off like a carrot.'

From *Colombo*, 15th November 1939:

'During this period the whole of the upper deck below the level of the fore-and-aft bridge was unsafe. The Marine butcher was swept overboard by one wave, but the next one brought him back, and he was recovered safely ; the chief baker was swept off his feet down the waist, but fortunately did not go overboard. The beef screen, the bakery, and the officers' galley had to be vacated, while the movement of the ship precluded the use of the ship's galley for cooking purposes.'

From *Caledon*, 18th November 1939:

'I was hove-to from 1300 for twenty-four hours . . . even though hove-to, it was dangerous for men on the upper deck, and the seas came over "green." The cutter was lifted at the davits, and fractured the disengaging gear; six depth charges and one shell were lost over the side as seas swept over the quarterdeck, the securing eyebolts, wooden chocks and one fixed chute being drawn from the deck. The sixteen-foot skiff was smashed beyond repair.'

From *Ceres*, 18th November 1939:

'. . . 32-foot cutter, port 25-foot whaler, and starboard skiff swept away during the night.'

From *Dragon*, 20th November 1939:

'Most electrical fittings exposed above the upper deck were water-logged, one magazine practically flooded, and a sea finding its way into the main W/T office had temporarily put out of action the main transmitting.'

From *Cardiff*, 12th November 1939:

'The ventilation of the mess decks is inadequate for the number of men borne, and when battened down (i.e., under sea conditions) ventilation is virtually non-existent as intakes are exposed to the weather and ventilation trunks become flooded.'

From the Commodore, 11th Cruiser Squadron (C Class), 13th November 1939:

13th November 1939.
'In all ships the conditions under which men are living are extremely bad. Due to their low freeboard upper decks are permanently awash in the normal Northern Patrol weather. . . . Sleeping accommodation

is quite inadequate; men, most of whom have been living in their own homes, have to sleep on and under mess tables; every slinging berth is occupied. Mess decks are wet, and drying room facilities are very poor (in the *Colombo* the drying room is always wet at sea) with the result that watchkeepers come down from their watch as lookouts, etc. (often in northerly gales and blizzards), to great discomfort and little opportunity of drying their clothes.'

All this damage and discomfort was suffered in one gale only, and, as B.B.C. listeners well know, 'gales in the sea area Iceland, Faeroes, Fair Isle' follow one another with monotonous regularity. Maintenance facilities in the Orkneys and Shetlands did not exist, so temporary repairs had to be done by the ships' companies during their short spells in harbour when all were in need of rest and recreation.

The arrival of armed merchant cruisers, armed trawlers, and boarding steamers eased the strain to some extent. Their fuel endurance enabled them to stay at sea for a much longer time than the small cruisers, while in bad weather they could ride the sea more comfortably, keeping dry between decks. On the other hand they were vulnerable to U-boat and air attack: besides, it was a waste of shipping to use valuable liners and their large complements for purely naval duties when they could be more usefully employed in transporting troops and supplies.

It was only a question of time before the U-boats would take their toll. In an official letter, Horton wrote:

'Any patrol line designed to intercept neutral merchant ships on well known tracks must inevitably be readily found by enemy submarines. . . . As an old submarine officer, there is nothing I should like better than to find my target reappearing in a few hours after I had failed to get in the first attack.'

Fortunately for Horton the Germans at this time had available fewer than fifty U-boats; as these were being conserved for future campaigns, no more than eight were operating at any one time. The ships of the Northern Patrol were able therefore to carry on their work effectively. In consequence, neutral shipping preferred to comply with the order to put into a British port for examination, rather than submit to being boarded at sea. In the course of a few months most neutral ships sought the protection of the British convoy system, thus obviating the need for a strong surface patrol. Close watch, however, still had to be kept for enemy merchant ships and warships. This was work more suited to reconnaissance aircraft than armed passenger ships, and in February 1941, when Coastal Command of the R.A.F. had obtained the machines they so urgently needed, the armed merchant cruisers were withdrawn. These gallant ships had served their purpose in stopping German overseas trade, but, as Horton had foreseen, their losses were heavy. After June 1940 ten were sunk by U-boats in the North Atlantic in less than a year.

CHAPTER FIVE

1940

'THE COBBLER RETURNS TO HIS LAST'

'Northways.' Norway, Horton's intuition. Hazards of the Skagerrack.

THE coming of the New Year held bright prospects for Max Horton. On the 7th December 1939 while pacing, like a caged lion, the floor of his Kirkwall office, worried about the *Rawalpindi*, and vainly hoping that some means might be found to strike a blow at the enemy, he received this letter:

ADMIRALTY,

WHITEHALL.

Dear Admiral Horton,   *7th December* 1939.

I have much pleasure in offering you the appointment of Vice-Admiral Submarines to date 9th January 1940.

I am offering you this appointment in consequence of the Board's decision that the Admiral Submarines in wartime should be an ex-submarine officer who has commanded submarines with distinction in the last war.

Their Lordships desire to take this opportunity of expressing their appreciation of the efficient manner in which you have organised and commanded the Northern Patrol.

Yours very sincerely,

(Signed) WINSTON S. CHURCHILL.

And so the weapon was placed in his hands. Indeed it was the only weapon which in those days of the 'phoney' war was ready and available to seek out and destroy enemy warships in their own waters. British surface warships and aircraft of the Coastal Command were fully employed in the vital duty of defending trade and preserving the lifelines of the Empire, while the Royal

Air Force was building up its striking power for bombing Germany. Nobody knew better than Horton that the offensive power of the Navy could never be developed to the full without the co-operation of the Royal Air Force, and in the dark days to come nobody worked harder to achieve it.

The post of Flag Officer Submarines was normally held by a Rear-Admiral. Horton was a fairly senior Vice-Admiral, so the First Sea Lord (Admiral Pound), when discussing his appointment on the telephone, said to him, 'I know the job is not commensurate with your seniority, but we want you. Your great knowledge and experience will be invaluable.' Horton said: 'I don't care a damn about the seniority as long as I have a free hand!' Pound replied: 'I will guarantee that you shall.'

In his enthusiasm Max wrote to a friend:

'The new job is taking over the Submarine Branch again. . . . H.Q. said that they must have someone who commanded a submarine in war to take charge of them in wartime—hence me. Always told you when things got bad I hoped they would send for me, and it looks like they have done it. I am so happy, happy, happy at the prospect of what lies ahead. I am almost falling over myself with excitement. I haven't forgotten all I knew and I hope to bring them luck anyway.'

Although Horton was naturally delighted with his appointment, the officers and men of the hard-worked cruisers were sorry to see him go. Here are a few extracts from many farewell letters.

One Captain wrote:

'With your departure we all felt that we had lost a friend in high places. I know you expected a lot of us, but we all accepted that gladly because we knew that in any ultimate issue you were always on our side, and that makes service easy. . . .

'But fighting the Germans is child's play to fighting the Arctic winter!

'With every good wish and good luck and our thanks for the way you always took our interests to heart.'

And another:

'We have been confident, proud and happy serving our country under your flag and are grateful for your continuous concern for our welfare.'

And again:

'Thank you very much, Sir, for your keen appreciation of the conditions of service of the ships' companies, when you always had so much work on a higher plane to contend with.

'THE COBBLER RETURNS TO HIS LAST'

'We shall indeed remember the days on Northern Patrol under your flag with pride.'

A few days after he had taken over his new command at Aberdour on the Firth of Forth, Max wrote:

'I have been terrifically busy here getting the hang of things, and haven't had one minute's exercise, but shall try and play a few holes today.

'I am seriously afraid that my joining has coincided with some bad luck to the craft. The Germans announced on Thursday at a Press conference in Berlin that they had sunk a British submarine, and I am almost sure this is true. It happened the day before I joined, I think, and this is not the only cause of my anxiety either.'

Horton had reason to be anxious, for on the 7th January the submarine *Undine*, when fifteen miles off Heligoland in sixty feet of water, was blown to the surface by depth charges dropped from anti-submarine trawlers. The crew abandoned her whilst she sank. Two days later the *Starfish* was sunk in the same area and the *Seahorse*, which was due to relieve her, did not return from patrol. Thus Horton, at the very moment when he returned to the service he loved so well, was faced with the loss of three submarines. He was heartened by this letter from the First Sea Lord:

My Dear Horton,

I must write and tell you how we all regret the loss of so many gallant lives in *Seahorse*, *Undine* and *Starfish*. I do hope however that it may be found that there are a considerable number of survivors. Losses will occur from time to time, but three submarines from one flotilla in a week is a heavy blow. I cannot say how glad I am that you are V.A.(S.) [Vice-Admiral Submarines] because it is in times such as these that your knowledge and reputation will be so invaluable to the S/M Service.

I trust that your Command may soon have a great success to set off against this heavy loss.

With the best of good luck to you and the gallant officers and men serving under you.

Yours very sincerely,

ADMIRALTY, S.W.   (Signed) DUDLEY POUND.
16th January.

The cause of loss (anti-submarine patrols) was not known at the time and Horton spent days and nights with his staff investigating every possibility. The most worrying factor was that although the submarines were operating in widely spaced areas there was a portion of their approach which had been traversed by all three, so it was natural to suspect an anti-submarine mining trap.

A staff officer writes:

'Although there was no suggestion of any loss of morale in the Submarine Service but rather a desire for revenge, patrols in these areas were discontinued. Max frequently visited the flotillas and his presence and bearing inspired them. He was a tiger to his staff, and we realised it within a few hours of his joining. But a tiger in whom we all had supreme confidence, and though he could and did bite hard when bites were needed, and though his growl was exceedingly fierce, to the trained ear that growl had a distinct note of friendliness on many occasions. His staff had to know their job or had quickly to learn it. If a mistake were made and frankly confessed with full reasons for making it, Max would be as tolerant as anyone, provided the mistake was not made through slackness. He worked hard himself, very hard, but he rightly saw to it that his staff worked harder. Yet he did not *make* work and was very critical of any action by his staff that might lead to making unnecessary work. He had always kept in close touch with the Submarine Branch and had a tremendous store of submarine knowledge and experience. Within a few days he was able to pick up the threads on all submarine matters and quickly spanned the interval that had elapsed since he was last an active submariner (as Captain of a flotilla in 1925).

'He would personally delve into the minutest problem connected with submarines, and woe betide any officer who tried to bluff that he had more knowledge of a subject than he in fact had. When any signal was received requiring action, no matter how trivial or without urgency, it was a cardinal maxim that the action required should be initiated at once.

'Anything that could be done now was to be done now, and not put off till the afternoon, much less till tomorrow.'

Fifty-seven submarines divided into five flotillas were available for service. All were concentrated in the North Sea except one flotilla in the Mediterranean reinforced from the Far East, and a small training flotilla at Portsmouth. The bases from which they operated were Rosyth, Blyth, Harwich, and later Dundee.

Horton as Vice-Admiral Submarines was responsible under the Admiralty for the general administration of the Submarine Branch of the Royal Navy, and under the Commander-in-Chief Home Fleet for the operational control of submarines (except Mediterranean and Far East). In the Mediterranean and Far East the Captains of submarine flotillas were responsible to their own Commanders-in-Chief for the operations of their flotillas.

It was because the Vice-Admiral was responsible to the Commander-in-Chief Home Fleet for submarine operations in the North Sea and Atlantic that the operational headquarters of the Submarine Command had been moved from Fort Blockhouse to Aberdour (Fife). The control of operations was thus separated from administration and material.

Both Horton and his predecessor felt strongly that Aberdour was too far away from the Admiralty. It was obvious to Max that he could not use the striking arm of the Navy with full effect unless he could work in close co-operation with the Naval Staff and the Coastal Command of the Royal Air Force. The First Sea Lord saw the wisdom of this, and suggested that Submarine Headquarters should be inside the Admiralty. The idea did not appeal to Max at all, for he wished to have full scope to use his initiative and freedom to make his dispositions within the framework of the Naval War Plan, while conforming with the intentions of the Commander-in-Chief.

He knew Admiral Pound well and admired his qualities, but could only give of his best when entrusted with a reasonable measure of independence.

The outcome of it all was that Horton took over three floors of 'Northways,' a large block of flats near Swiss Cottage in Hampstead, far enough away from the Admiralty to give him a free hand, and close enough for day-to-day contact with the Naval Staff.

By keeping outside the Admiralty machine, Max was able to achieve a much more effective and independent position. He had easy access to the latest intelligence which might affect the submarine campaign, he was available for immediate consultation with the Admiralty, his staff could work in the closest co-operation with the Admiralty staff divisions, and he was less than half an hour away from the Headquarters of Coastal Command at Northwood. He was also able to keep in close touch with fleet movements, changes in higher policy and happenings outside the Submarine Branch. Furthermore, he was just as accessible to the Commander-in-Chief Home Fleet as he had been at Aberdour. If the Commander-in-Chief Home Fleet wished some particular submarine operation to be carried out, he knew that Horton was in a position not only to obtain Admiralty reactions, but also to give him a fully considered opinion before the matter was officially proposed to the Admiralty. Similarly Max was in a far stronger position when putting up ideas of his own.

In addition, the whole of the Submarine Command, operational, personnel and material was again merged into an efficient whole at Northways instead of being separated. In one of the few personal reminiscences which Horton had written he has this to say about the position:

'The position of the Flag Officer Submarines in war had been the subject of countless proposals between the wars. No decision having been reached, the Flag Officer Submarines, at the time being in command of all S/Ms in Home Waters under C.-in-C. Home Fleet, sought an H.Q. in the Firth of Forth with his operational staff, whilst the material side remained at Portsmouth—thus the majority of papers had to make a nice little trip of 450 miles each way to be minuted, and the personal touch between the two divisions of the staff was almost completely lost. Further, the Flag Officer Submarines, as personal adviser to the Admiralty on S/Ms, was also quite out of touch, and his own operational supervision was not so good.

'I couldn't bear such an organisation, despite the golf course just outside the front door, and decided to move nearer the Admiralty where one would be at least in close personal touch with one of my masters. It resulted in an organisation which I am proud to say was the envy of every other naval organisation of similar character. Though I say it myself, it was unexampled and beautiful, although its real beauty could only be appreciated silently in some of its aspects.

'The Admiralty very kindly regarded us as inside their fold, inasmuch as all dockets referring to S/Ms were marked to Admiral (S)—one knew (what no Flag Officer Submarines had ever known before) all the objections and snags that various departments found in carrying out his desires—in fact, letters from myself to the Admiralty came back in a docket for my remarks after they had been round the departments. The silent advantage was—when one thought that the Admiralty might disagree with Flag Officer Submarines one could usually get the C.-in-C. Home Fleet to back me up. If C.-in-C. Home Fleet was difficult it was often possible to square the Admiralty, and two to one are always good odds, especially when our case was good.'

The move to Northways was therefore to everyone's advantage, especially to the Air Officer Commanding-in-Chief Coastal Command, R.A.F. The fear of the Coastal Command airmen of not knowing where and when British submarines might be met, and whether they could attack or not, was largely ended; from now on, any query about a submarine's position could be answered at once, and Coastal Command were able to have prior knowledge of intended submarine movements and dispositions.

Horton soon found that he saw eye to eye with the Air Officer, Commanding-in-Chief, Sir Frederick Bowhill (himself an old sailor) on all problems, but both were handicapped by shortage of suitable aircraft.

Bowhill says:

'I always went to see him or he came to see me as neither of us were very enamoured of correspondence. . . . We had a very close, and in my opinion perfect, co-operation. . . . I found Max a naval officer of tradition, perfectly charming to work with, he had a thorough understanding of our problems as well as his own, fearless in his decisions, knowing them to be of the best, and a perfect comrade-in-arms.'

The naval liaison officers R. T. Bower, C. W. Meynell, and D. V. Peyton-Ward on the staff of Coastal Command were themselves experienced submarine officers and the co-operation between the two operating staffs was close and happy.

The firm basis of friendship between the two Services, the one above and the other beneath the sea, continued throughout the war, and the absence of friction between otherwise contrasting forces bears witness to the solidarity of the initial co-operation. When, in later years, Horton took over the command of the Western Approaches, the influence of this previous understanding probably had much to do with the rapid solution of inter-Service problems in the Battle of the Atlantic.

During the first six months of the war, British warships in their operations against enemy merchant ships were obliged to conform to International Law, which meant that 'a submarine may not sink or render incapable of navigation a merchant vessel without having first placed passengers and crew and ship's papers in a place of safety. For this purpose the ship's boats are not regarded as a place of safety unless the safety of passengers and crew is assured in the existing sea and weather conditions by the proximity of land or the presence of another vessel which is in a position to take them on board.'[1] In December 1939 Lt.-Commander E. O. Bickford, R.N., in the submarine *Salmon*, while patrolling in the North Sea, raised his periscope and found himself looking at the *Bremen*, a huge liner and pride of Germany's merchant fleet. She was about to pass within close range of his torpedoes. He could hardly fail to hit, but the Admiralty orders were quite definite—a merchant ship must not be sunk unless she refused to stop. So Bickford, cursing lawyers and their works, brought the *Salmon* to the surface and made the signal 'stop instantly.' The *Bremen* paid no heed. Before Bickford had time to fire a warning shot with his gun, German aircraft appeared. The *Salmon* went deep, and the *Bremen* raced on.

The First Lord, Mr. Churchill, had stated that the effectual stoppage of the iron ore supplies from Narvik to Germany ranked as a major operation of war. This important pronouncement did not reach Horton till some days later, and it came in a roundabout way. When he heard of it he remarked sarcastically: 'Of course, I am the last to be told that iron ore is a first objective as I am the only one who can do anything about it!'

Iron ore was vital to German war production. In the winter months, when the Baltic port of Lulea was ice-bound, it was carried by rail from the Swedish mines to Narvik, and transported from there through the Norwegian fjords to Germany. The only time these ore ships could not enjoy the sanctuary of territorial waters was in the short run across the Skagerrack and Kattegat, so it was here that British submarines were placed to intercept them. It was here also, as might be expected, that the Germans had massed their anti-submarine craft on the sea and in the air.

The chances of sinking an ore ship without being sunk himself, after having politely allowed the crew to take to the boats, were

[1] Article 22 of London Naval Treaty 1930.

74

about as slim for a British submarine commander as those of the proverbial celluloid cat in hell. Nevertheless, some successful results were achieved in seemingly impossible conditions.[1]

On the night of 21st March 1940, Commander G. C. Phillips in the *Ursula* sighted a darkened merchant ship and ordered her to stop. The ship took no notice until a shot was fired across her bows. Then she stopped, protesting that she was Estonian although the name *Hedderheim* of Bremen could now be read on her stern. Phillips ordered her to send a boat. On learning that the ship carried 7,000 tons of iron ore, he told the Captain to abandon her as she would be sunk in fifteen minutes. At the same time he expedited the operation by firing another shell over her funnel; when the crew were in the boats, he sank her with a torpedo, but only just in time. Within a few minutes, in answer to flares from the boats, patrol craft were on the scene. *Ursula* escaped, taking with her some Germans for interrogation. Two nights later Lt.-Commander C. H. Hutchinson in the *Truant* had a similar experience with the merchant ship *Edmond Hugo Stinnes*. On this occasion the German ship, having refused to stop, continued to send S.O.S. messages undeterred by the customary shot across the bows. Hutchinson then blew her bridge away with his gun, whereupon the ship scuttled herself and the crew took to the boats. After picking up the Master for interrogation he told the remainder to pull for the shore. Phillips and Hutchinson were mildly reprimanded by their Admiral for exceeding their instructions, but no steps were taken to restrain the others.

Captain B. W. Taylor, R. N., at that time commanding the *Severn*, a large submarine of 2206 tons, writes:

'The Admiralty directive was "Sink at sight except in a narrow lane leading up the Skagerrack." Sir Max's orders were "Sink at sight anywhere!" I met a merchant ship at dawn in the lane. Obey Admiralty or Sir Max? I compromised, surfaced, and stopped her. She turned out to be the Swedish S.S. *Monark* with a German prize crew aboard. Calm day—prize crew removed by ship's boats—quite safe. Prize crew spent ten days on patrol with me. Very unhappy when explosions

[1] Horton was highly indignant at the supine attitude of neutral countries to flagrant breaches of International Law by Germany, and expressed his views in strong terms to the First Lord, Mr. Churchill. See Appendix IV.

heard around us. More unhappy when greeted at Dundee by "Jocks" in kilts with fixed bayonets!'

In an attempt to force shipping out of territorial waters the Admiralty had planned a mine-laying operation ('Wilfred') to be carried out by surface ships and submarines in the northern Norwegian leads. The date selected was the 4th April. Horton was informed on the 29th March, whereupon he immediately summoned to Northways all the Captains of North Sea submarine flotillas. He explained to them that, although he had had no information from Intelligence sources, he was quite certain that 'Wilfred' would bring enemy counter-action, probably the invasion of Norway. He told them that every available submarine, regardless of rest periods, was to go to sea at once and take up allotted patrols in the Kattegat, Skagerrack, off the Danish coast and in the Heligoland Bight. Submarines at sea were told to sink transports if encountered, thus indicating that something unusual was afoot.

'Wilfred' was postponed until 8th April, and on the morning of that day, thanks to Horton's prompt action, nineteen submarines were either in or near their patrol areas. Meanwhile, reports began to come in that they had seen an unusual number of northbound merchant vessels flying neutral flags. As the restriction on sinking at sight did not apply to transports, the Polish submarine *Orzel*, belonging to the British 2nd Flotilla, sank the German troopship *Rio de Janeiro* off the south coast of Norway. Thus, at one stroke, the *Orzel* not only destroyed a large body of German soldiers, but also confirmed that Norway was about to be invaded.

In most cases, however, merchant vessels flying neutral flags could not readily be identified as transports. Many submarine commanders speak bitterly of the frustration suffered during the forty-eight hours which elapsed before permission was given by the British Government to sink *all* northbound traffic. Horton had protested violently, and it was largely due to his efforts that the leg iron clamped on his Commanders was eventually removed. The welcome order to sink without warning all German merchant ships encountered in the Skagerrack was received by Lt.-Commander J. E. Slaughter in the *Sunfish* on the afternoon of 9th April.

'THE COBBLER RETURNS TO HIS LAST'

At that very moment he sighted a German merchant ship. He says in his report 'Just as the sights came on the Vice-Admiral's [Horton's] signal was read out to me, so I fired.'

Horton, with his long experience of submarine warfare and local knowledge of the Baltic Approaches, had disposed his submarines so effectively that seventeen enemy transports and supply ships were sent to the bottom during the period 8th to 29th April 1940. In addition, four ships are known to have been sunk by mines laid by the *Narwhal* (Lt.-Commander R. K. Burch). Horton had wanted to place two submarines in Oslo Fjord off Horten, for he had a hunch about the name, but the Government for political reasons would not allow it. The losses inflicted on the enemy would have been far more severe if political considerations had not weighed so heavily. Nevertheless Allied submarine successes compelled the enemy to organise a convoy system for the delivery of supplies and troops to Norway, thus delaying the German advance and locking up destroyers and aircraft urgently needed to hinder the Allied landings at Narvik, Namsos, Andalsnes and other points on the Norwegian coast.

Rear-Admiral Darke[1] writes:

'As Flag Officer Submarines Max was superb in his operational and administrative actions. He had an intuition of what the Hun would do, which was quite uncanny. As an instance I take the German invasion of Norway; Max told me at the time he had made certain dispositions to cover that very eventuality, but was overridden and made to alter them by the Naval Staff at the Admiralty. When asked by the Naval Staff why he had made dispositions to cover Oslo he replied "Because that is what the Germans obviously intend to do, and it is equally obvious that it would do the Allies the greatest possible harm at the moment." The Naval Staff replied that Intelligence did not lead them to think so. I am sure that this uncanny intuition was the basis of his great success later as Commander-in-Chief Western Approaches.'

Speaking of Horton's intuition, the late Sir Charles Craven, Chairman and Managing Director of Vickers-Armstrongs Ltd., said: 'I firmly believe there is no man in this country who has studied war so closely—every kind of war. People talk about

[1] Rear-Admiral R. B. Darke, D.S.O., commanding submarines at Portsmouth.

"intuition"—to my mind it is sheer knowledge with a brilliant mind to use it, and so get in one ahead of the enemy. Maybe a bit of intuition as well, but it would be useless without knowledge.'

The British submarines were also successful in their hunt for bigger game. On 9th April, Lt.-Commander C. H. Hutchinson in the *Truant* sank the German cruiser *Karlsruhe* off Kristiansund. The warship was screened by three destroyers, and the counter-attack with depth charges was vicious and prolonged, compelling Hutchinson to remain submerged for nineteen hours. His compass had been damaged, and when he came to the surface at midnight he found himself surrounded on three sides by the enemy coast and no stars to guide him. He managed however to feel his way to the open sea and when the clouds cleared, he was able to steer by the stars.

On the following night the *Spearfish* commanded by Lt.-Commander J. H. Forbes, R.N., torpedoed the pocket battleship *Lutzow*, damaging her so severely that she took no part in naval operations for over twelve months.

On 15th April the *Sterlet*, commanded by Lt.-Commander Haward, torpedoed and sank the German cruiser *Brummer* full of troops in the difficult waters of the Kattegat. The *Sterlet* was never heard of again, and probably met her end under severe counter-attack.

The submarines had more than their share of ill luck. Lt.-Commander Ben Bryant, in the *Sealion*, who had been given the position of honour at the entrance to the Sound, had withdrawn to charge his batteries when a German squadron passed through. This was the force which went to Oslo, and if Horton had been allowed to follow his 'hunch' another submarine would have got them off Horten. Lt.-Commander J. E. Slaughter, R.N., in the *Sunfish* off the Swedish coast, sighted and reported them, but they were too far away for him to attack. Lt.-Commander E. F. Pizey, R.N., in the *Triton*, off the Skaw, fired a full salvo at one of the German battle cruisers, allowing for a speed of fifteen knots. As he fired, he heard the enemy revolutions increase to twenty-five knots. His torpedoes missed astern, but he came to the surface and reported the enemy by radio. The battle cruisers were on their way to North Norway, and during the night in dense fog passed close to three submarines which Horton had placed between the Skaw and S.W. Norway. They heard the enemy, but, having no radar, could not attack on account of the fog. The wireless reports, from *Triton* and *Sunfish*, however, were of great value to the Admiralty and the Commander-in-Chief Home Fleet.

Thus, in the early days of the Second World War, the Germans learned to their cost that once again they had to reckon with Max Horton. But this time his activities were not confined to an isolated unit in the Baltic, for his leadership now inspired the whole of the British Submarine Branch, and his knowledge and skill were at the disposal of every Commander. His personality was so closely knit by common interest to them all, he could picture in his mind their difficulties and assess their chances of success. When he reviewed on the operational chart the dispositions he had made, he would see in each paper flag the submarine it represented, and his thoughts would go out to her gallant Captain and crew. Once, when Horton had advised a submarine commander to go under the ice to avoid depth-charge attack, a Minister said to him: 'When I heard of that order I got down on my knees and prayed for them.' Max replied: 'Sir, I pray for them all every night.'

He knew from his own experience the navigational hazards of the Skagerrack and Kattegat, where the tides are tricky and the flow of fresh water from the Baltic brings rapid changes of density. He knew that a submarine passing submerged in perfect trim from fresh water to the greater buoyancy of salt water might find herself breaking surface unintentionally at a critical moment. Above all, he knew that the efficiency of anti-submarine measures and the weight of counter-attack to be expected had increased far beyond anything that he had experienced himself. Destroyers and anti-submarine vessels with listening devices patrolled the narrow waters, and low-flying aircraft armed with depth charges scoured the surface of the sea in search of a patch of oil, a ripple or a shadow. Generally they searched in vain, for the British submarine crews were war-minded and wary. They were too well trained to allow bilge water and other little things to betray their presence, but they would cheerfully accept any risk to

79

bring about the destruction of targets prescribed in their operation orders. The master mind had seen to that.

A submarine Captain writes:

'I know he spent many miserable hours thinking about us, and he was terribly cut up when a submarine was lost. He would not show it, but would concentrate on the job even more fiercely than usual. He wished to make certain that training and good material would minimise future losses.'

Another commanding officer who was getting on in years, finding that his nerve was giving way, felt that in the interest of his ship's company he must ask to be relieved:

' I went down to Northways to see him, anticipating a cold reception and curt dismissal. It was quite otherwise; he asked me what were the causes of my trouble. I haltingly explained that I could not put my finger on any one item, but that sleeplessness, over-sensibility to noise and smell were among the factors. He at once became sympathetic, remarking that commanding officers suffered the same way in the First War. Instead of dismissal I found myself employed for a time on various staff jobs, and later was given command of a surface ship.'

Mr. Churchill, feeling that the strain on the submarine crews might be beyond human endurance, suggested that a system of relief crews for submarines in the Skagerrack would give some easement. Horton said that the idea would be unwelcome to the officers and men, for no crew would wish to be separated from their own boat. Success depended upon the efficiency of the weapon, and since their lives were also at stake, the care and maintenance of its intricate parts must be in their own hands. The spirit of the crew was closely integrated with their environment. They had a deep affection for their submarine and any idea of handing her over to anybody else, even for a short spell, would be abhorrent.

Here is an extract from a letter he wrote to Mr. Churchill:

> NORTHWAYS,
> SWISS COTTAGE,
> LONDON, N.W.3.
> *29th March* 1940.

Dear First Lord,

. . . I have considered the question of using relief crews but all Captains (S) and commanding officers whom I consulted were dead against such a proposal, even if it were possible to provide the extra officers and crews. I fully share their views, for it is no more possible to expect efficiency in such circumstances than might be expected if it were tried in a battleship, cruiser, or destroyer.

I keep a specially close watch on the state of the officers and crews of the small submarine flotillas from the point of view of fatigue and strain. I am fully convinced that the system we are now working is not too great a strain on the human factor and is in fact providing us with a tough and war-experienced personnel whose high standards will spread and inspire the whole Submarine Branch with the happiest results.

I do hope that you may be able to find time to visit Harwich; you would find there a morale and spirit which would explain better than any words of mine the undesirability of changing the system which has produced it. The French submarines who recently arrived at that port would also feel greatly honoured and inspired by a visit.

I venture to enclose for your consideration some notes as to our position at sea vis-a-vis the neutrals. [See Appendix IV.]

(Signed) MAX HORTON.

The story of the *Tetrarch* is an example of the ordeals which many submarine crews endured in the Norwegian campaign. It is told here, not with intent to harrow the reader, but as a true picture of success achieved by good leadership, patient training and perfect discipline.

On an afternoon of breathless calm in the Skagerrack the *Tetrarch*, commanded by Lt.-Commander R. G. Mills, R.N., while patrolling at periscope depth, sighted a large German transport escorted by three destroyers. Being well aware that his periscope, cleaving the glassy sea, would betray his presence, Mills decided to strike at once, but must 'keep his head low.' He had no time to see the result of his attack, but caught a glimpse of three destroyers coming straight at him in line abreast at high speed. He went deep. Almost immediately the depth charges came down. For three hours the destroyers kept up their intensive underwater bombardment, while the *Tetrarch* tried every known device to put them off the scent. At nightfall, when they had expended all their depth charges, a flotilla of anti-submarine trawlers took over the hunt.

The conditions in the *Tetrarch* were becoming unbearable. Owing to bright moonlight on the previous night and a watchful enemy, she had been submerged for over nineteen hours. The air was foul and the batteries were low, so Mills decided that he must at all costs come to the surface and get some air into the submarine. He hoped to elude the enemy vessels in the darkness, intending to engage them with gunfire, if necessary. When the *Tetrarch* broke surface, the air pressure in the submarine was so great that a lashing inside the hatch parted, and it flew open. Mills who was underneath and a man holding him by the legs were lifted off their feet, but neither was hurt. The gun's crew rushed to their station and the tube's crew stood by their torpedoes. In the moonlight, two trawlers were seen approaching. Mills fired two torpedoes at them, recalled the men from the gun and dived to 300 feet. Depth charges exploded uncomfortably close, causing the submarine to 'porpoise' between 400 feet and the surface. The situation was tense; the *Tetrarch* could not re-charge her batteries, and their dwindling power had to be conserved. With great skill, Mills succeeded in trimming the submarine so that she held her balance stopped at 300 feet. This delicate operation demands the utmost concentration from the Captain and perfect discipline from the crew. Everyone must remain still. When the submarine tends to become heavy forward a man is moved aft to re-adjust the balance and vice versa, as on a see-saw. If she starts to sink, the periscope is raised to displace more water and keep her depth. Thus, the *Tetrarch* held 'stopped trim' for twelve weary hours, while her crew lay still and silent in the darkness. Their discipline was rewarded, for the searching trawlers, hearing nothing on their hydrophones, gave up the hunt.

Fortunately, while holding 'stopped trim,' the *Tetrarch* was carried by a sub-surface current in the opposite direction to her pursuers, so when Mills brought her to periscope depth in the morning, nothing was in sight. This was by no means the end of the ordeal. The submarine was still in enemy waters, and any attempt to re-charge the batteries was bound to be observed. Mills had no choice but to creep away on what little power remained. It was not until after dark that he felt he could come to the surface with a reasonable chance of not being disturbed while re-charging.

'THE COBBLER RETURNS TO HIS LAST'

Apart from her few hectic minutes on the surface on the previous night, the *Tetrarch* had been submerged for forty-two hours and forty minutes. The fresh air made the crew sick and dizzy, but they and their ship soon regained strength and mobility, ready to fight another day.

Horton's concern about the conduct of the war was not confined to the narrow limits of submarine operations, albeit their success was the one bright spot in a dim campaign. He was opposed to frittering away partially trained military forces in a country where the enemy was already established in strength, and he felt also that the R.A.F. must play a greater part in the war at sea. At midnight on 26th April 1940 he wrote:

'I am seriously alarmed at the Norwegian situation in relation to our soldiers ashore there and their rapidly worsening situation. All the large defended ports being in the hands of the Hun, our forces have had to use small and inefficient ports in the face of complete air superiority and heavy bombing. Transports could only berth and unload at night (very short at this stage of the year). Ashore, bombing without means to resist or defend has resulted in loss of stores and broken-up organisation—country is under heavy snow—communications are difficult—the usual water transport is also entirely commanded by the Germans—again solely due to their air superiority which prevents our warships contesting the area in which our troops are having such a terribly difficult time.

'The enemy, comfortably installed at Oslo-Trondheim, Bergen, and Stavanger, is carrying out his plan to order and in accordance with his carefully worked-out scheme—he is pouring forces into the country from modern quays with all material assistance that properly equipped ports can give—he is relatively unmolested from the air and only our S/Ms have been able to take a toll of shipping—during the last few days of moon all S/Ms have had to be withdrawn—not *only* for moon, *but because they had come to the end of their torpedoes, or fuel endurance.*

'Under these conditions the enemy can undoubtedly reinforce his troops quicker than we can. He has properly defended bases to work from whilst we have none. To be constantly bombed without redress is destructive of morale—we can neither dig in nor advance—the result is inevitable—we shall have to evacuate under circumstances more difficult than Gallipoli and with, I fear, far more serious losses —I think it is useless to pursue a hopeless task—*we must cut our losses now* in every area S. of Narvik at once—whatever the effect on neutrals —a bigger disaster in a month's time will not help us.

'We could I think hold Narvik for the summer if we concentrated all available troops there and dug in properly, besides doing everything to make iron ore transit impossible to Germany.

'The effect on neutrals of proposed evacuation must be endured since we cannot change the circumstances as related above so—cut our losses at once.

'Unless we can do something soon to make the best use of our Air Force we shall *be done*, that definitely is our most crying need and it has been obvious to every observer since the *war started*.

'P.S. On 1st May, Prime Minister announced that Andalsnes was evacuated—Namsos on 2nd May. Actual evacuation started on 28th April—two days after this appreciation.'

With the whole coast of Norway now in their hands the Germans could use freely the inner 'leads.' Horton thereupon re-arranged his dispositions so that some of his submarines could ravage enemy shipping in the fjords, while others kept up their attacks on the convoys in the south.

The plan worked well, and the more fortunate submarines in the north, finding themselves free from air supervision, were able to use their guns. Many people living around Kors Fjord will remember a May morning when they stood on the hills and watched the *Trident* open fire with her gun on a German supply ship. They will remember their feelings of hope and joy when they saw the British shells exploding on the enemy ship, forcing her to beach herself at the eastern end of the fjord. Then there was that terrific explosion which shook the houses for miles around as the *Trident*'s torpedo blew her to pieces. It was the first sign to these good people that the Germans were not having it all their own way. The *Trident*'s Captain, Lt.-Commander G. M. Sladen, R.N., however, viewed his success in a different light: 'Realising that retribution would soon be upon me and wishing to be clear of restricted waters, I made a somewhat undignified exit to seaward, steaming down Kors Fjord at full speed.'[1]

This game of hide and seek in God's good air was a pleasant recreation after the days of hell and hazard they had suffered in the Skagerrack.

---

[1] Official report.

CHAPTER SIX

1940
ANXIOUS DAYS

The Free French submarines. Need for R.A.F. co-operation at sea. Anxiety at the Nore. Hitler's plans frustrated. Submarine losses. Horton's broadcast. He is offered Command of the Home Fleet. Promotion.

THE march of events opened up new opportunities, bringing variety and change of scene. By midsummer the western coasts of France, Holland, Belgium, and Scandinavia were in German hands. The Baltic was free of ice, and the enemy could get their much-needed supplies of iron ore from the port of Lulea in the Gulf of Bothnia. A strong concentration of British submarines was no longer necessary in the Skagerrack, so only one patrol was retained off the coast of Norway for reconnaissance and for attacking enemy warships.

Late in June 1940 the *Clyde* was on this duty when her Captain (Lt.-Commander D. C. Ingram, R.N.) sighted the battle cruiser *Gneisenau*.[1] The sea was very rough and it was difficult to see the target at periscope depth without breaking surface. He pressed in through the destroyer screen to a range of 4,000 yards and hit her with one torpedo, which compelled her to return to Germany where she spent many months being repaired; vital months from the German point of view, as this powerful warship was badly needed to assist in the execution of Hitler's plans for the invasion of England.

At the time of Dunkirk, Horton applied himself with characteristic energy to the task of finding and equipping small craft to assist in the evacuation.

[1] *Gneisenau* and *Hipper* were on their way to attack shipping.

MAX HORTON AND THE WESTERN APPROACHES

At the height of the emergency, when time meant so much, a message came at 1.0 a.m. from Sheerness that the engines of a Diesel lighter, which had been on the mud for ten years, could not be started. Horton acted at once, and quickly got the telephone number at Grantham of the managing director of the firm who had built the engines. Max roused him and the man was on his way to Sheerness within an hour. The lighter went to Dunkirk.

The fall of France brought many problems for Horton. The British Government, acting on the principle that 'those who are not for us are against us,' decided that French warships which had sought sanctuary in British ports were to be given the choice of throwing in their lot with the British Navy or being interned. Among those were two French submarines, *Rubis* and *Surcouf*. The *Rubis* was at Dundee, and had carried out many successful minelaying operations under British direction. Horton immediately sent a message of sympathy to her commanding officer, at the same time expressing the hope that the *Rubis* would continue to serve under his command. Her Captain, Lieut. de Vaisseau Cabanier, and his crew responded with enthusiasm. On the other hand the *Surcouf*, having recently returned from the West Indies, had done no operations with the Royal Navy and had no wish to continue the fight. She was at Devonport, and when some British officers went on board to take her over Lt.-Commander Sprague was shot and killed, while talking to the Captain.

At midnight on 3rd July 1940, Max wrote:

'The situation has now become perfectly beastly—two of my experienced submarine officers, including the C.O. of *Thames*, were, I fear, mortally wounded when taking over the *Surcouf* at Devonport this morning. It is sure that our relations with France after these and other incidents will become embittered to the last degree. I think it probable that when other factors operate in France—great distress and probably famine, also the feeling of the French (played on of course by the Germans)—may result in their giving facilities to those we are fighting, if not actually taking up arms against us. The war will take on a far more bitter aspect. The whole of Europe and North Africa besides Spain and Portugal (both of which are almost sure to be overrun by Germans very shortly) will be ranged against us—some odds indeed.

'I am sending out all available submarines today and tomorrow as a result of Admiralty signal that invasion is to be expected this coming weekend, Saturday 6th–Sunday 7th July. Personally I do not believe it—but perhaps there may be feints or raids from Norwegian ports, and I am covering them all on the W. Coast. I think it more likely they will continue their preparations for a large-scale landing in Kent —shortest sea passage—as well as for an attack on S. Ireland from Brest and Biscayan ports, but these things take time, and I now postpone the likelihood of serious attack until the end of July. Meantime they will be ranging their aircraft against us—preparing aerodromes, etc., along northern France and intensity of air raids is bound to increase. They will not start on invasion until their arrangements are perfected, but I expect the Iberian push to start in a week.

'The only hope of relief in the situation lies in the realisation in Germany that Russia is making good use of her opportunities in the Near East and that the rift between these two countries will lead to dispersion of German forces.'

When the Free French forces were formed in Great Britain under General de Gaulle, the submarines *Rubis* (Lieut. de Vaisseau Cabanier), *Minerve* (Lieut. de Vaisseau Sonneville) and *Junon* (Capt. de Frigate Querville) came under the operational control of Admiral Horton. When presenting decorations to the officers and men of the *Rubis*, Horton said:

'I am very happy to be here today on this rare and special occasion, and to have the opportunity of telling you personally how much I appreciate and admire what you, Captain Cabanier, and the officers and men under your command in *Rubis* have achieved against the enemy since you joined us at Harwich on the 1st May; achievements that I am able to assess and value better, perhaps, than most officers because the reports of all the work done by submarines come to me, and also because I am a submarine officer myself. . . .

'This occasion arises at a moment when we are fighting a battle of life and death with our common enemy, and it is a source of comfort and inspiration to me to know that in this fight I have in my command men of such courage, ability, and character as I see before me now.

'In my own name as Vice-Admiral (Submarines), and in the name of my countrymen and our other Allies, of which we have such fine representatives present here today, I congratulate you, Captain Cabanier, officers and men of the *Rubis*, on your brave deeds and splendid example.'

Horton took a personal interest in Cabanier and his men, striving, through the Governor of Gibraltar, to have their families, where accessible, moved out of the clutches of the Vichy Government. They responded heartily to his leadership, and in each little wardroom his portrait hung beside that of General de Gaulle.

The French submarines became part of the 9th Flotilla, which included two Polish, four Dutch, several Norwegian, and three British submarines, all based at Dundee. They were a happy party, the Scottish people did their best to make them feel at home, and it is said that the lassies had an interesting time.

One day, Horton sent for Cabanier to discuss his last patrol. On the night before the interview, the Admiral studied carefully the *Rubis'* report which as it happened was not the one in question. Next morning, before Cabanier arrived, Horton told his Flag Lieutenant to bring the charts and the patrol report.

'The report of *Rubis'* last operation has not been received, Sir!' 'Nonsense,' said Max, 'I read it last night.' The young man then pointed out, with all the tact he could muster, that the Admiral had been reading the report of the previous patrol.

'Don't be silly,' said Max, getting angry. 'Bring it here at once!' As he left the room, the Flag Lieutenant, thinking he was out of earshot, muttered 'I'll bet I'm right.' Max called him back, and smiling broadly said: 'Ah! You will bet?—and how much will you bet?'

'Five pounds, Sir—ten if you like.'

'What odds will you give me?'

'This time, Sir—five to one.'

'The bet's off. You are too damned sure!'

At that moment Cabanier entered the room and apologised for intruding. 'Not at all!' said Max. 'I thought my Flag Lieutenant had made a mistake, but as usual my staff are right!'

'Not always!' said the Frenchman.

The Flag Lieutenant writes:

'From then onwards I knew that nearly all acrimonious incidents could be turned to good-natured argument if only a bet could be introduced, and I often took advantage of this. Sir Max did not always accept the bets, and I never won a penny off him, but it could be guaranteed to change the atmosphere.'

Although Horton did not think that invasion was imminent he was seriously alarmed at the apparent lack of a co-ordinated plan to counter it. On 3rd July 1940 he wrote to a friend:

'At the conference at the Admiralty this morning called by C.-in-C.

ANXIOUS DAYS

Nore[1] representatives of all Services including "Bomber" and "Fighter" and "Coastal" Air Commands were present. C.-in-C. Nore said that the greatest battle in the history of our island was drawing near (referring to invasion) yet none of the senior officers particularly concerned had ever met in conference until he called this one! His true statement shows how little co-operation means to those who control us—lip service, nothing more. C.-in-C. Nore asked for assurance from the fighters that they would be on the spot to engage enemy bombers who were sure to attack our defending surface forces. Fighter representative said their role was *defence of Britain* and not defence of our ships—this remark again shows the total absence of co-operation—C.-in-C. Nore asked that *some* fighter squadrons should be earmarked for this duty. The Air said they would of course do what they could, but flexibility demanded that they had a perfectly free hand. It will be seen therefore that neither the Army nor Navy can rely on any definite measure of air support or co-operation. Once again I say the Air are fighting a war of their own and divided control can in my view only result in disaster. Logically, the Air must take over both Navy and Army and control the battle as Commander-in-Chief Combined Forces, or else a proportion of the Air must be given to Army and Navy to be used in conjunction with their own forces. C.-in-C. Nore said in a pleading voice: "Do you think it could be made possible for me to meet A.O.C. Fighters? I have never met him." He was told to put his points on paper and send it to "Fighter Command" with a copy to Air Ministry. *What a system.* What a disgrace that such things can be when we are engaged in a death struggle.'

Four days later he feels that his worst fears are confirmed:

7th July 1940. 2345.

'The disgraceful episode of Convoy 178 is a blatant indication of the complete absence of co-operation by Air Force and perils of divided responsibility—this convoy coming down Channel was attacked by relays of bombers off Portland between 1 and 2 p.m.—six at a time for two hours—some ten ships were sunk, fired or damaged. At midnight—E-boats torpedoed two more of the wretched convoy. Yesterday they were bombed again—two ships in Portland Harbour also damaged —a total of fourteen or fifteen ships with valuable cargoes! No fighters and no escort worth talking about. With our system there is nobody to appeal to if the Air don't turn up—it is a criminally inefficient system: the German aircraft take more or less the same routes every night to N.E. Coast and spread out over industrial areas there—from Wash across to Liverpool—down Channel and across by Poole to Avonmouth, Cardiff and Swansea. Do the people realise that, with the enemy Air Force based along the French coast, no Channel routes can

[1] Admiral the Hon. Sir R. P. Ernle-Erle-Drax, K.C.B., D.S.O.

M.H.—4*
89

be used and that the whole of the southern approach between Land's End and Ireland will shortly be controlled by enemy aircraft—that route will probably have to be abandoned, and up to now it is our principal route for supplies. All shipping will have to come N. of Ireland and down Irish Sea (that part that don't go to Clyde)—a proportion will go round N. Scotland and down E. Coast, but only a small one—the W. Coast ports then available will be Clyde, Liverpool, and Avonmouth—now we understand that these practice flights of the Hun, training his pilots in the routes to be taken when the hour is struck, will be multiplied by 100. Can we distribute and feed the country from those ports alone—and what about when they are mass bombed in Liverpool and Avonmouth? *Again I state that my opinion is that the Hun's principal weapon to be used against us is blockade and not invasion.*

'Is our Air Force sufficient in numbers to compete? I have grave doubts even on that score—it may be they are overwhelmed by what they realise is in store for the country and therefore do not want to waste any aircraft in supporting us on the sea—but it is all part of the same problem.'

In the above letter, Horton is referring to Convoy OA 178 which was the last ocean convoy to take the Channel route. It had passed Dover on 3rd July and was attacked off Portland on the 4th. Aircraft sank four ships and damaged nine, while E-boats sank one and damaged two. Thereafter, ocean shipping from the Thames and East Coast ports was sailed in convoy up the East Coast, and round the north of Scotland.

Horton's bitterness is understandable, for he may not have been aware of the measures that had been taken to protect shipping by the meagre air forces then available. The Royal Air Force was stretched to its limit, and in fairness it must be said that three fighter squadrons had been diverted for the defence of Scapa Flow and one to the Tay-Montrose area. In addition daylight patrols were being maintained over the East Coast convoys and occasionally over the North Sea.

The primary task of the Royal Air Force was the air defence of Great Britain. In an attempt to include the protection of shipping within this commitment, fighter aircraft were moved in October 1939 to airfields near the coast. The difficulty was that no proper provision had been made before the war for the defence of shipping by aircraft, and when the test came, this responsibility could only be met at the expense of the main commitment. The colossal wastage of shipping and its repercussions on the economic life of the country were largely due to this pre-war policy.

Horton's views on strategy and the direction of war deserve attention. He believed in the old British strategy of keeping open the seaways, so that military strength could be built up rapidly and used offensively at the right time and place. Command at sea was the paramount requirement, and as long as we could hold it in the English Channel, he felt sure that Hitler would not attempt the crossing.

As a submariner, Horton believed that U-boats, if used ruthlessly in large numbers, could bring trade to a standstill in the Atlantic, thus reducing the Army and Air Force to a state of impotence. He was convinced that the Germans would adopt this policy, and was correct in his forecast that 'the principal weapon to be used against us is blockade and not invasion.' The production of U-boats was increasing every day, and they could approach unopposed the Atlantic supply lines from bases ranging from the North Cape to Finisterre. To Horton's mind it was a matter of urgency to destroy U-boats near the convoys before their numbers could swamp the defence. This was a task that the Navy could not do alone.

Horton had reason to be anxious about the attitude of the Royal Air Force in regard to the war at sea. While commanding the Northern Patrol he had asked in vain for more long-range reconnaissance aircraft to co-operate with warships on his attenuated patrol lines. He felt that some of the large armed liners could be employed more usefully in carrying troops and cargoes than offering themselves as targets for German cruisers and submarines. The experience of his own submarines in the Norwegian campaign had confirmed his opinion that aircraft were a vital factor in anti-submarine defence.

Although the German airmen were not accustomed to working with warships they learnt quickly how to use depth charges. In July 1940, *Orzel*, *Shark*, *Salmon*, and *Thames* were lost. These submarines, having insufficient darkness in which to charge their batteries, were located and possibly sunk or disabled by flying-boats, who also directed A/S craft to the point to make sure of the kill. The unpleasant lesson learnt was that submarines cannot operate without great risk in high latitudes under enemy air coverage during the long daylight of the summer months.

Owing to the shortage of aircraft with crews trained in naval duties, British submarines were being used for reconnaissance in the central and southern North Sea to give warning of the approach of German invading forces. Horton thought that this was a waste of effort as R.A.F. planes passed over the area every day. He wrote 'my submarines are charged with reconnaissance duties in the middle and southern North Sea. No other force visits this area except Bomber Command and since they are fighting a private war with Germany they don't tell anybody what they see in time to be of any use.'

He appreciated that the Royal Air Force had a great task to perform in the general strategic plan, but he believed that victory ultimately would depend upon keeping open the sea highways. Bomber crews could be quickly trained in their thousands for attacking industrial areas, but it took some time to train aircrews to work over the sea, to talk the same language as the sailors in the ships below them, and to know the difference between a battleship and a trawler. He understood quite well that Fighter Command would soon be stretched to the limit in defending London and the ports, but his experience so far had led him to believe that the Air Ministry was half-hearted in its efforts to make provision for the needs of the Royal Navy in its heavy task at sea. Coastal Command, while co-operating to the full, was severely handicapped by lack of suitable weapons, aircraft and personnel.

Every day while on his way to the Admiralty he would pass long queues of young men waiting to enter the R.A.F. transit depots in St. John's Wood. 'How many of these,' he asked, 'would eventually find themselves out on the broad Atlantic helping the Navy to bring in the convoys?' For this task they would have to be sea-minded, and even with the enemy at the gates, Max could see no reason why the training of an adequate number of airmen in sea warfare should not start now.

He profoundly disagreed with the optimistic views prevailing in some quarters that existing anti-submarine measures would master the U-boat. Patient research had brought the 'Asdic' to a high state of efficiency, but the results to be expected from it had been overrated. Its range was short, consequently many hunting craft were required to cover the area where a U-boat was lurking.

Nelson had said 'only numbers can annihilate,' and it was plain to see that the German Admiral Doenitz intended to apply this principle in his submarine warfare against commerce. The Germans had already discovered that heavy losses could be inflicted on convoys by submarines working in packs, so they were feverishly building more and more submarines. In Horton's view there could be no other counter to this than numbers of destroyers, numbers of frigates, numbers of aircraft and, above all, numbers of officers and men in the Royal Navy and the Royal Air Force, fully trained and highly skilled in the use of anti-submarine weapons. While thinking of these things he would stand at the window of his office and see beneath him London, spread out like a vast carpet with its pattern of roof tops, church spires, railways, parks and factories merged into a haze of smoky blue. The thought of the visitation soon to come appalled him, but he agreed with Mr. Churchill that London seemed 'too vague and large a target for decisive results.'[1] His lofty viewpoint helped him to see the war in true perspective, strengthening his belief that the greater danger lay in the waters of the Atlantic.

Admiral P. Ruck-Keene writes:

'I was working with him at the time and I remember he was scheming and planning about the Battle of the Atlantic long before anyone had ever thought or heard about it. He and C.-in-C. Coastal Command were as thick as thieves, and he sent me over to Ireland to hunt submarines by the very methods that afterwards brought us such success . . . aircraft and destroyers working together . . . . In a few months his personality had pervaded the whole of the submarine flotillas and their morale rose to the very top and stayed there all the war. . . . Few realised what a great man he really was.'

One day he sent for a staff officer and said 'Produce a graph showing the total tanker tonnage available and the losses sustained by U-boat attack.' He became very gloomy when he saw the rate at which the tonnage was falling.

[1] *The Second World War*, Vol. II, p. 332. Winston S. Churchill.

During the summer and autumn of 1940 the submarine flotillas in home waters were employed on anti-invasion patrol. The old H-boats were used for the dangerous task of landing officers and agents on the coasts of the Channel Islands and France. By sinking the *Karlsruhe* and torpedoing the *Lutzow, Gneisenau* and others the Submarine Service had already contributed in no small measure to frustrating any hopes that Hitler may have had of invading England. In the critical month of August, when the German need of a fleet was greater than at any time in her history, he had only one pocket battleship, four cruisers, and a few destroyers fit for service. It was British command at sea in those fateful days that caused Hitler to abandon the project in favour of unrestricted attack by bombers and U-boats.

British submarine losses had been severe, but not out of proportion to their achievements and the risks they had taken. The following extracts from the report of a conference held at the Admiralty on 6th August 1940 throw some light on these losses, and also lay stress on the growing importance of aircraft in anti-submarine operations:

'The First Sea Lord expressed concern over recent submarine losses. He believed we had lost five submarines in the Mediterranean and six or seven in home waters during the past few weeks. Thus our loss of twelve submarines was exactly equivalent to the programme of new construction for 1939–40. He was anxious to know if there were any new factors that would account for the rise in our losses.

'He gave our total losses during the war as nineteen; this did not include three Allied submarines. The Mediterranean losses were largely due, in his opinion, to the fact that the Italians had laid minefields in deeper water than we had expected. The recent losses in home waters were largely due to the operations of enemy aircraft at night. Vice-Admiral Submarines [Horton] pointed out that probably four of the last six submarines lost in home waters were sunk by aircraft dropping depth charges in the semi-light conditions at night off the Norwegian coast. In this light, low-flying aircraft could always sight our submarines on the surface before any look-out, however keen, could sight the aircraft. The loss of the *Narwhal*, a minelaying submarine, was so far entirely unexplained; no claim to her destruction had been made by the enemy. There appears little doubt that *Spearfish* has been recently sunk by a U-boat. Such a sinking must be accepted as the normal hazard of naval warfare. In the submarine versus submarine campaign up to date both the enemy and ourselves have lost two submarines.

'The First Lord questioned why we cannot produce as good results in attacking U-boats with our aircraft as the enemy has achieved. The First Sea Lord replied that recently we have maintained a heavy concentration of submarines off the Norwegian coast, where the enemy have also concentrated very large numbers of aircraft and surface vessels who have little to occupy them except to hunt our submarines. Our problem, involving maintenance of our trade over wide areas, is a very different one.

'Admiral Horton considered that the enemy probably uses a low-flying and slow-flying aircraft, possibly of the flying-boat type, for anti-submarine purposes at night.

'The First Sea Lord stated that the depth charge had the advantage that it could be dropped from a very low height, thus reducing errors of aim, whereas a bomb must be dropped from at least 400 feet to safeguard the aircraft from its explosion.

'Admiral Horton instanced two cases in which our submarines have been attacked by aircraft with depth charges and have been blown to the surface from periscope and greater depth, escaping serious damage. Continuing, he pointed out that our submarines have constituted our first line of defence on anti-invasion patrol. To maintain the required reconnaissance, they have had to be concentrated in the unhealthy waters off the Norwegian coast during periods of no moon early in July and early in August when invasion was most probable. Analysing our seven losses, Admiral Horton said that the Dutch submarine O.13 had been sunk off the Skagerrack about thirty miles north of the German declared area, by enemy surface forces. The *Salmon* had been sunk in a similar position, probably by air attack; the *Shark* had been sunk off Utsire (Norway)—she had been brought to the surface, disabled by air attack and subsequently finished off by surface forces. The Polish submarine *Orzel* had been sunk further south-west of the German declared area, probably by air attack. The loss of the *Thames* may have been due to German air attack on her outward passage, the enemy having claimed to have sunk a submarine which would fit in with this theory. On the other hand she may have been undamaged by this attack and have continued her passage, to be lost, subsequently, in the newly laid German minefield off Norway.

'The First Lord asked for information if these deductions provided sufficient explanation of our losses or whether it was possible that the enemy had evolved something new in anti-submarine measures.

'Admiral Horton considered our losses were fully explained.

'The First Lord asked what change in our submarine dispositions had thus become necessary.

'Admiral Horton explained that our submarines are being withdrawn from the anti-invasion patrols in Norwegian waters as a result of the growing moon. He said that a decision will be called for later, when the next dark period comes along, whether our submarines are to take up these patrols again. The increasing hours of darkness will make things easier. He was absolutely confident that neither German material nor personnel were anything like as good as our own. Our losses were due to the weight of numbers the Germans could bring to bear, both air and surface forces, in a big anti-submarine effort in a small area.

'It was unanimously agreed that the main trouble was shortage of aircraft. If the numbers allocated to the Coastal Command could be doubled, or even trebled or quadrupled, we might hope to achieve far better results. As an example of the difficulties faced by the Coastal Command, it was pointed out that the A.O.C.-in-C. has no striking force at his disposal. The 'Beaufort' aircraft that are supposed to constitute his striking force have been grounded for the past six weeks, owing to engine trouble.

'If an increase comparable to that achieved for the Fighter and Bomber Command could be forthcoming we should be well on the way to a solution of our problem.'

In this matter of air support and co-operation the Navy was fighting a very one-sided battle. The airmen had constantly told the country how deadly aircraft could be to ships at sea, which was perfectly true in all cases where there was no counter-attack from the air. The Germans, virtually unopposed, were inflicting serious damage on our submarines and also on our surface ships and merchant vessels with bombers and dive bombers, while the R.A.F. was unable either to counter these attacks or to make similar attacks on German merchant ships and warships, which would have helped to balance our losses. Worse still, except for the small number of air crews in Coastal Command, the R.A.F. had been given no training to enable them to do such work and there was a serious shortage of weapons suitable for the purpose. Our aircraft, for instance, were not supplied with fully effective depth charges until the autumn of 1942.

For security reasons the public had been told practically nothing about the work of British submarines. Only a fragment of the story could be unfolded, so the Admiralty asked Admiral Horton if he himself would give a talk on the B.B.C., as he would know better than anyone else the exploits that could be safely disclosed. Here is the script of his broadcast:

'Nearly eleven months of war have passed since our submarines first set out to take their share in the great struggle against Nazi tyranny. From that day to this they have been in the front line. Tonight I want to tell you what I can about their work and about the officers and men who sail in them.

'Were you permitted to visit one of our ports, where our submarines are based, you would notice there were varying numbers in harbour from day to day. To all, except those who are connected with this branch of the Navy, that would be the sum total of your knowledge, but behind these silent movements there is a wealth of romance and adventure.

'The submarine, as you are probably aware, can operate against the enemy unseen and often unsuspected. With these advantages it can approach the enemy's coasts far closer than our surface forces, and what is more it can remain in that advanced position for a very considerable time. It carries a sting far more deadly than any other ship of equivalent size, and it can direct that sting from a few hundred yards' range. These simple facts at once bring home the nature of the work involved. To advance against the enemy's coasts means threading a way through seas which have been infested with every hazard that modern war can devise. To remain in that advanced position means more exposure to attack by night and day from air and surface forces. To achieve success means approaching within a few hundred yards of the enemy, when one slip by any member of the crew may mean disaster and even when the attack has been completed the crew know that they stand the risk of retaliation by depth charging for some time afterwards.

'Against these odds, often under the most severe weather conditions, our submarines have achieved successes far beyond our early expectations. It is hardly necessary for me to point out that these successes have been against legitimate targets such as enemy warships and transports. Two of their most valuable warships have been struck by torpedoes and put out of action for some time to come, two cruisers have been sunk and others damaged. In addition, the immense total of over 200,000 tons of transports has been sent to the bottom, representing the destruction of approximately two divisions of soldiers and their equipment. Such figures speak for themselves. To them must be added the constant flow of intelligence of the greatest value, the knowledge of which might otherwise be denied us.

'The life of those who sail in these ships is a full one indeed. In a matter of two or three weeks they experience almost every sensation known to human beings and some many times over. Adventure, hardship, boredom, intense excitement, comradeship, elation and a host of others, crammed into this short space of time. Let me give you some illustrations. When on patrol, at any moment an enemy ship may be sighted through the periscope. The crew go quickly and quietly to their stations, the torpedoes are brought to the "ready" and the attack begun. Enemy aircraft and surface forces protect the target. Meanwhile the submarine is manœuvred to a position from which the torpedoes can be fired. There are few occasions which could be more exciting and none where coolness and perfect training are more vital. The result may well be trumpeted throughout every capital in the world. That is *adventure*. *Hardship* has not the same romance but it is none the less present. Those nights in the winter when high seas and driving winds take command and you and I are safely in our beds our submarines, under the very nose of the enemy, are enduring the cold, fatigue and discomfort which inevitably accompany such weather. Nor do the confined quarters inside the vessel help matters, when clothes need drying and weary bodies call for rest. Sometimes, however, *boredom* is the lot of a submarine's crew for the whole of a patrol, especially when fighting an enemy who spends so long in harbour. The hours when the submarine is dived, generally throughout the entire day, are very tedious. A cigarette would help but that is forbidden, conversation is lacking after ten days or a fortnight, and even Ludo loses its charms. *Intense excitement* may come at any moment, and I believe that the depth-charge attack takes first place. Many feet below the surface of the sea the submarine may have to hide from his enemy. Suddenly the whole vessel is shaken like a cocktail. Lights go out, loose objects break and rattle. Sometimes the very hull pulsates with each explosion. Only magnificent material under skilful hands saves the vessel. These sensations and many others lead to a spirit of comradeship which is particularly marked in all submarine crews, and which is assuredly one of the greatest rewards of the life these men lead. The climax of a patrol is reached of course on the return to port and here *elation* knows no bounds, those who have made history by their exploits and joked about the Portsmouth football team while depth charges burst around them appear, like some strange people of another age, from the shell which has been their home for so many days, unshaven, heavy-eyed and unbathed; but they are fit and well, and they have done their job successfully and bravely. Their spirits and courage are an inspiration to those who direct their operations and already in this war their deeds have received the personal congratulations of His Majesty the King, the Prime Minister and the whole Board of Admiralty.

'In such a team it is perhaps invidious to mention any one individual, but I feel the submarine commanding officer deserves a special word. Besides shouldering the responsibility for his ship, his work is unique in that by one single act on his part he may influence the very course of the war. No wonder it is the aim and endeavour of every young Lieutenant in the Submarine Branch of the Navy to rise to command his own ship as soon as possible. The opportunities held by such a position are greater than in any other branch of the Navy, and I believe it is fair to say in any of the three Services.

'In the work of our submarines we are being assisted by our Allies. Under my command I have Dutch, Norwegian and Polish crews, and I am glad to say one of my most efficient units is manned by officers and men of the Free French forces. I find these splendid submarine crews animated by the same spirit as our own, and I look forward to adding to their numbers as time goes on.

'Some of the stories one hears when these brave men return from patrol illustrate the wonderful spirit of which I have spoken. These are the "shoreside" yarns and good hearing they make, but I would like you to know the stories which will go down the ages in naval history. I cannot possibly tell you them all, as fresh deeds occur almost daily, but those which spring to mind in the order of their occurrence are: firstly, that magnificent exploit by the Polish submarine *Orzel*, whose determination and dash led to their escape from internment in Tallin in the Baltic. With nothing better than a map of Europe they worked their way through the Kattegat and Skagerrack to England, braving a hundred unknown dangers on their passage. Then came the epic patrol of the *Salmon*—two Nazi cruisers severely damaged, a submarine sunk, and a "pass" at the *Bremen*, all crowded into two or three glorious days. This patrol will go down to history, and years hence, when this war is on the bookshelf, people will tell the tale of this very gallant ship. These events were hotly followed by the news that *Ursula* had penetrated closer to the enemy's shores than had hitherto been attempted. She was rewarded by a cruiser venturing across her path. Next came the great events of the Norwegian invasion when our submarines, disregarding the most destructive measures the enemy could bring to bear, sank warships and transports almost faster than we could credit possible.

'On a dark night last February in the Heligoland Bight, one of our submarines captured the iron ore ship *Hugo Stinnes*. The German Captain declared that he had never left territorial waters but the commanding officer of the submarine knew he had. In this submarine there was always a sweepstake on the time of arrival in harbour from patrol and since this subject of navigation had been much to the fore, the commanding officer allowed the German Captain to enter and in addition paid for his ticket. Sure enough that ticket was the winner.

'On another occasion the navigator of a submarine had scaled the periscope to obtain a better view of something on the horizon. Suddenly an aircraft came out of the sky—there could be no delay and the submarine was crash dived. The commanding officer soon realised they were one short inside the submarine. The vessel was immediately brought to the surface. There was found a most irate and indignant officer still clinging to the periscope who wanted to know what all the fuss was about because the aircraft was friendly!

'I would like to give you more details of these submarine exploits which became a thorn in Hitler's side, but there are very good reasons for withholding them at present, and I am confident that one day you will hear their stories, told far better than I could tonight.

'Today our submarines are as much in the front line as ever and their work in these dangerous waters will continue until final victory. Of our victory I have no shadow of doubt, and to anyone who may not be quite so sure as I am, I would say to him: "Meet some of the officers and men of the submarines; there you will find that knowledge of victory which is inspired by faith in our cause. You will also find an unconquerable valour which has been our heritage through the ages and it is alive today as it was at any time in the history of this island".'

One day in early October the First Lord, Mr. A. V. Alexander, sent for Horton and offered him the command of the Home Fleet. While they were talking, Admiral Pound put his head round the door and said jokingly 'Well, has he refused it?' Pound knew that Horton had refused appointments before and how stubborn he could be when matters of principle were at stake, so was not surprised when the First Lord replied 'He hasn't jumped at it.'

Horton's first reaction was to refuse, because he had always felt that the Commander-in-Chief Home Fleet was too much under the thumb of the Admiralty, was out of touch with the higher direction of the war and had no power to direct the operation of the aircraft of Coastal Command. He felt also that it would be impossible for him to conduct sea and air operations effectively from his flagship when wireless silence had to be enforced.

After twenty-four hours reflection he sent this letter:

VICE-ADMIRAL (S),
NORTHWAYS,
LONDON, N.W.3.
10th October 1940.

Dear First Lord,

I appreciate to the full the very high honour attaching to your offer of yesterday morning, but, after deep thought and much heart-searching, I have come to the conclusion that I cannot accept.

The chief reasons that have led me to this decision are the conditions under which the Commander-in-Chief Home Fleet has to carry out his heavy responsibilities. I spent the first four months of the war in close contact with the Home Fleet and since then have maintained this contact.

The difficulties which C.-in-C. Home Fleet suffered when endeavouring to make contact with important enemy forces or units when the enemy were active at sea before and during the Norwegian campaign led me to form very definite conclusions. I expressed some of these views to the Prime Minister when he was First Lord and also to V.C.N.S.[1] at various times.

In brief my views are as follows:

I think it essential that the Commander-in-Chief Home Fleet should have directly under his orders adequate air forces—

(a) For reconnaissance;
(b) For sea bombing;
(c) Fighter protection.

To carry this into effect bomber squadrons would have to be placed under C.-in-C. H.F.'s orders, not only for bombing enemy forces at sea, but to supplement the inadequate reconnaissance machines which is all that the A.O.C.-in-C. Coastal Command can supply.

Shore-based fighter protection for the Fleet is also necessary and must be under the Commander-in-Chief's orders in certain areas.

These forces should work and train together and with the Fleet continuously, and the personnel should not be subjected to constant changes.

Only if the above measures are put into force do I see a chance of the Home Fleet successfully fulfilling its functions.

I also formed the opinion, and expressed it to V.C.N.S. some months ago, that the C.-in-C. Home Fleet should be shore based and that the Admirals of individual squadrons should be considerably younger. Generally the age of responsible officers at sea should be reduced.

In the lull in surface warfare at sea during the last months some of the above needs may not have been so apparent, but I am sure that they will emerge again directly the enemy resumes activities with his larger units.

Lastly, I formed the opinion that the Commander-in-Chief Home Fleet did not enjoy that degree of independent judgment and action which seemed to me to be essential to the full discharge of the responsibilities of this Command.

Feeling so strongly as I do on the above matters, and realising that there is little or no hope of the principal requisite changes being made in the near future, I could not undertake with any confidence

[1] V.C.N.S.: Vice-Chief of Naval Staff.

the Commander-in-Chief Home Fleet's onerous responsibilities to
the Board and to the country.

It is with real pain and regret that I feel compelled, for the reasons
stated, to renounce the high honour which you have offered me.

Yours sincerely,

(Signed) MAX HORTON.

THE RT. HON. A. V. ALEXANDER, M.P.,
First Lord of the Admiralty.

This courageous decision was typical of Max·Horton. He made
it with the full knowledge that he was throwing away his chances
of becoming an Admiral of the Fleet. He had, already stated his
opinion officially to the Admiralty that 'Fleets cannot operate
without the close co-operation of air power' and he was willing
to sacrifice his future career in support of that principle. Furthermore he was certain that he could serve his country best in a
post where his knowledge and experience of submarine warfare
would be used with full effect. He had been brought up in submarines, he had fought in submarines, and he had seen the results
of his leadership and administration as Flag Officer Submarines.
Although he had been given no hint where his destiny lay, his
intuition told him that 'when things get bad they will send for me'
—and with that thought he was content.

Towards the end of 1940 it became clear that the enemy had
failed in his attempt to gain air superiority over the British Isles.
Had there been no English Channel this resounding British success
would not have prevented the German hordes from pouring into
the country and overwhelming the ports and airfields. It was fear
of blue water that stopped Hitler, and since it was unlikely that
he could ever gain command at sea in home waters the threat of
invasion faded away. Britain, although she stood alone, turned
at last to her traditional strategy and planned to use her sea
power to enable the Army to strike where the enemy was weakest.

Twelve months after Horton had taken over the command of
British submarines, the Battle of Britain had been won, the Italian
Fleet had been severely crippled by the Fleet Air Arm at Taranto,
and a British Army was advancing in Libya. Nevertheless, the
menace of the U-boat was growing greater every day, and
the Battle of the Atlantic had still to be fought.

ANXIOUS DAYS

At the end of the year 1940 the Admiralty in a tribute to the Vice-Admiral Submarines said:

'The high percentage of successful submarine attacks, and the low number of material failures, contributed a remarkable achievement.'

Horton was promoted to Admiral on 9th January 1941 at the age of fifty-seven. Ever since his exploits in the First World War his name had been known to the British and German public, and there were many pertinent comments in the Press:

'In past years Horton was universally regarded as a man with a great future should war come, but without one if peace continued. It is his complete mastery of every aspect of submarine warfare which gives him at the present moment a unique position.'

'From his earliest days he has been "unorthodox" in many of his views and ways, and his strong personality, if it has not made him always popular, has earned for him the universal respect of the Navy as one of its outstanding men, and one upon whose judgment the country could always rely in any great emergency.'

'His personality has undoubtedly been a source of inspiration to the younger generation of submarine officers.'

'His reputation as a seaman and tactician is second to none; but it is in the sphere of underwater warfare that his knowledge and experience are supreme, both of which are reflected in the deeds, accomplished in this war by the younger generation of submarine men.'

Vice-Admiral James Fife, U.S.N., who came to England in the early days of the war, has recorded this impression of Max Horton:

'I first knew Sir Max at the time of the blitz in London. I was one of the American "observers" sent to England after Dunkirk. Upon arrival, the U.S. Naval Attaché—Alan Kirk—turned me over to Sir Max at his headquarters at Northways, Swiss Cottage. With the atmosphere of those days, when England was fighting it out alone and the going was tough, my first and lasting impression of Sir Max was that he was an officer and gentleman of the old school who was carrying on the traditions of Drake and Nelson. Absolutely fearless for his personal safety he had only one thought—how to damage the enemy. A man of the highest personal integrity, he was ruthless and intolerant of mediocrity. Since he was a perfectionist himself, he would have no part of anyone who did not give his all for the common cause. As I grew to know him better I found that he had a superb loyalty downward to those whom he could trust and who served him well. Later on, during the Pacific War, occasionally when I faced a particularly knotty problem I would sometimes ask myself "How would Sir Max handle this?"'

CHAPTER SEVEN

MEDITERRANEAN OFFENSIVE

Horton visits the flotillas. Their work and the results. The bombing of Malta and its effect on submarine operations. Loss of the 'Medway.' Correspondence with Captains. Prime Minister's tribute.

WHEN Mussolini committed his country to war on 10th June 1940 there were only twelve British submarines in the Mediterranean, four at Malta and eight at Alexandria. Two were mine-layers and the rest were large ocean-going types of 1,780 tons recently recalled with their depot ship *Medway* from the Far East. They were too big for inshore operations in the translucent waters of the Mediterranean, and on their very first patrol off Italian ports three of the four which had sailed from Malta, *Grampus*, *Odin*, and *Orpheus*, were lost. Speaking of this disaster, the Commander-in-Chief, Admiral Sir Andrew Cunningham, says:

'At the time we had no information as to the cause, but were aware that the Italians had laid extensive minefields off their ports in depths up to 150 and 200 fathoms. We knew that our submarine Commanders, superbly trained and without thought of danger, would push right in. I did not consider it was fair on them, so gave orders that they were not to get inside the 200 fathoms line unless in actual pursuit of important enemy units.'[1]

Owing to commitments in home waters these large submarines were all that could be spared for the Mediterranean, yet, in spite of this initial setback, they achieved many successes. The *Parthian* sank an Italian submarine ten days after war was declared.

When the danger of invasion had receded at home, submarine

[1] *A Sailor's Odyssey*, p. 238, by Admiral of the Fleet Viscount Cunningham.

reinforcements came to the Mediterranean. The existing flotilla based at Alexandria was strengthened by boats of the T class (1,430 tons) and re-formed as the 1st Flotilla under Captain S. M. Raw, R.N. By the end of January 1941 five brand new submarines of the U class (650 tons) had arrived at Malta and formed the 10th Flotilla under Captain G. W. G. Simpson, R.N. Each flotilla was kept to an operational strength of eight to ten submarines. Although the little submarines of the U class had comparatively low speed and fuel capacity, they proved to be very suitable for their work. Malta being so close to enemy naval bases and convoy routes these handicaps did not matter. Indeed, their small size was an advantage in heavily patrolled waters, and it was found possible to keep an average of four of them at sea throughout the war.

In April 1941 the depot ship *Maidstone* (Captain G. W. Voelcker) was stationed at Gibraltar with the 8th Flotilla, including three Dutch submarines. Their duty in those early days was to patrol the western basin of the Mediterranean, thus giving submarines experience of operational conditions before they moved east to reinforce the 10th and 1st Flotillas. All submarines from England destined for the Mediterranean were given a final work-up on the 'nursery slopes.'

The operations of British submarines in the Mediterranean were directed by Admiral Cunningham, the Commander-in-Chief, but Admiral Horton as Flag Officer Submarines in London was responsible for the initial training of the crews, the administration of the flotillas, their supply and equipment.

Max, as one of the pioneers of submarine warfare, had helped to found the traditions of the branch and to create the magnificent esprit de corps which permeated it. He was the 'Master Submariner.' A brief reference to the part played by submarines in bringing about the decisive British victory over the Axis powers in the Mediterranean is not therefore out of place in his biography.

In September 1941 Horton proposed to the Commander-in-Chief that he would like to visit the Mediterranean flotillas and got the reply 'Welcome—no objection.' He flew in a Sunderland flying-boat via Gibraltar and Malta to Alexandria, staying about three days at each place. While with the Commander-in-Chief he sought to obtain more publicity for submarine work and there was some straight talking on the subject.[1] Cunningham agreed to more publicity, subject to certain reservations about security, which resulted in Anthony Kimmins visiting the flotillas and afterwards giving a broadcast.

Shortly after Horton had landed at Malta from his Sunderland, he addressed a parade of all the officers and men of the submarines in harbour. Being well aware that his speech would make a deep impression, he confined his remarks to four vital points:

RESPONSIBILITY

'You have joined a Service where responsibility—heavy responsibility—rests almost immediately on its youngest officers—any man in a submarine by a mistake at a critical moment can finish himself and all his shipmates—the opportunity of an officer doing likewise are correspondingly increased.'

KNOW YOUR JOB

'It is essential that you know your job—it isn't just a matter of making good in your profession, it is simply a matter of survival. Don't be satisfied by knowing what happens if certain things are done, be sure you understand why it happens. Don't be satisfied in yourself if any part of a submarine is still a mystery—bother your instructors until you *understand*.'

LOOKING OUT

'The first order I issued on returning to submarines was one referring to look-out. More than any other single factor, a sharp and efficient look-out is likely to lead to success in war and survival of it. No one with experience doubts the truth of this statement—look-out of the standard required implies a tense concentration which requires a strong effort of will to maintain. A feeling of responsibility is a big aid to look-out—that is why the C.O. nearly always sees an object first. An indifferent look-out spells death. Don't forget it ever. I have said enough maybe to make you realise anew that you have joined a Service where great prizes are to be won with corresponding risks.'

STANDARDS

'It is essential to keep the standard high—nothing can be neglected—it is not a kindness to overlook slackness or mistakes, it is really great cruelty to do so—cruelty to the wives and relatives of the man you let off, and his shipmates and to yourself. There is no margin for mistakes in submarines, you are either alive or dead.'

[1] Q.v. *A Sailor's Odyssey*, p. 410, by Admiral of the Fleet Viscount Cunningham.

Horton could speak to technicians with a knowledge equal to their own, and so could expose their theories and claims. He was tireless in his efforts to get to the bottom of any problems, strategical, tactical and technical. Captain Simpson gives this account of the Admiral's visit to Malta:

'He held a conference of C.O.s to discuss current problems and had a two-hour discussion alone with Wanklyn and Tomkinson.[1] to enquire first hand about their attack technique.

'I had a long interview with him the first evening. Having covered the ground pretty thoroughly, I remarked that we had had trouble with the steering unit of our torpedoes, and gave him my idea of the cause. His eyes lit up, he clasped his hands on the table in front of him and said "Why does this occur?" I explained in detail. "Where are the drawings?" he asked. I went and fetched them. After a few minutes study he remarked "Who told you this story?—because it's nonsense." He then said that, whatever the failure, it was nothing to do with my explanation. He added "Do you agree you were talking nonsense?" to which I readily and genuinely assented. He then remarked that Rear-Admiral Boyd[2] who had been Captain of Vernon [torpedo school] was travelling with him; so I was to have a typical steering unit, showing the defect, available next morning at the torpedo preparing shop, where he and Admiral Boyd would inspect it. Next morning Horton led the inspection and proved to all of us that the *design* was not at fault. Due to length of patrols with a torpedo sitting in the tube, a certain amount of verdigrese would form and interfere with the delicate mechanism. He remarked that, since we were committed to this in all torpedoes, the only solution was for the steering element to be cleaned and re-assembled in every submarine the day before sailing, and also on patrol if it lasted more than two weeks. He sat down, and sent a signal to that effect to all flotillas then and there.

'Two days later Wanklyn in the *Upholder* sailed for patrol, fired twice at destroyers and sank one. While on patrol with three torpedoes left, the *Trieste* and *Trento*, Italian cruisers, passed him at high speed. He attacked from 2,000 yards, and although his estimates of course and speed were practically exact, all torpedoes missed. I learnt about this some days later when *Upholder* came back from patrol. I then discovered that, since the torpedoes were already in *Upholder* two days before sailing, they were not overhauled; only those embarked after Horton's order were so treated. This was inexcusable, so I signalled to the Admiral, who had returned home—"Regret to report that due to

[1] Distinguished submarine Commanders.
[2] Later Admiral Sir Denis Boyd, K.C.B., C.B.E., D.S.C.

lack of precision in promulgating and executing your order, *Upholder* has just missed a *Trento* class cruiser due to centre and vital torpedo of a spread of three circling." To this I received no reply, but Kimmins, who happened to be interviewing him after receipt of this signal, told me his reactions. Sir Max was apparently delighted that the lesson had been rubbed in so soon and so effectively.

' I have told this in full to give a picture of his complete self-confidence and mastery of technical matters. What impressed me was his superior knowledge to artificers and technicians on the job—this was quite obvious.'

Recalling his interview with Horton at Northways, Anthony Kimmins says:

'He suddenly dived to his desk and handed me a signal. "What do you make of that?" he asked . . . I looked up from the signal to find him watching me closely . . . "Not too good, is it, Sir?" I said rather lamely. "Not too good?" he barked. "It's damned bad. Good targets missed because of carelessness in the care and maintenance. Bad? It's. . . ." And then in a flash his voice changed. The bark had been replaced by that same tone which he had used before he showed me the signal. "But that's not the point," he said. " What delights me is that when they've made a bloomer they don't try and cover it up. They admit it frankly and tell me all about it." It was the proud father again— the father whose boy had written from school and admitted candidly that he had been in the wrong. . . . "Each of these submarine Captains is a potential Derby winner, only a thousand times more so," he went on in his enthusiastic way. "Nothing must be spared to keep them in good health and trained to the minute. Nothing must be spared to give them every encouragement. You could help a great deal." '[1]

From the strategic point of view, we have seen how the damage inflicted on enemy warships by British submarines in home waters deprived Hitler of any hope he may have had of landing his armies on British soil. Two years later Rommel's army was brought to a standstill at El Alamein owing to loss of petrol and ammunition. 'Of this overall loss the enemy attributes 45 per cent. being due to submarines, 11 per cent. to naval and 26 per cent. to R.A.F. aircraft, 8 per cent. to surface ships and 7 per cent. to mines.'[2]

Space will only permit a brief glance at the submarine disposi- tions which brought about this remarkable result, and only a few

[1] *Half-time*, by Anthony Kimmins, p. 80.
[2] *A Sailor's Odyssey*, p. 674, by Admiral of the Fleet Viscount Cunningham.

examples can be selected from many individual exploits which for daring, skill, and versatility are unsurpassed.

In January 1941, when General Wavell's army went over to the offensive, the U class submarines at Malta were in an ideal position for striking at the Italian supply route between Sicily and Tripoli. This was work for which many years of patient training had fitted them. All targets were legitimate. The commanding officers could sink at sight without having to worry about the counterclaims of reconnaissance and the restrictions of International Law. In consequence, the sinking of enemy supply ships on their rigid convoy routes commenced in late January and increased in tempo with experience of conditions.

Retaliation came swiftly. Rommel was about to land in Tripoli, and his supplies across the Mediterranean were vital to him. Malta must therefore be made untenable as a base for British warships and aircraft, so the Luftwaffe came to Sicily, and the raids on Malta were stepped up to a rate of a hundred a month.

In addition to this, the enemy kept their supply routes under air supervision, and laid mines in the Sicilian Channel. The Italian convoys were usually limited to a small number of fast ships, escorted by destroyers and torpedo boats, and supported by cruisers—the warships often outnumbering the ships in the convoy.

Yet even when the enemy was at his strongest, the submarines of the 10th Flotilla relentlessly kept up their attack and took a heavy toll. After reviewing their successes, the First Sea Lord said in a letter to Horton: 'I thank God I do not have to run a convoy system in the face of your submarine commanding officers.' It is not surprising that the Germans preferred to travel by air rather than by sea, although this threw a heavy strain on their transport machines and used up precious petrol.

The submarines engaged on these strenuous patrols had little hope of a happy release on return to harbour, because the flotilla base at Malta, naturally enough, was a priority target for the Luftwaffe. As relaxation was essential, arrangements were made for the crews to go to rest camps in the country while repair parties attended to the machinery and hull.

Meanwhile Malta was running short of supplies, so the largest and oldest submarines of the 1st Flotilla were used to carry vital commodities from Alexandria. In July 1941 this underwater freighter service brought to the beleaguered island 126 passengers, 84,280 gallons of petrol, 83,340 gallons of kerosene, 12 tons of mail, 36 tons of stores and munitions, including torpedoes for submarines and aircraft. Shortage of torpedoes was a great anxiety to Horton and the submarine officers. In 1941–42 the Malta flotilla fired 600 torpedoes, and their replenishment was too precious to risk in heavily bombed convoys. The inadequate supply was always a serious restriction, and submarines had to hold their fire occasionally against enemy shipping returning home in ballast.

Whilst the 10th Flotilla at Malta kept up its attack on enemy supply routes and warships, the 1st Flotilla at Alexandria covered the Levant, the Aegean, the Adriatic–Benghazi routes and coastwise traffic from Benghazi to the east. The 1st Flotilla's score steadily mounted, and when activity slackened in the eastern basin, one or two submarines would make the long passage from Alexandria to reinforce the 10th Flotilla in the central basin. For instance, the *Triumph* (Commander W. J. W. Woods) torpedoed the Italian cruiser *Bolzano* north of Messina, the *Rorqual* (Lt.-Commander R. H. Dewhurst) sank an Italian U-boat south of Stromboli and the *Torbay* (Commander A. C. C. Miers, V.C.) attacked ships in Corfu harbour.

Although the British people have cause to remember the German U-boats, few realise that the standard of professional skill in their own submarines was far higher than that of the enemy. The German U-boats and their crews, having been mass-produced for the sole purpose of sinking (without warning) slow-moving merchant ships in convoy, proved to be singularly ineffective against high-speed targets. Consequently the British Admiralty were able to transport troops and vital supplies in large liners across the Atlantic without loss. The Italians, hoping to benefit by British experience, adopted the same method for reinforcing the Axis armies in Libya, but they were quickly disillusioned. The officers and men of the British Submarine Service, having been trained to attack fast-moving warships protected by every form of anti-submarine defence, sank five liners averaging 17,000 tons in the short space of three months. The following abridged account of one of these successful operations is taken from the official report of Captain G. W. G. Simpson commanding the 10th Flotilla, dated 25th September 1941.

'In the early morning of 18th September, three submarines of the 10th Flotilla were patrolling about eighty miles east of Tripoli. They had been ordered to attack a fast Italian troop convoy which was expected to arrive at Tripoli from the eastward at about 9.0 a.m. Lt.-Commander M. D. Wanklyn in the *Upholder* had placed himself on the probable course of the enemy with *Upright* five miles to the north and *Unbeaten* five miles to the south.

At 3.7 a.m. Lieut. Woodward in the *Unbeaten* sighted three large liners escorted by destroyers about eight miles to the north and immediately informed *Upholder*. Realising he was too far away to reach an attacking position ahead of the convoy, Woodward decided to follow in its wake in the hope of overtaking any ships disabled by his consorts. Wanklyn in the *Upholder*, having closed the enemy at full speed on the surface, reached a good position to attack. Unfortunately, his gyro compass had broken down, and he was obliged to steer by magnetic compass with the helmsman down below. It was difficult to hold a steady course as the submarine was yawing badly. At 4.6 a.m. he fired four torpedoes aimed individually at three very large ships (later identified as *Neptunia*, 19,500 tons, *Oceania*, 19,500 tons and *Vulcania*, 24,500 tons). Then he dived. Owing to the yaw, he had to spread his torpedoes over the full length of the convoy anticipating the amount of swing between the order "fire" and the torpedo leaving the tube. By skilful timing he covered the target with accuracy and two ships were hit. At 4.15 a.m. the *Upholder* came to the surface; in the dawn light Wanklyn saw one liner stopped with a destroyer standing by, and another very large ship escaping to the westward. The third liner had evidently been sunk. While reloading, he took up a position whence he could attack the damaged ship with the sun behind him. Meanwhile, the *Unbeaten*, who had been following the convoy, had the same idea, and both submarines unknown to each other dived to attack the enemy from the same side. Just at the moment that the *Upholder* was about to fire she was put deep by an escorting destroyer. Undismayed, Wanklyn dived under the liner and fired two torpedoes from the other side at a range of 2,000 yards. Both torpedoes hit, and the transport broke up and sank. Thus Wanklyn killed his wounded bird a few seconds before the *Unbeaten* fired.'

In a private letter to Horton, Captain Simpson said:

H.M.S. *Talbot*.

27th September 1941

Dear Admiral Horton,

... I send this letter by air mail with my account of what occurred—Wanklyn is a most remarkable man, and seems to get phenomenal results, in adversity as well as out of it—for instance to sink two liners [*Neptunia* and *Oceania*] of 20,000 tons each in a night attack with the Sperry gyro compass broken down—out of a total of three ships with only four torpedoes must be mighty hard to beat for records.

Again thanking you, Sir, for all your help.

Yours,

(Signed) GEORGE SIMPSON.

Shortly after this successful operation, Wanklyn was awarded the Victoria Cross for 'valour and resolution' on a previous occasion when he had sunk another 18,000-ton troopship, the *Conte Rosso*, in the face of strong counter-attack. Altogether he sank 97,000 tons of Axis transport shipping, one destroyer and three U-boats while in command of the *Upholder*. There was the time when he was travelling east from Palermo along the north coast of Sicily on a moonlight night. He had sunk one ship but she had cost him seven torpedoes, and he had only one left. Suddenly, gun flashes stabbed the darkness from under the background of the land. This proved to be the Italian submarine *Saint Bon* which had seen him in the moonlight and opened fire. When Wanklyn reached the bridge the enemy was getting the range, so the British submarine dived immediately. The Italian, deprived of his target, altered course at right angles to the *Upholder*, Wanklyn fired his one torpedo by eye through the periscope and hit the enemy under the conning tower at about 1,000 yards. This snap shot in the dark, without the aid of instruments, was one of many examples of his amazing judgment and split-second decision in emergency.

In August 1942, he and his gallant ship went on their last patrol, and met their end while attacking a heavily escorted Italian convoy. In a letter to the Admiralty reporting the loss, Captain Simpson said, 'their brilliant record will always shine in the records of British submarines. . . . The *Upholder* would have returned to the United Kingdom on completion of this patrol . . .

it seems to me that Wanklyn was a man whom the nation can ill afford to lose.'

Certainly no man could have done more to uphold the traditions of the British Submarine Service, and there could be no epitaph more fitting than the name of the ship destined to be his last command.

The First Submarine Flotilla, commanded by Captain S. M. Raw, R.N., at Alexandria was conveniently placed for the main task of disrupting enemy supplies to Libya, but the conditions varied according to the fortunes of the opposing armies. When Rommel drove Wavell back to the Egyptian frontier in the spring of 1941 he opened up terminal ports for the Axis army on the coast of Cyrenaïca. This enabled him not only to disperse his maritime lines of supply, but also to use small craft in coastal waters to take the burden off his mechanised transport on shore. Raw says in his report: 'Most of these ships (coastal craft) are very small, not worth a torpedo, and they stick to the ten-fathom line. Attack with the gun necessitates an approach into shallow water with a sandy bottom, which leaves the submarine in a hazardous position in the event of an air attack. As, however, no craft other than submarines are suitable or available for interception of this traffic these risks have perforce to be accepted.'

The submarines of the 1st Flotilla were stretched to the utmost. In addition to covering Libyan coastal waters they were urgently needed for operations on the other side of the Mediterranean. They rescued many survivors from Crete, and were continuously employed on offensive patrols in the Aegean and Ionion Seas, where they had to contend with strong anti-submarine forces and intensive air activity. In their single-minded endeavour to destroy enemy supply ships they did not hesitate to enter enemy harbours and sink them at anchor. It was for valour in operations close to the enemy coast that Commander A. C. C. Miers in the *Torbay*, Lieut. P. S. W. Roberts and Petty Officer T. W. Gould in the *Thrasher* were each awarded the Victoria Cross. Admiral Cunningham while giving an account of these cases of great bravery also says that 'every submarine that could be spared for service in the Mediterranean was worth its weight in gold.'[1]

[1] *A Sailor's Odyssey*, p. 445.

During the summer months of 1941 there had been a slight easement in the bombing of Malta, but at the end of the year the German Air Force was reinforced. The assault continued in crescendo throughout the spring and early summer of 1942 at an average rate of 250 raids a month.

In April when the bombing was at its height, repairs to submarines of the 10th Flotilla could not be carried out in the dockyard, so they had to be submerged during daylight hours either in the harbour or just outside, coming to the surface at night for overhaul at the base. The Luftwaffe had a good idea what was going on; two submarines were sunk in harbour, some were damaged whilst lying on the bottom, and two more were mined in the approaches.

The rest camps were no longer sanctuaries, as the German airmen were picking them out and attacking them with dive bombers and machine-gun fire.

The problem of maintenance and repairs was difficult enough, but there came a time when all the minesweepers were put out of action, and the submarines had to take the risk of passing through unswept channels in order to get in and out of harbour. The chief concern of Simpson and his men was to be able to keep up their offensive against the enemy supply ships. Rather than give up Malta as an operational base he made proposals to the Commander-in-Chief for running a system of relief crews and informed Horton that he had done so. Max, as we know, disliked the idea, and in a letter to the Admiralty said:

'The effect on crews of continually changing from one submarine to another is bound to have an adverse effect on morale, which, in turn, will show itself during operations at sea. The esprit de corps engendered in a submarine crew by pride in the individuality of their vessel and of its achievements will not apply under the new proposals, and their corporate pride in their flotilla will not fully take its place.'

While discussing the question at the Admiralty, he ruefully recalled how he and others at the time of the Abyssinian crisis had urged that bomb-proof shelters for submarines should be tunnelled in the soft rock.[1]

[1] Rock shelters were first proposed officially in 1934 by Captain G. D'Oyly Hughes, R.N., then commanding submarines at Malta. Horton supported the scheme and strong representations were made to the Admiralty by successive Commanders-in-Chief. The Government however would not sanction the expenditure.

It was hoped that a reinforcement of forty-seven Spitfires flown from carriers on 21st April 1942 would ease the situation. Unfortunately, most of these were knocked out on the ground soon after they had landed.

Major repairs, which only the dockyard could do, were becoming increasingly urgent, and there was danger that the submarines might be hemmed in by mines. So the Commander-in-Chief decided that the 10th Flotilla must be moved temporarily to the Eastern Mediterranean, where it could share repair facilities with the 1st Flotilla at Alexandria. The submarines, while operating against enemy supply lines, were to continue to use Malta as an advanced base for fuelling and re-arming as long as they could get in and out. Horton fully agreed with this decision.

In spite of all difficulties in these critical four months, the 10th Flotilla never ceased to harass the enemy. Between 1st January and 1st May 1942 they sank a cruiser, four Italian submarines, one U-boat, thirteen transports, two schooners, a salvage ship, a trawler, and blew up an Italian goods train.

On 5th May, Simpson reluctantly withdrew his flotilla, and with a heavy heart set course for Alexandria. Horton, sensing the feelings of these noble young men, wrote to their Captain on 5th June:

'I do appreciate your forethought and the splendid work done by you all to prepare for the intense scale of air attack to which you were subjected, and I had never any doubt but that the flotilla was prepared to stick it to the bitter end and at the same time continue to render an excellent account of itself.

Under present conditions, however, I am sure the 10th Submarine Flotilla will prove of greater value during its enforced change of base to Alexandria than it could have done under the conditions with which it would have had to contend at Malta.

I hope it will not be long before the submarine base at Malta, which you have all worked so hard to establish, will once again welcome you back to continue the fight under less exacting conditions.

I am passing your letter to all flotillas so that they can learn valuable lessons from your experience.'

(Signed) MAX HORTON,
Admiral.

The 10th Flotilla operated from Alexandria for about two months, but at one time it looked as if it might be a case of 'out of the frying pan into the fire.' The German army under Rommel had been halted at El Alamein only sixty miles from Alexandria, and there was a possibility that they might overrun the base. General Auchinleck felt confident that he could defeat Rommel, who in any case was short of supplies. Admiral Harwood, the naval Commander-in-Chief, thought nevertheless that it would be a wise precaution to move the submarines to Haifa, from whence they could carry on their attacks against the enemy supply ships without danger of interruption. So on 29th June 1942 the 1st and 10th Flotillas sailed from Alexandria. The submarines went on ahead followed at dusk by the depot ship *Medway*, commanded by Captain P. Ruck-Keene, R.N.[1] The destroyer *Sikh*, with Captain Simpson on board as a passenger, was also in company, a prudent arrangement to avoid having both Captains in one ship. The *Sikh* narrowly missed a mine outside the harbour, and a few hours afterwards three torpedoes struck the *Medway*. This valuable ship, with her workshops, stores and over a thousand men on board heeled over and sank in the short space of ten minutes. Fortunately several destroyers were close at hand, and nearly everyone was saved, although twenty-one were killed and eight wounded. A full description of this incident and the steps taken to establish a submarine base at Beirut is given in a private letter to Admiral Horton from Captain Ruck-Keene. [See Appendix IX.]

Meanwhile the situation at Malta was improving rapidly. With the arrival of air reinforcements, British fighters had gained air superiority over the Luftwaffe, consequently the approaches could be kept clear of mines and the dockyard freely used. On 19th July, the 10th Flotilla returned and immediately resumed their attack on the enemy supply lines where the prospects were good because, as Simpson put it, 'the ground had not been shot over for some time.'

Although the results achieved by British submarines had surpassed even Horton's expectations, the losses had been heavy and the strain had been great. On 14th August 1942 he wrote to Simpson:

[1] Captain Ruck-Keene had succeeded Captain Raw in command of the 1st Flotilla.

'I expect —— is probably in need of a rest and we will try to make arrangements to relieve him shortly.

'The problem of filling up the quotas is far from easy to solve. We shall not press you. I think it may be necessary to enter some more senior experienced Lieutenants of the right type with a view to training them to become commanding officers, without going through the more junior roles. If we can raise a few out of the Admiralty I shall probably start an experiment in this direction very soon. I shall be interested to have any ideas you may have on this subject regarding their training generally.

'I am so glad you managed to get in a little leave at Beirut and are happy to be back again at Malta. I am quite sure Malta is happy to see you again too.'

Horton, foreseeing the inevitable expansion of the Submarine Branch, had opened it in 1940 to officers of the Royal Naval Reserve and Royal Naval Volunteer Reserve. Many of these became First Lieutenants and some achieved command. On the whole they reached a standard equal to that of the Regular officers and consequently solved the problem which he mentions in the above letter. By the end of the war more than half the submarine officers came from the R.N.R. and the R.N.V.R. The success of this experiment reflects the greatest credit not only on the officers themselves, but also on the professional officers of the Royal Navy who inspired and trained them.

Horton corresponded regularly with the Captains of all three flotillas, and the close and happy relationship between them stands out clearly in their letters.

The commanding officers were not afraid to speak their minds, telling him of their troubles down to the smallest technical detail. A few of these letters, being mainly of interest to professional readers, will be found in the Appendix. Horton's reply to a letter from Captain G. B. H. Fawkes, R.N. (then commanding the 8th Flotilla at Gibraltar), is quoted here as an example of the general tone of the correspondence:

NORTHWAYS.
24th October 1942.

Dear Fawkes,

Many thanks for your letters. I do appreciate so much being kept in the picture. I understand what a sweat it must be when you are so busy.

I shall be very interested to hear in due course how ——— gets on under her new C.O. I daresay if her previous C.O. had been more carefully watched and criticised in his methods very firmly, he would have made good. Meantime I am happy he should remain with you for the present.

I got your full report about ——— and we are considering action to prevent similar occurrences. The whole show makes bad reading.

P.48's[1] signal reporting her flooding of auxiliary machine room seemed a very stupid and rather panicky one, although I have some sympathy over the initial mistake with regard to the log, *since I did the same thing myself in 1915 and nearly sank my boat.* Why on earth could P.48 not have shut off his ventilation trunks or bunged them up? However, I expect you will give me the answer to this very soon.

In new construction there is a possibility of a store-carrying submarine design being progressed. The general idea is to use a T class hull, no internal tubes, two battery sections; carrying about 250 tons internal cargo and 120 tons externally. Your views would be appreciated, especially as regards the hatch.

I am passing your remarks about congestion at Gibraltar and taking the defence of Gibraltar on an inter-Service basis to a higher quarter. I am sure you are right on this subject.

I gather you are very hard worked in comparison with your easy time here. I wish I had known of the latter—I am sure I'd have found something more for you to do!

Let me know what I owe you and address of your bank—I am looking forward doubly to P.31 or *Otus* arrival. Have just seen Marsh who brings your letter of two days ago—Roper and Frew are looking into what we can do to help you with repair parties.

Very best of luck to you in your highly responsible job and to your flotilla. If there is anything you want personally or otherwise, do not hesitate to let me know.

Yours sincerely,

(Signed) MAX HORTON.

Max did not hesitate to criticise himself to junior officers if he felt that they might benefit by his own mistakes. He was severely critical of others and occasionally harsh in his judgment when officers failed to reach the high standard he expected of them. He did not suffer fools gladly and would often quote Herbert Spencer's words, 'The ultimate result of shielding men from fools is to fill the world with fools.' On the other hand he was

---

[1] Mr. Churchill, for reasons of morale, disliked the idea of submarines being named by letters, so directed that they should all be given proper names.

always tolerant when mistakes were freely admitted, and sympathetic when weakness was openly confessed.

In the late summer of 1942, the 8th Flotilla became fully operational at Gibraltar where it was well placed for work in the early stages of the Allied assault on North Africa (Operation Torch). In December the whole flotilla was moved to Algiers, and just before the depot ship *Maidstone* sailed, Horton, recalling the fate of the *Medway*, told Fawkes 'not to get torpedoed on the way!' Horton may have had a hunch, but more likely it was an ordinary hazard of war, when the *Maidstone* was attacked on passage by a U-boat. The torpedo hit the screening destroyer *Porcupine*, splitting her in two. Both halves remained afloat and were safely towed into harbour having been re-christened respectively the *Pork* and the *Pine*.

The submarines played a major part in the final defeat of the Axis Powers in North Africa. The flotillas were concentrated in the central basin of the Mediterranean and operated consistently against the main enemy supply lines to Bizerta and Tunis. Among many of those in the 8th Flotilla who fought with distinction were *Safari* (B. Bryant), *Sahib* (J. H. Bromage), *Saracen* (M. G. Lumby), *Splendid* (I. L. McGeoch), and *Seraph* (N. L. A. Jewell).

Viscount Cunningham writes:

' In the last two months of 1942 these fine young men of all three flotillas, working in conditions of great hazard in mined areas covered by the enemy's light surface forces and aircraft, sank fourteen merchant vessels, two destroyers, one U-boat and two small craft. Another ten merchant ships with a cruiser, a destroyer and a torpedo boat were all damaged. . . .'[1]

On 23rd January 1943, the day that Tripoli fell to the Eighth Army, the Commander-in-Chief announced that British submarines in the Mediterranean had sunk their millionth ton of shipping.

Apart from the main task, so successfully accomplished, the submarines were often required to undertake individual operations of amazing variety. The stories of some of these exploits have

[1] *A Sailor's Odyssey*, p. 510.

become legendary, and there is no need to recount them. A short summary should be sufficient to show the wide field of activity covered by British submarines in the Mediterranean and the versatility of the crews engaged:

They took vital supplies to Malta.

They helped to evacuate the army from Crete, and later landed Commando troops on that rocky coast under the noses of the Germans.

They laid mines to fill up gaps which the enemy had left in Italian minefields as channels for his own ships to use.

They blazed trails through suspected minefields.

They bombarded trains, bridges, floating docks, gas works and factories, and landed Commandos for demolition of trains, tunnels and aircraft.

They served as marks for bombarding warships, and as inshore beacons to guide landing craft to their allotted beaches which submarines had previously reconnoitred.

On 8th July 1940 a signal from the submarine *Phoenix* brought about the first encounter between the British and Italian Battle Fleets.

In April 1941 Lt.-Commander H. C. Browne, R.N., in the *Regent*, having passed through two minefields in the Straits of Otranto, reached Kotor in Jugoslavia at the same moment as the district had come under Italian control. Jugoslavia had signed an armistice and he had been instructed to embark the British Minister, Mr. Ronald Campbell. While waiting to get in touch with the Minister the *Regent* was bombed by low-flying German aircraft, and also machine-gunned from the shore. Under heavy fire Browne managed to extricate his submarine with an Italian hostage on board, but without the Minister.

On 19th October 1942, Lieut. N. L. A. Jewell, R.N., in the submarine *Seraph*, embarked General Mark Clark and a party of U.S. officers at Gibraltar, and landed them secretly at night on the Algerian coast for important conversations with the French High Command. A fortnight later the same submarine picked up General Giraud from a small boat twenty miles east of Toulon and later transferred him to a flying-boat for passage to Gibraltar.

General Clark was much impressed by Jewell and also by the

co-operation which was evident in the British fighting forces. He was a good friend to the British submarines ever after, and went out of his way to provide amenities for them, including an amphibious jeep for their recreation.

Lieut. M. B. St. John, R.N., in the *Parthian*, stopped a small sailing vessel carrying a party of Greek soldiers and a pretty girl escaping from the Germans. While the soldiers embraced St. John in gratitude for their rescue, the boarding party from the submarine embraced the girl.

Lt.-Commander R. H. Dewhurst, R.N., in the minelaying submarine *Rorqual*, attacked with his single gun an Italian floating battery of three guns mounted on a lighter in tow of a tug. He sank the tug and closed the battery to a range of 500 yards. The heavy fire from the battery forced him to dive. He fired a torpedo set to run on the surface, but it circled and he had to go deep to avoid his own torpedo. When he last saw the battery it was ablaze amidships and had a heavy list.

In dealing with a branch of the Navy where so many excelled, it is perhaps invidious to mention names. Those already mentioned have been selected to show the nature of the tasks which for them and many others were all in the day's work. In the gallant company of those who won the Victoria Cross, Commander J. W. Linton cannot be overlooked:

'In a night attack on a convoy of two supply ships escorted by two destroyers he waited for his sights to come on the target, while a destroyer was racing towards him with the obvious intention of ramming. He had just time to fire his torpedoes and take the *Turbulent* deep before the destroyer passed directly overhead . . . "it looked revolting and occupied the entire periscope". . . . Both the supply ships were hit. . . . After many successes the *Turbulent* set out once more and did not return. . . . She is believed to have become the victim of a minefield. The Victoria Cross was added posthumously to the awards her Captain had already gained (D.S.O. and D.S.C.). He had sunk a cruiser, a destroyer, a U-boat and 22 supply ships, some 100,000 tons in all; he had destroyed three trains by gunfire. . . . In mourning him let there also be remembered the many great men of His Majesty's Submarines who have shared the same end in the performance of their duty.'[1]

[1] *His Majesty's Submarines*, p. 60. H.M.S.O.

Horton wrote: 'One of the worst of the many knocks the submarines have had. I feel very distressed. It was his last trip, I am told, before coming home.'

Although Horton had had nothing to do with the control of operations in the Mediterranean, he had reason to be satisfied with the manner in which the officers and men of the Submarine Branch had responded to every call.[1]

The highest tribute of all came from the German Admiral serving with the Italian High Command: 'Now as ever the British Fleet dominates the Mediterranean. . . . The most dangerous weapon is the submarine.'[2]

And in the House of Commons the Prime Minister said:

'I have often looked for an opportunity of paying tribute to our submarines.

'There is no branch of His Majesty's Forces which in this war has suffered the same proportion of fatal loss as our Submarine Service.

'It is the most dangerous of all Services. That is perhaps the reason why the First Lord tells me that entry into it is keenly sought by officers and men.

'I feel sure the House would wish to testify its gratitude and admiration to our submarine crews for their skill and devotion, which have proved of inestimable value to the life of our country.'

---

[1] During the war with Italy, British submarines sank 1,335,000 tons of enemy shipping in the Mediterranean, and 41 of their own number were lost.
[2] *The Second World War*, Vol. III, p. 433. Winston S. Churchill.

CHAPTER EIGHT

1940-42
MANY WATERS

Convoys. The watch on the Azores. 'One Against Three.'
Russian interlude. Arctic Patrol. The Black Sea. 'Midgets
and Chariots.'

THE British submarines played their part in the Battle of the Atlantic, not only by attacking enemy warships, U-boats and tankers, but also by supplementing weak convoy escorts. Their objectives naturally varied according to the tasks entrusted to them, but submarine Commanders were sometimes bewildered (and so was Max) by political and tactical restrictions. Horton, having suffered himself, paid great attention to the framing of his operation orders so as to leave no doubt in the minds of those who had to carry them out. It was particularly difficult to define the task of a submarine on convoy duty; she is not designed for the purpose and must have freedom of action to develop her attack. As a rule, the best position for a submarine is ahead of the convoy where she is favourably placed to deliver a torpedo attack against enemy heavy ships. On the other hand she is liable to be overrun by the merchant ships and mistaken for a U-boat. If the submarine is stationed in the rear she is well placed for dealing with U-boat packs coming up from astern, but may get mixed up with stragglers from the convoy. Horton was opposed to the use of submarines as escorts, but after the loss of the *Jervis Bay* in November 1940 he agreed, at the request of the Admiralty, to send a small flotilla to Halifax to reinforce weak escorts and to act as a deterrent against pocket battleships in the Western Atlantic. He flatly refused to allow submarines to escort convoys in the Western Approaches where there was little danger of attack by surface warships and where the submarine herself would be an embarrassment to British anti-U-boat forces.

The submarines of the Halifax Flotilla escorted convoys as far as the middle of the Atlantic until July 1941, when, under pressure from Horton, they were withdrawn for important duties elsewhere. Although they had inflicted no damage on the enemy their presence with the convoys had a good moral influence on the sorely tried crews of the merchant ships. Submarine escorts were used again as protection for the Arctic convoys against German warships lurking in the fjords of Norway.

In the winter of 1940–41 it was feared that the Germans might establish a base for replenishing surface raiders and U-boats in the Azores. The Admiralty directed that a submarine patrol, based at Gibraltar, was to be maintained off Ponta Delgada (the principal port in the Azores), 'to detect and report on a sea-borne attack.' As the political situation with Portugal was delicate the Admiralty, to Horton's fury, took over the control of this operation. According to Admiralty orders every effort was to be made to avoid the presence of the submarines being reported. At the same time each commanding officer was reminded that 'nothing in these orders prevents the submarine from attacking enemy surface warships or submarines,' and also that any ship approaching Ponta Delgada, not reported to him in advance, was to be treated with suspicion. Finally, the Admiralty stated: 'It is realised that unexpected situations may arise and the commanding officer is given full authority to act as he thinks proper.'[1]

Unexpected situations did arise: on the night of 27th December 1940 the *Trident* (Lt.-Commander G. M. Sladen) sighted a darkened ship moving near the entrance to Ponta Delgada. The *Trident* challenged. On receiving no reply, she fired a shot across the stranger's bows, and ordered her to stop. The ship paid no attention, and as if to show her contempt, turned her stern to the *Trident*, lifted her skirts and ran for the harbour. *Trident* fired five torpedoes at her. They all missed. Which was fortunate, as the ship proved to be the S.S. *Router* of Panama. Two days later the *Trident* sighted a troopship escorted by a

---
[1] Admiralty records.

cruiser and some smaller vessels. The submarine, being in a good position to attack, was about to fire, when the Captain noticed that the cruiser had a familiar look. On further investigation he identified the 'enemy force' as H.M.S. *Berwick* and some corvettes escorting the *Empire Trooper* damaged, in convoy.[1] The submarine *Otus* on the same patrol, having stopped and boarded a darkened steamer, found she was the British ship *Lindsay*. The Captain of the *Otus* in his report said: 'Short of stopping every unreported merchant vessel entering harbour and thereby continually disclosing the presence of the submarine, it is considered impossible to carry out a patrol rendering Ponta Delgada one hundred per cent. safe from invasion.'

Horton strongly supported this view, so the patrol was withdrawn. It was the first and last time in six years of war that operation orders to submarines were issued by the Admiralty.

There were some tough encounters in the Battle of the Atlantic between British submarines and U-boats. They were more in the nature of battles of wits than duels in the grand manner of the *Shannon* and *Chesapeake*, and perhaps the most remarkable of them all was the *Clyde*'s fight with three U-boats.

This large submarine of 1,850 tons, commanded by Lt.-Commander D. C. Ingram, R.N., was designed for ocean patrol work, and could attain a speed of twenty-one knots. On 25th September 1940, while off Santa Cruz in the Canary Islands, casting longing eyes at a German tanker inside the harbour, Ingram got a signal from Horton ordering him to go, with all dispatch, to Tarrafal Bay in the Cape Verde Islands, about a thousand miles to the north. He had also been told that U-boats were in the habit of refuelling there.

By virtue of *Clyde*'s speed he reached the entrance to the bay on the evening of 27th September, and at about midnight sighted a U-boat (U.68) leaving the anchorage. Just at the moment when the *Clyde* was turning on to her firing course he sighted another U-boat (U.111) on his port beam. The *Clyde* was now in a vulnerable position both from the danger of ramming and being torpedoed, so Ingram broke off his attack on U.68 and turned to

[1] *Empire Trooper* had been shelled by the German cruiser *Hipper* on Christmas Morning 1940.

deal with U.111. He brought his gun into action and tried to ram. The U-boat dived quickly, and the bows of the cumbersome *Clyde* passed over the top of her. The other U-boat, for some reason known to herself, remained on the surface. The *Clyde* fired a salvo of six torpedoes at her. These were seen by U.68, who dived immediately, leaving the British submarine in the awkward position of being on the surface while two angry opponents groped for her unseen and uncomfortably close. The *Clyde* then dived, reloaded and tried to get Asdic contact. Two hours passed, and as nothing was heard, the *Clyde* came to the surface. At about 3.0 a.m. a U-boat was seen surfacing. The *Clyde* tried to ram. So did the U-boat, but the German, being in a better position, struck the *Clyde* right aft causing only minor damage. Both submarines dived, and there was no further contact. Although Ingram did not know it, his opponent in the last encounter was yet another submarine, U.67. The three U-boats had made a rendezvous at Tarrafal Bay for transferring torpedoes. All three were eventually destroyed in the Battle of the Atlantic.

Although Horton's responsibilities as Admiral Submarines were specifically defined, he felt that his knowledge of U-boat warfare entitled him to express his anxiety about the position in the Atlantic. After eighteen months of war, he was more than ever convinced that the number of aircraft in this decisive theatre fell far short of the need. On 8th March 1941 he wrote to the First Sea Lord:

'Our shipping losses on our principal line of communication seriously threaten the successful prosecution of the war.

'Although the officially quoted figures of weekly sinkings are bad enough, they do not record the large number of ships damaged. Neither do they show how our ports are cluttered up and hampered by the constantly increasing number of such ships whose repairs cannot be undertaken because all the yards are fully occupied already. The simplest and quickest way to reduce our losses is radically to increase the number of long-range aircraft working in North-west Approaches, so as to maintain incessant attack on enemy submarines and to force them to remain submerged by day, thereby decreasing their effectiveness by at least fifty per cent.—the effect on the Focke-Wolfe menace would be equally great.

'In my opinion the minimum number of additional long-range squadrons necessary are six, i.e., seventy-two aircraft.

'I am aware there is a programme of reinforcement of the Coastal Command approved which is due to be in operation in June or July —this may be too late.

'Coastal Command could be reinforced almost immediately from Bomber Command by turning over six squadrons of Wellingtons and Stirlings lock, stock and barrel (including personnel), *if* the Cabinet chose to give the order now.

'Of course the transference would entail repercussions to our war effort elsewhere. This must be accepted, since weakness in the vital area means final loss of the war, however near we may get to winning it in other areas.

'Given the extra squadrons the sole difficulty relates to personnel trained and experienced over the sea to navigate them. It is suggested this difficulty could be overcome at certain expense elsewhere.'

Horton then makes detailed proposals for finding these officers and men, and concludes:

'. . . I appreciate the above means a bit of an upheaval and that there are likely to be strong objections from many quarters, but unless anyone can think of a better way of getting essential reinforcements to the vital area in as quick a time, these objections should be ruthlessly overruled.'

* * * *

Shortly after the Germans invaded Russia, Mr. Churchill told Stalin that owing to commitments in the Middle East and elsewhere the only speedy help he could give would be in the north. Accordingly Horton was directed to send a small flotilla to reinforce the Russian submarines at Murmansk on the north coast of Russia. Although British submarine resources were stretched to the utmost, the *Tigris*, Commander H. F. Bone, and *Trident*, Commander G. M. Sladen, reached this station in late July 1941 and were allotted patrol areas well within the Arctic Circle between North Cape and Varanger Fjord. Their task was to destroy German transports which were using the coastal route to supply their army on the North Russian front. In the words of Commander Bone 'conditions were most unfavourable for submarines.' On account of enemy air supervision in perpetual daylight they could seldom remain on the surface long enough to charge their batteries. The enemy transports hugged the coast and were difficult to detect against the background of snow-covered rock. Towards the end of the year *Sealion*, Lieut. G. R. Colvin, R.N., and *Seawolf*, Lieut. R. P. Raikes, took over the patrol.

For them the conditions were worse; practically no daylight, very poor visibility in the short hours of twilight, and violent storms with snow and sleet most of the night. Air reconnaissance being absent, the submarines could keep their watch on the surface, but everything was frozen solid.

Yet the results achieved were remarkable. Bone sank a large supply ship on his first patrol, causing the enemy to put their shipping into convoy. Bone and Sladen kept up their attacks in spite of all counter-measures, and on several occasions sank or damaged more than one ship in the same convoy.

Meanwhile in July 1941, the Soviet Admiralty asked if they could send two observers to the Home Fleet, in exchange for two British officers to be attached to the Black Sea Fleet. In view of the Russian submarine strength in the Black Sea and Horton's natural desire to explore the possibilities of future co-operation with the Russian submarine service, he obtained permission for one of the two officers to be a submariner. Captain G. W. G. Simpson seemed an obvious choice as he was an interpreter in Russian, but he could not be spared from his important post at Malta. Horton therefore selected Commander G. B. H. Fawkes, R.N., who was given the rank of acting Captain and went out as Naval Attaché Sevastopol and 'Senior British Naval Liaison Officer' to the Commander-in-Chief Black Sea Fleet. Commander G. W. Ambrose, who had spent most of his time in destroyers, was appointed as assistant. Fawkes's main role from the Admiralty was to act as an observer of events in South Russia. For this purpose he had personal cyphers enabling him to communicate (via Sevastopol radio) direct with the Admiralty, the Commander-in-Chief Mediterranean and the Head of the British Naval Mission in Moscow. His other role, given him by Horton, was to establish close contact with the Russian submarine force and help them in any way he could.

The party, which included other officials bound for Moscow, left Scotland on 11th August 1941 by Catalina for Archangel, and then by Russian plane to Moscow. Here they reported to General Mason-Macfarlane and Admiral G. J. A. Miles, who warned them not to be disappointed if they found that they were able to see little and learn nothing, because that had been their own experience in Moscow. After a very cordial interview and reception at the Russian Admiralty, Fawkes (accompanied by a commissar) and Ambrose flew on to Sevastopol. Although Horton was well known to the Russian Navy, Headquarters in Sevastopol said that they had not been told these officers were expected and at first seemed at a loss to know what to do with them.

Fawkes wrote:

SEVASTOPOL.
27th August 1941.

Dear Admiral Horton,

I must be frank and admit that I have achieved practically nothing to date. The reasons for this are:

(1) Everyone is so pre-occupied and worried by the present state of affairs, that Ambrose and I are more of a nuisance than an asset. Though the U.S.S.R. Admiralty were very keen to send two officers to our fleet, I don't think the local authorities down here are over-keen to see us. I think the situation is somewhat akin to a Russian naval officer arriving at Blockhouse not being able to speak a word of English) in the middle of an invasion scare!

(2) The difficulty of finding an interpreter for me, who can translate technical terms, etc. I'm glad to say one arrives today, but up to now the lack of one has been a real obstacle.

(3) The fact that everything is centrally controlled from Moscow Admiralty, of whom the local people are in dread. Communication is apt to be interrupted, and anything I ask has to be referred to Moscow!

Ambrose, of course, speaks Russian, so they pushed him off to a destroyer and he is no worry to them. The interpreter cannot be spared, and they tried at first to push me off to a cruiser that left here a week ago and hasn't returned since! The Captain spoke slight English, and I feel sure they didn't want to be bothered with me during the present serious situation at a time when they are undoubtedly very harassed.

However, I dug my toes in and told them that is not what I was sent out for. I regard my job as Submarines, and by virtue of being Senior Officer, as link between this part of the world and the Admiralty, etc., I am now attached to the S/M base.

I have throughout adopted the attitude that I fully sympathise with their pre-occupation, etc., and I don't want to make myself a nuisance in any way, but if I can be of any help, etc. etc. Of course one has to be very careful not to give them the slightest suggestion of patronage or that I am here to tell them what's what, and of course I have stressed that I am not a Naval Intelligence expert, nor am I thirsting for most secret information. I think I am succeeding in winning their confidence, and though this may sound a despairing letter, it isn't by any means, now my interpreter has arrived (or rather is due today) I hope to go ahead.

Every job has its difficulties to be overcome, and I am only reporting that to date I have achieved very little. I have been told that after my interpreter arrives I shall be consulted on operational matters (not only S/Ms), but this may only be eye-wash. However, I am doing my very best, and exasperating though it is, one cannot achieve quick results.

I hope all is well with you, Sir, and that the caviare arrived. I get no news at all here as yet, but hope to get a wireless. Somebody told me we had marched into Iran. Can't establish communication with C.-in-C. Mediterranean yet, however that is being arranged in Moscow.

Yours very sincerely,

(Signed) G. B. H. FAWKES.

There is no lack of cordiality, I get on very well with all the N.O.s I have met; they are just extremely busy and harassed.

However, things were soon to change. After protesting strongly to the Commander-in-Chief Black Sea Fleet that they were not pulling their weight, Fawkes and Ambrose found to their amazement (and also to the surprise of the Military Mission in Moscow and the Admiralty) that they were receiving the Soviet Commander-in-Chief's daily summary of events. This document is normally issued only to Flag Officers, so a useful liaison was established. Although they were the only two non-Russians in South Russia, completely cut off from the outside world, they had interesting experiences. Ambrose went to sea in Russian cruisers and destroyers, and witnessed the evacuation of Odessa, while Fawkes visited almost daily the two Soviet submarine flotillas at Sevastopol and Balaclava, and established cordial relations with their Captains. He even visited them on occasions without being accompanied by his attendant commissar. Fawkes eventually persuaded the Russian authorities to let him do a patrol in an M class submarine. While patrolling in shallow waters close inshore between Constanza and Varna, the submarine attacked a small convoy screened by German manned escorts, and he had the unique and unenviable experience of being depth-charged in a Russian submarine in less than sixty feet of water. Fawkes says:

'It was a glassy calm day; we had been sighted before we fired, due to too free use of the periscope. We broke surface on firing, and after firing went to the bottom and stayed there. Apparently this was the doctrine amongst Russian submarine commanding officers. A similar incident had occurred in the Baltic when a submarine commanding officer, having stubbornly endured eight hours depth-charging, surfaced to find only one German trawler left. He sank her with his gun, thus becoming a hero of the Soviet Union. In my case despite language difficulties I managed to persuade the commanding officer that there was absolutely no future in staying put and being depth-charged, so to my relief he crept slowly to seaward and eventually escaped. We then had to return to base as we had sustained a certain amount of damage including putting the one and only periscope completely out of action.'

Soon after this incident, the Germans overran the Crimea. Fawkes and Ambrose escaped by air; Fawkes, after visiting Moscow, returned in H.M.S. *Suffolk* to the United Kingdom by way of Archangel. On reporting to Northways, he was greeted by a growl from Horton: 'Who the hell said you could go to sea and get depth-charged in a Russian submarine? You exceeded your instructions.' Then, with his well-known smile and a twinkle in his eye: 'Come and sit down and tell me all about everything out there.'

In the early days of 1942, Hitler provided some interesting targets for the British submarines by concentrating German surface warships in Norway ready to pounce on convoys taking supplies to Russia. In February the *Prince Eugen*, on her way to join the *Tirpitz* and *Scheer* at Trondheim, was torpedoed by the *Trident* (Sladen) and put out of action for eight months.

The British patrols were specially reinforced when Allied convoys were passing through Arctic waters. And at the beginning of July, while the ill-fated convoy PQ 17 was in the area, nine British and two Russian submarines were disposed by Horton to intercept the German heavy ships.

The submarines had been well placed. On 5th July *Tirpitz*, *Scheer* and *Hipper*, while making for the convoy, were sighted and reported by British and Russian submarines off Alten Fjord.

The German High Command, having picked up these reports, and fearing that British heavy warships might be met, ordered the squadron to return to harbour. Unfortunately the British Admiralty had ordered the convoy to scatter before learning of this withdrawal, and the scattered merchant ships, defenceless in perpetual daylight, became an easy prey for U-boats and aircraft. Of the thirty-four ships which left Iceland twenty-three were sunk.

This tragic story has been told by Mr. Churchill,[1] and need not be repeated.

Meanwhile the Russians haa been increasing their submarine strength in Arctic waters by reinforcements from the Baltic via the Stalin Canal, so in January 1942 the British submarines were withdrawn from the Murmansk patrol. The Senior British Naval Officer at Polyarnoe (near Murmansk) remarked: 'The success of British submarines . . . has firmly established our prestige with the Russians . . . while it would be wrong to suggest that they [the Russians] were glad that their submarines are no longer to operate alongside ours, there is a feeling of relief that they have no longer to compete against such efficient units.'

During the time when British submarines were operating in the Arctic, many transports, including troopships, were sent to the bottom. The Germans were obliged to strengthen their convoy escorts, thus locking up destroyers and aircraft which could have been used to supplement the attacks on British convoys taking supplies to Russia. On 17th September 1941 Admiral Raeder reported to Hitler: 'At present troop transports are unable to proceed east of North Cape; supply steamers can only do so at very great risk. The submarine danger is being reduced as far as possible by the addition of more submarine chasers and escort vessels . . . but only at the expense of other areas.'

* * * *

The idea of using submarines to destroy capital ships in defended harbours appealed strongly to Horton. His own experiences in 1914, when he lay on the bottom inside the harbour of

[1] *The Second World War*, vol. IV, page 235.

Heligoland, had convinced him that such an operation stood a good chance of success if a small submarine could be designed specially for the purpose. The crew would have to be expendable, albeit highly trained, and should not exceed four men willing to accept all hazards.[1]

One day in 1940, his Chief Staff Officer, Captain E. R. Gibson, R.N.,[2] told Horton that he had learnt that a midget submarine was being built privately on the Hamble by Commander C. H. Varley, R.N., a retired submarine officer of the 1914–18 war. 'We must go there at once,' said Max. 'Order the car and tell him we are coming.' Varley was not at all pleased. This midget submarine had been his pet hobby for some years, and he hoped to be able to complete the prototype in secrecy without interference from official quarters. Horton convinced him that time was the most important factor, and arranged that Varley should have every assistance from naval sources to develop the prototype. It did not fulfil all requirements, *but it worked.* The Director of Naval Construction then improved the design, and after exhaustive trials several operational submarines called 'X craft' were built by Messrs. Vickers-Armstrongs. The midget submarines had many teething troubles. Horton, however, had no intention of using the new weapon until these were overcome and the crews had been trained to the highest pitch of endurance and efficiency. As it happened, this standard was not reached by the time he hauled down his flag as Admiral Submarines.

The objective that he had in mind was the new battleship *Tirpitz*, and in the meantime officers and men had been selected from volunteers for 'special and hazardous service.' Their training was entrusted to Commander T. I. S. ('Tizzy') Bell, R.N., and later to Commander D. C. Ingram, R.N. In April 1943 six 'X boats' were formed into a special flotilla under Captain W. E. Banks. The final plans for the attack (based on experience with the 'Human Torpedo') were prepared by Commander G. P. S. Davies, R.N.

---

[1] The original proposal was put forward in 1912 by Lieutenant, now Commander, G. Herbert, D.S.O., R.N., who was a friend of Horton's. He assisted Horton in developing the new type.

[2] Later Vice-Admiral Lord Ashbourne, C.B., D.S.O.

Absolute secrecy was essential, and it is very much to the credit of all concerned that the existence of British midget submarines was not disclosed until 23rd September 1943, when an enormous explosion lifted the huge bulk of the *Tirpitz*. This was caused by very powerful charges laid under her bottom by two of these craft which had penetrated the elaborate defences of Alten Fjord.

On such an occasion Horton was not sparing in his praise. In a signal to his successor he said:

'Will you please convey to the 12th Submarine Flotilla my warmest congratulations and profound admiration for their unique and successful attack on the *Tirpitz*.

'Having been closely associated with the inception and early trials of the "X craft" I fully realise the immense difficulties which have had to be surmounted and I know also what devoted service has been given by those who designed the craft and its special equipment, by the original trial crews, and by those responsible for training the operational crews and for planning the operation itself.

'The long approach voyage in unparalleled conditions culminating in the successful attack on the target, called for and produced the highest degree of endurance and seamanlike skill.

'While deploring with you the loss of officers and men whose gallantry is unsurpassed in the history of the Submarine Service, I rejoice at the success which crowned this magnificent feat of arms.'

Admiral Claud Barry replied:

'I have passed on your signal to those concerned. May I thank you most warmly from them all and say how particularly we all appreciate receiving such a high tribute from you who have done more than anyone else to make the Submarine Service what it is and who was the mainspring of this great venture.'

In a letter to his nephew, written after the facts were known, Horton said:

'The two-ton charges, of which three were placed under the *Tirpitz* by the little craft, lifted her bodily five or six feet out of the water when they went off, and that was that—no more use as a ship and all her turrets chucked out of line.'

As the *Tirpitz* was no longer a fighting unit, she was removed later to Tromso Fjord, where she became a sitting target for

R.A.F. bombers who eventually destroyed her more than a year later, after careful training. Thus the career of the most powerful battleship in the world came to an inglorious end. In two years of war service she had taken part in only one offensive operation, when she bombarded a meteorological station and damaged some coal mines in Spitzbergen.

Horton was also responsible for the development of the 'Human Torpedo,' based on an Italian model used in the First World War and called a 'Chariot.' It was manned by a crew of two who sat astride its body wearing special diving suits. Driven by electric batteries, it could creep slowly and silently underneath the target. When in position, the crew would detach the explosive head and fix it by magnets to the ship's bottom. After setting the time fuse, they would remount and ride submerged to a safe distance.[1]

Several 'chariots' were ready for service by the summer of 1942. As the *Tirpitz* had not emerged from the Norwegian fjords Max, feeling that 'a chance lost in war may never recur,' decided to send two 'chariots' in a Norwegian fishing boat to Trondheim, where the *Tirpitz* spent most of her time. On arrival near Trondheim Fjord, the 'chariots' were to be put over the side and towed underneath the fishing vessel, which would then go up the fjord hoping to pass through the German control with false passports. It was planned that she should reach a point about eight miles from the *Tirpitz* shortly after dark, when the charioteers would emerge from their hiding place and ride their machines to the target. As soon as they had gone, the fishing boat was to scuttle herself.

The Norwegian fishing vessel *Arthur* was selected for the task. She was commanded by Skipper L. A. Larsen and manned by a Norwegian crew. The charioteers, all British, were commanded by Sub-Lieut. W. R. Brewster, R.N.V.R. The Commander-in-Chief Home Fleet, Sir John Tovey, approved the project, and arranged that one of his battleships should play the part of the *Tirpitz* in a dress rehearsal. The ship was moored

[1] The operational development of the machines and training of the crews were entrusted to Commander G. M. Sladen, R.N., and W. R. Fell, R.N., q.v. *Above us the Waves*, by Warren and Benson.

head and stern near the steep-to shore of a lonely Scottish loch in the same manner as the *Tirpitz* at Trondheim. All the 'stage props' required to complete the scene, such as nets, mines, and other obstructions, were placed in their correct positions relative to the target. Fishing vessels for rescue and shore parties representing the Norwegian 'underground' were briefed for the task of helping prisoners to escape. The crews selected for the assault had already been trained and exercised to the limit of physical endurance. Nothing was left to chance and several rehearsals were required before Horton was satisfied.

The little expedition finally sailed from the Shetland Islands on 26th October 1942. The weather was very bad and *Arthur* did not reach the fjord till four days later. The 'chariots' were hoisted out, trimmed heavy and slung under her bottom. On reaching the enemy control point, *Arthur* was stopped by a German patrol vessel and carefully inspected while the British crews lay hidden behind a false bulkhead. After much prevarication by the redoubtable Larsen, a pass was issued and instructions given to surrender it to the authorities at Trondheim. *Arthur* was then allowed to carry on towards the port. The fjord is ten miles wide in places. It was blowing hard with a nasty steep sea. *Arthur* was 'bucketing' about wildly and it was feared the 'chariots' might break adrift and sink. A lee was found near the point where the riders were to mount for the last lap of their perilous voyage. Here their worst fears were confirmed. The 'chariots' had gone. *Arthur* was immediately scuttled, and the whole party went ashore, making for the Swedish frontier. All got safely across except Able Seaman Evans, who was wounded in a brush with a German patrol. He was eventually shot by order of Hitler.

No further operations were carried out by 'chariots' in home waters, but they were used successfully in the Mediterranean, where they sank a cruiser and severely damaged a transport in the strongly defended harbour of Palermo. Later they entered Spezia, while the port was under German control, and sank the large Italian cruiser *Bolzano*.

Nothing pleased Max more than to hear nice things about the officers and men of the Submarine Branch. Their deeds were the measure of his inspiration and the reward he sought. He was particularly encouraged when he received this letter from Captain H. H. G. D. Stoker, a retired submarine officer of distinction, who had been instructed by Max on board A.1 in 1905:

21st September 1942.

My Dear Admiral,

Very many thanks indeed for letting me visit the *Forth* from where I have just returned.

I was honestly and genuinely thrilled by everything I saw and every officer and man I spoke to. The general spirit, efficiency and lively earnestness of everyone seemed to me to have attained the highest possible standards—all the very best points of the old days retained and developed, and none of the worst. In fact I felt quite bursting with pride ever to have been in the "Trade"; and was so overcome I made a rotten shot at giving, by request, a short talk on Sunday morning.

Amongst a hundred impressions, I particularly noticed the complete absence of envy or "lucky" suggestions when feats of others were being recounted, and the unbounded loyalty, respect and appreciation they all have for you personally.

Ionides (whom I'd never met) and all his officers frankly astonished me with the warmth of their welcome, and their hospitality and friendliness undoubtedly contributed to my overcoming. Roper, too, was politeness and patience itself when I saw him about arranging the visit.

Don't, please, look on this as a "fulsome" letter; I *feel* every word of it, and am writing both Ionides and Wevell in similar terms.

Yours ever,

H. G. STOKER.

Max replied:

OFFICE OF ADMIRAL (SUBMARINES),
NORTHWAYS,
LONDON, N.W.3.
24th September 1942.

My Dear Stoker,

Your letter has given me the greatest pleasure and I am delighted that you as a veteran submariner should have been able to form such a high opinion of the modern brand.

I agree they are good—very good—and *Forth* has always been a happy ship.

137

MAX HORTON AND THE WESTERN APPROACHES

My visit to the Mediterranean at the end of last year showed the finest spirit I have ever encountered in my life. The discipline and "calling to account" is pretty strict but I like to think it is administered with a human touch which doesn't worry about mistakes—only their repetition!

I am just off for a trip up north and I hope you will come and have lunch on my return.

Thank you again for your cheering letter.

Yours,

MAX HORTON.

Extracts from Stoker's letter were circulated by Horton in orders throughout the Submarine Branch.

CHAPTER NINE

1941-42

THE SEA AND THE AIR

The watch on Brest. R.A.F. and sea power. Appointed
Commander-in-Chief Western Approaches.

WHILE the British forces were pressing the Italians in the Mediterranean, the submarines in home waters, like the frigates of old, were keeping a close watch on Brest and the French Atlantic ports. Their task was formidable, as the Germans used these ports not only to bring in supplies, but also as bases for their submarines and surface craft.

In carrying out blockading duties the submarines were still expected to provide for the safety of the crews of merchant ships. Lt.-Commander H. A. V. Haggard, R.N., in the *Truant*, had an interesting experience while complying with this convention. One day while on the surface in the Bay of Biscay he sighted a heavily laden merchant ship making for Bordeaux. In the approved manner he ordered her to stop, and send a boat with the Captain and ship's papers. At the same time he kept the submarine's gun trained on her bridge. An unusually large number of men took to the boats, and while Haggard was searching among them for the Captain, the merchant ship blew up and sank. The Captain of the merchant ship, when eventually found, turned out to be a German officer commanding a prize crew. The ship was the Norwegian motor vessel *Tropic Sea* which had been captured by a German raider some four months before. She was carrying in addition to her own crew the Captain and twenty-two survivors of the British S.S. *Haxby* sunk by the raider. Haggard had only room for twenty-five passengers, but the sea was calm so he left the remainder in the ship's lifeboats, reporting their position by radio. Soon afterwards, they were rescued by British flying-boats.

In spite of the difficulties experienced by Allied submarines in trying to conform to International Law, the British Foreign Office would not agree to merchant vessels being sunk at sight in the open waters of the Bay of Biscay. Consequently for nearly a year after the fall of France, a considerable quantity of fuel and Spanish iron ore reached the enemy through Biscay ports. Submarines were permitted to sink at sight eastward of a line joining Brest and Biarritz. This was too close to the enemy coast to maintain an aircraft patrol, and too far off the beaten track of enemy vessels approaching Brest for submarines to intercept them.

In the autumn of 1940, when most of our new submarines (small U class) were needed in the Mediterranean, Horton suggested that the 'sink at sight' zone might be extended a hundred miles to the westward, so that they could spend a few days hunting in the Bay on their way out. This, he said, would give them opportunities to sink a few tankers, and at the same time make the best use of his slender resources. Without waiting for Government approval, he extended the zone for individual submarines and informed the Admiralty that he had done so. Nobody objected, but it was not until July 1941 that the Bay of Biscay became a 'sink at sight' area, except for a 'chastity belt' of twenty miles round the north coast of Spain. The British Government was anxious to preserve the neutrality of Spain and there were certain difficulties about reducing the width of the belt. Coastal Command of the Royal Air Force could not be certain of identifying Spanish merchant ships from the air; furthermore, aircraft at a long distance from their bases were not able to navigate with the same degree of accuracy as surface craft and submarines.

From Horton's point of view all these political niceties were somewhat academic, as he had only eight submarines available for operations in home waters. By midsummer 1941 a total of thirty-one, including three Allied, had been lost. Twenty-five new submarines had done their acceptance trials, while eight Dutch, five Greek, three French and one Norwegian had come under

British control. In fact, for operational purposes in all theatres, we were no better off numerically than we had been at the outbreak of war. Horton regarded the Biscay patrol as one of his most important commitments. As a general rule he kept two of his best submarines in these turbulent waters, for the approaches to the French coast held good prospects of intercepting German war-ships, U-boats and tankers.

This disposition proved to be a valuable contribution to the British war effort in the Atlantic. Between September 1940 and April 1941, four tankers and several supply ships were sent to the bottom, including the 10,800-ton tanker *Franco Martello* from Pernambuco, sunk by Lieut. E. P. Tomkinson, R.N., in the new submarine *Urge* on passage to the Mediterranean. On the night of 2nd April 1941 Lt.-Commander H. F. Bone, R.N., in the *Tigris*, had a spirited gun duel with a German tanker of 5,500 tons, seventy miles from St. Nazaire, and after damaging her severely, finished her off with a torpedo. The German War Diaries betray the anxiety of the enemy about the shortage of fuel for U-boats; in December 1941 Doenitz admitted that the 'shocking destruc-tion of supply tankers for U-boats had rendered it inadvisable to attempt further supplies from surface vessels until the situation could satisfactorily be dealt with.'

The Biscay patrols were kept up till the end of the war, but little could be done to stop the Spanish iron ore trade to France; much of the voyage took place in territorial waters and the Foreign Office restrictions were designed 'to keep incidents within manageable proportions.' Four large German merchant ships, however, were put out of action on 7th December 1942 by Royal Marine Commandos under Major Hasler, R.M., who were landed at the mouth of the Gironde by the submarine *Tuna*. This and other operations of a similar nature were planned in co-operation with the Admiral Submarines.

Towards the end of 1941 the increasing demands for sub-marines on the Norwegian coast and in the Mediterranean left few to spare for the watch on Brest. The German battle cruisers *Gneisenau* and *Scharnhorst* had been located there in March, immediately after their return from successful operations against the Atlantic convoys. During their cruise they had sunk 115,000 tons of shipping, and it was a matter of vital importance to prevent them breaking out again.

Horton, by scraping the barrel, managed to collect a motley force of ancient submarines including three Dutch and five British boats of the H class, built in 1918—'anything that could dive and fire a torpedo.' They had been used for training and none of them was fully operational. Ten took up their allotted positions in the teeth of a south-westerly gale on an arc covering the approaches to Brest. Gale followed gale and nearly all developed defects. Some were bombed by our own aircraft and others by the enemy, but they clung to their patrol lines until most of them had nearly run out of fuel and water.

When it became known that the German heavy ships had entered dry dock, the patrol was withdrawn, and the little H boats went back to their training duties. Horton was thankful, because he regarded training as an overriding requirement and it was against his principles to disturb it. He felt also that the destruction of the German battle cruisers should now be a Royal Air Force commitment, and that Brest could be watched effectively by land-based aircraft. During 1941 Horton kept two submarines near the approaches to the English Channel so that they could be quickly moved towards Brest if the emergency arose. In May when it was thought that the *Bismarck* might make for St. Nazaire, they were ordered with four others to patrol off that port. Contrary to expectations the *Gneisenau* and *Scharnhorst* remained in Brest; no one could understand why these fast and powerful battle cruisers should stay idle for nearly a year, when they could have created chaos and havoc on the convoy routes in co-operation with the *Bismarck*. It is now known, however, that the *Gneisenau* was torpedoed in Brest on 6th April 1941 by an aircraft of Coastal Command which was lost with all its crew, and that the *Scharnhorst* was severely damaged by bombs from an R.A.F. bomber three months later.

In February 1942 it became evident that the two ships were about to put to sea, and it was expected that they would carry out exercises in the approaches to the harbour. Horton had too few submarines at his disposal to make sure of intercepting the enemy when they reached the open sea, so he decided to place one submarine inside the exercise area. Lt.-Commander G. R. Colvin, R.N., in the *Sealion*, was selected for the task. After negotiating successfully the well-known navigational hazards of this dangerous coast, he spent two days inside the exercise area constantly diving to avoid anti-submarine patrols and aircraft.

On the night of 11th–12th February 1942 he withdrew from the area to charge his batteries, and, as luck would have it, the German battle cruisers made their escape on that very night.

These ships, as is well known, passed through the Dover Straits under strong fighter cover in broad daylight and reached home apparently unscathed.[1]

The news, naturally enough, astonished the British public. Max was perturbed because it seemed to confirm his view that the machinery for co-operation between the Royal Navy and Royal Air Force was not geared to deal with an emergency at sea. He had in fact prepared a paper on the subject which he had not yet forwarded to the First Sea Lord, but after the Channel incident he had no hesitation in doing so. He had not seen the findings of the official court of enquiry, but he knew that the only aircraft which had made close contact with the enemy before they had passed through the Straits were six Swordfish of the Fleet Air Arm. Slow and ill-equipped as they were, these antiquated aircraft with no fighters to protect them pressed home their attack—doing, alas, mortal injury to themselves without hurting the enemy. Horton knew also that a large number of R.A.F. bombers had been in the air, but none of the crews had been trained to locate and identify enemy warships at sea. Those who eventually found the battle cruisers attacked with great gallantry, suffering heavy casualties but inflicting no damage.

Horton's paper finally took the form of a general appreciation of the war situation leading to the conclusion that the sea communications of the Empire were gravely threatened, and that the R.A.F. must share with the Royal Navy equal responsibility for their defence. In his concluding remarks he said:

'Recent events have proved that fleets cannot operate without the close co-operation of air power. If we are to hold our own during this

[1] It was learnt afterwards that the *Scharnhorst* had been damaged by mines laid by aircraft.

vital year, and wear down the enemy before we ourselves are exhausted, it is essential that the whole of our naval and air force strength should be concentrated and employed in the battle for sea power. If we lose our sea power, we lose the war.' [Horton's paper is quoted in full in Appendix VIII.]

Being wise after the event, it may be said by some that he was unduly pessimistic in his outlook. But, at the time of writing, he had good cause for anxiety. There were no escort carriers in commission,[1] and consequently no means existed for providing fighter cover for convoys in the open ocean. The number of aircraft suitable for operating against U-boats was quite inadequate, and the provision of air crews for Coastal Command was far short of requirements. Max's deep concern about air support at sea was prompted by knowledge and experience, for he knew better than anyone else that existing anti-submarine measures were ineffective without it. His urgent plea for better co-operation was therefore timely, and may have had some effect in influencing the Government to take appropriate measures. Indeed it would have gone hard with the Allies if a number of the suggestions in his sound and valuable paper had not been adopted.

The Prime Minister took steps to increase the number of long-range aircraft for Coastal Command, and with the co-operation of Mr. Mackenzie King he established air bases for them at Goose in Labrador and Gander in Newfoundland. In November 1942 he created the Anti-U-boat Committee to allot priorities and take action on a Ministerial level.

In the same month, Horton was appointed Commander-in-Chief of the Western Approaches.

He wrote to Admiral Darke:

'I simply hate leaving Submarines. No Admiral could possibly have been better and more loyally served than I have been, and the way morale and the offensive spirit have withstood the bitter casualties is a source of overwhelming pride. . . . Whatever else befalls in the short time I have left to serve, nothing can exceed the pride I feel in having run this show for nearly three years, or the poignancy of the extremes of happiness and grief that have happened so frequently, resulting from our victories and losses. I am deeply grateful for your help and advice (even though the latter was not invariably taken).'

[1] The escort carrier *Audacity* was lost in December 1941.

THE VICTORY SMILE
Hoylake, 1943

NOSTALGIC MEMORIES

THE BATTLE OF THE ATLANTIC

A tense moment in the Operations Room at Derby House, Liverpool. Admiral Horton and Air-Vice-Marshal Slatter are standing at the foot of the ladder

And also a letter to Captain Simpson:

'A line to say farewell to you and the 10th Flotilla. Leaving Submarines is the most damnable wrench but circumstances left no alternative. I have done what's possible to implement matters referred to in your last letter. There is little I can say more about your glorious party [the 10th Flotilla]—there have naturally been many changes and grievous losses but the spirit, than which there is none higher in any flotilla in the world, survives; and when we have regained command of the Mediterranean, and I have high hopes it will not be long delayed —a big proportion of the credit must go to you and your flotilla.

'I want to thank you personally for the frank way you have always written to me and maintained such close touch—it has been of great help and shows a confidence which in the Service generally is more often spoken about than actually displayed. In the normal course, Phillips will be relieving you about Christmas and I hope to see you some time, even though my H.Q. is at Liverpool. . . .'

During nearly three years as head of the Submarine Branch, Admiral Horton had laboured unceasingly to improve and develop his charge to the topmost peak of efficiency. That he was successful in this can be judged from the work of British submarines during 1940–42 and afterwards, when the weapon he forged continued to harass the enemy under the able direction of his successor, Rear-Admiral Claud Barry. The first official recognition of Horton's services to the Allied cause came from the Dutch who, from the experience of their own submarines, had reason to appreciate the quality of his leadership. In May 1942 the Queen of the Netherlands personally conferred on him the Grand Cross of the Order of Orange Nassau. Apart from the pride he felt at receiving such a high honour, so graciously bestowed, the beauty of the 'insignia' delighted him. On return to Northways after the ceremony he could not resist the temptation to put it on for his staff officers to see. The glittering emblems, and the broad orange ribbon across his chest, harmonising perfectly with the brass buttons and gold braid, stood out in sharp contrast to the dark background of navy blue. Fully conscious of its effect he said wistfully: 'What a pity they don't give us these things when we are young.'

On 9th November, when he hauled down his flag as Admiral

Commanding Submarines, Max received this message from the Board of Admiralty:

'Their Lordships desire to express to you on relinquishing your command their high appreciation of the exceptional manner in which you have carried out the duties of Flag Officer Submarines for nearly three years of war.

'The outstanding successes achieved by British submarines in both Home and Mediterranean waters bear striking witness to the morale of the Submarine Service and to the efficiency of the training and skilful planning of operations carried out under your supervision.

'The prestige of the Submarine Service has never stood higher than it does at this moment, and for this their Lordships feel you are entitled to feel very just satisfaction.'

In Horton's opinion the success achieved was due entirely to the high quality of the submarine officers, and he welcomed the opportunity to tell them so in a speech, when they entertained him at dinner after the war:

'Quite frankly and speaking from a long experience of the Service in all its aspects, I do really and truly regard submarine personnel as being the finest in the Service. I don't mean they are better types on entry, for entry is common to us all generally speaking, but I do mean that conditions of life aboard a submarine and the training and experience given by the day-by-day life in submarines develops qualities which no other type of Service engenders to a like degree—this may be arguable so far as the lower deck is concerned, but so far as the officers are concerned in my opinion it admits of no doubt whatever. Qualities of decision and leadership and ready acceptance of responsibility can only be developed by their exercise; I am sure that in no other type of craft is there greater opportunities for such exercise at such an early age—further than that, the duties of either First Lieutenant or Captain demand a practical knowledge of engineering, electricity, hydraulics, etc., in addition to their deck executive duties which is only less than that of specialists. Such specialists lack the everyday exercise of the other qualities and these facts make the submarine officer the best all-rounder in the Service in the middle ranks. . . .

'I think the proudest signal I ever received, and there were many during my time as Flag Officer Submarines, was from Dudley Pound when he said words to the effect:

"Thank God we have not to guard our convoys against the attacks of your submarine Commanders."

'The best German commanding officers were no slouchers (and I would still like to know how Prien[1] got into Scapa) but I reiterate here and now—as one who had experience of both our own and German submarine commanding officers in the war—every word of Dudley Pound's signal.'

And now, when the Atlantic life-line was stretched to its utmost limit and the U-boats were increasing their stranglehold, the call came for Max Horton to save his country from the deadly peril.

---

[1] Kapitän Leutnant Gunther Prien, a famous U-boat Commander, who by careful watching found a gap in the defences of Scapa Flow and sank the battleship *Royal Oak* with four torpedoes early in the war.

CHAPTER TEN

November 1942–February 1943

THE BATTLE OF THE ATLANTIC

'It was the job of the little ships and lonely aircraft, a hard, long and patient job, dreary and unpublicised, against two cunning enemies —the U-boat and the cruel sea.'[1]

Derby House. Horton v. Doenitz. The 'wolf packs.' Captain Walker's counter. The Support Groups.

ON 17th November 1942, Sir Max Horton, after a week's leave, took over the Command of the Western Approaches from Admiral Sir Percy Noble, who had been appointed Chief of the British Admiralty Delegation in Washington.

When the war began, Admiral Sir Martin Dunbar Nasmith, as Commander-in-Chief Plymouth, was responsible for the protection of shipping in the North-western and South-western Approaches to the British Isles. Although handicapped by shortage of escort vessels and suitable aircraft, he established the convoy system and kept it running for six months without serious loss. U-boat construction, however, was going ahead apace, and after the collapse of France the full weight of the German submarine offensive fell upon the Atlantic supply lines north-west of Ireland. The shipping losses in June 1940 were nearly equal to the total sustained in the first six months of the war. During the month, fifty-eight merchant ships were sunk: eleven of these were in convoy, forty-four were sailing independently, and three were stragglers. The losses continued at an average rate of about 400,000 tons a month until the following summer, while attempts

[1] Lees-Knowles Lecture, Cambridge, 1951—Captain G. H. Roberts, C.B.E., R.N.

to hunt U-boats anywhere except in the close vicinity of convoys proved to be ineffective.

The threat to our national existence caused Mr. Churchill to remark 'The only thing that ever really frightened me in the war was the U-boat peril.' The steps he took to counter it are described in his book.[1]

The shortage of destroyers and small craft suitable for trade protection became acute on account of casualties in Norway, the Channel after Dunkirk, and the Mediterranean. Most of the destroyers which had survived were required for defence against invasion. At the beginning of 1941, fifty per cent. of a total force of 146 escort vessels were out of action, and, owing to lack of suitably placed maintenance bases, repair work fell far short of requirements.

The number of escort vessels and aircraft available was not enough to protect the convoys using the two main approaches north and south of Ireland. Plymouth was under daily supervision of enemy aircraft based in France, and was unsuitably placed for operational control of the vast traffic using the Clyde and Mersey. The Prime Minister directed therefore that the north of Ireland route was to be the sole approach and that the headquarters of the Commander-in-Chief Western Approaches was to be at Liverpool. This move had been foreseen by Mr. Churchill, who, when he was First Lord, directed that the basement of Derby House, in the city, was to be reconstructed as a massive armoured and gas-proof citadel, wired and equipped for the needs of a modern operational nerve centre. Accordingly in February 1941, when all was ready, Admiral Noble was appointed to the new post, and installed with a large staff at Derby House.

Noble succeeded in convincing the Government of the deplorable shortage of everything and, supported by the Prime Minister's directive, gained 'priorities' for the construction of ships, weapons and suitable aircraft.

Under the able supervision of Engineer Rear-Admiral Sir Henry Wildish and other Engineer officers of the Royal Navy, repair bases and workshops were established during the course of the year at Londonderry, Liverpool, Greenock, Belfast, St. John's, Newfoundland, and on a smaller scale at other ports.

[1] *The Second World War*, Vol. II, p. 529.

By the spring of 1942 these had become really efficient, so by the time Horton had taken over the Command only sixteen per cent. out of a total of 180 escort vessels were out of action from all causes.

Noble's departure was deeply regretted by his staff, some of whom were apprehensive of Horton's reputation for promoting efficiency by ruthless driving. A staff officer writes:

'I remember our horror when we heard that Max was to succeed Percy Noble. P.N., of course, was liked and respected by everybody, including the Wrens, and his departure was greatly mourned.

'Max was quite ruthless and quite selfish, but I loved him dearly! If you knew your job, all was well; if you didn't, God help you! He knew everyone's job, but provided you knew your job a little better than Max did, you were all right.

'He had some maddening habits. He would play golf all the afternoon, then return, dine, play a rubber or two of bridge, and come down to his office (overlooking the Ops. Room) at 11.30 p.m. and start sending for his staff. His golf was a necessity to him. He would send for the "Met. Man"[1] in the morning to find out what it was going to be like at Hoylake that afternoon. I remember being present at the interview once. The "Met. Man" gave a theoretical exposition, all about "cold fronts" and "precipitation" and so on, and Max looked up and said: "D'you ever look out of the window?"'

When Captain G. W. G. Simpson became Commodore at Londonderry, Horton asked him if he intended to live in the official residence. The Commodore, surprised at the question, replied 'Yes, of course.' The Admiral then said 'Well, that won't suit me at all, because there is no "scrambler" telephone there, and it will take me at least twenty minutes to get you on the 'phone out of working hours. My routine is golf every day from two to six, and I usually finish my work at 1.0 a.m. I hope you will arrange your routine to suit.' So the Commodore put a bed in his office, and slept there. Three months later he achieved a little more comfort by requisitioning a semi-detached house next door.

Another staff officer writes:

'The scene in the great Plotting Room at Derby House, with every yard of the Atlantic marked and the walls covered with the symbols of convoys, U-boats, escorts and all sorts, changed with the arrival of Max Horton. The graciousness, the adept handling of overworked

[1] Meteorological Adviser.

personnel by P.N., was missing. Nobody could say that Sir Max was a boor, but he certainly was direct, and without any frills whatsoever.

'Battles were generally fought at night now. After dinner he would arrive in the Plotting Room to watch the battle develop, to order reinforcement, to build plans for the next time. His words were always direct. "Where is . . .?" "What is . . .?" "Why is . . .?" and sometimes "Why not?" or "Why the hell not?" Then having grasped the situation his decision would come in a flash. I remember one night when the battle was pretty serious. It had started later than usual, and Sir Max had already turned in. He literally roared into the "Plot" in rather worn and split pyjamas, hirsute fore and aft. Those present gave him plenty of sea room in anticipation of the coming storm. Then he settled down to work with us, drinking pints of barley water, and his serenity amazed us. He seemed to have an uncanny prevision of what the enemy would do next, which came of course from his long experience of submarines.'

In fact Max was being himself: a master of his profession, domineering yet not arrogant: vain, perhaps, but never pompous. Golf kept him fit, and battles were fought at night, so he arranged his routine accordingly.

Once, when a photographer from the American paper *Life* came to see him, Max said: 'Certainly, I'm just off to play golf. Come along.' On arrival at Hoylake he took a putter from his bag and, dropping a ball about thirty yards from the 18th hole, said to the Pressman: 'Watch me do this hole in one,' and—for the first and only time in his life—he did. The resulting photos appeared on the cover of a *Life* to say nothing of a whole series inside.

Anthony Kimmins says: 'When in the States, I discovered what an enormous impression those photos had made. His name kept cropping up everywhere I went. The fact that a British Admiral could be human enough to admit that he took time off in wartime for a round of golf had caught their fancy. The only photos of British Admirals they had ever seen before were either at their desk poring over a chart, or posing with one hand on a globe.'[1]

It was a comfort to Max to feel that in Admiral Noble he would have a colleague on the other side of the Atlantic who had borne the heat and burden of the struggle. Sir Percy Noble by his

[1] *Half Time*, by Anthony Kimmins, p. 81.

personality could be relied upon to promote good feeling between the Allied navies, thus accelerating new construction and the provision of vital supplies.

He had left behind at Derby House a staff of over a thousand officers and ratings of whom a large proportion were Wrens. A Lieutenant R.N.V.R. doubled the parts of Flag Lieutenant and pilot of the Commander-in-Chief's aeroplane, but he soon found it difficult to look after Horton as well as the aircraft. On the advice of the Secretary (Captain (S.) E. Haslehurst), a Wren officer was appointed as Flag Lieutenant to the Commander-in-Chief. She was Miss Kay Hallaran, specially selected by the Superintendent of W.R.N.S. Haslehurst says:

'We were very fortunate in getting her. Although her parents were British (or rather Irish) they lived in Cleveland, Ohio, and she had been brought up in the U.S.A. She must have been nearly thirty, fairly tall and slim, dark, and always faultlessly turned out. She had immense poise and savoir-faire and never got rattled. A very good "mixer" and equally charming to Admirals and ratings. She had so much tact and charm of manner that she was able to handle impatient senior officers much more effectively than any male junior officer could have done. I doubt if Sir Max ever realised how much she did for him. He never showed much consideration for his staff and she carried out an exacting job with immense patience and cheerfulness. After the war she decided to go home to Cleveland and died there last year under an operation. I do not think I ever heard anyone say a hard word about Kay, which is remarkable in such a job.'

Noble and his Chief of Staff, Commodore J. M. Mansfield, R.N., had created a smooth-running organisation, which included arrangements for directing, under the same roof, aircraft of Coastal Command and the warships engaged in the vital task of destroying U-boats.

The Commander-in-Chief and the Air Officer commanding No. 15 Group Coastal Command (Air Marshal Sir L. H. Slatter) occupied adjacent offices with a large plate-glass window, common to both, overlooking the operations room. Facing them on the opposite wall was an enormous chart of the North Atlantic showing the positions of everything, Allied or enemy, that flew, floated, or had recently been sunk. It was kept up to date quietly and efficiently by busy Wrens who flitted up and down telescopic ladders with the agility of trapeze artistes. Conveniently placed with access to the room were sections of the staff dealing with convoys, escorts, communications and operations, all co-ordinated by the Chief Staff Officer Operations Captain R. W. Ravenhill, R.N., and, in his absence, by the Duty Captain. Horton and Slatter lived on the premises.

The staff was organised as a trident, Operations–Administration–Material, with a Chief Staff Officer of Captain's rank at the head of each. All three were co-ordinated by the Chief of Staff, Commodore A. S. Russell[1], who succeeded Mansfield and became Horton's deputy and responsible to him for policy and general control.

With this organisation supporting him, Max felt confident he could eventually outwit and defeat his formidable antagonist Doenitz, a submariner no less experienced in submarine warfare than himself. The German Submarine Commander-in-Chief had proved himself to be a first-class strategist and had held the initiative from the start. He had probed for the soft spots and had applied successfully the old principle of concentrating his forces to strike where the defence was weak. In consequence, the Allied anti-submarine forces were always a lap behind. By the time they had mustered their resources to deal with an attack in one area, the U-boats were sinking merchant ships right and left in another.

In the first year of the war, the U-boats and Focke-Wulf aircraft[2] found a happy hunting ground off the West Coast of the British Isles, and we know now that they would have achieved even greater success if there had been any semblance of co-operation between them. In 1941, when British long-range aircraft began to appear on the scene more frequently, Doenitz moved his U-boats to mid-Atlantic where they could operate outside air supervision. At the end of the year, when the United States entered the war and the combined counter-measures seemed to be getting the upper hand in the North Atlantic,

[1] Commodore Russell became seriously ill and his place was taken in October 1943 by Commodore I. A. P. Macintyre, who had been Chief Staff Officer to Horton at Northways.

[2] Two-thirds of the ships sunk by aircraft were not in convoy.

Doenitz suddenly switched the whole weight of his offensive to the eastern seaboard of the United States and the Caribbean. He found there, as expected, a 'U-boat's paradise.' The United States coastal trade was not in convoy and anti-submarine measures were negligible. Ships and tankers offered sitting targets in open anchorages and undefended harbours. The tankers fell easy victims, as they steamed up the coast with their vital supplies from the oil ports of the Gulf of Mexico and the Caribbean. To make things easier for the U-boats, coastal pleasure resorts, such as Miami, continued at night to illuminate their seafronts with miles of neon-lighted beaches, against which the unfortunate shipping was mercilessly silhouetted. When the Navy Office complained, they got a blunt refusal to douse the lights, as it would ruin the tourist trade! After six terrible months, an efficient convoy system was got going, air cover was provided and the Miami tourists had to find their way in the dark.

Doenitz kept up his attack in the Caribbean and on the American coastal routes until the end of July 1942. In six and a half months his roving U-boats had sunk 495 merchant ships and 142 tankers, amounting to a total of 2½ million tons. Owing to her new commitments in the Pacific and her timely aid to Britain under Lease-Lend, the United States was short of anti-submarine vessels and aircraft. The construction of small craft had been neglected because it was believed they could be improvised and rapidly produced at small shipbuilding yards. But if the lessons of British experience had been followed earlier in the war, the United States Navy would have been better prepared to meet the U-boats. Great Britain, in order to assist in saving the precious oil, sent twenty-four anti-submarine trawlers, ten corvettes and a few aircraft of Coastal Command to the harassed area, a severe strain on her slender resources.

Meanwhile the offensive against North Atlantic convoys had waned. In fact during March 1942, 450 ships in nineteen convoys reached the British Isles without loss. But this was only a lull. In August, Doenitz, having been frustrated in U.S. waters by the introduction of convoys with air and surface escorts, decided that the time was ripe to come back to mid-Atlantic where he hoped to be beyond the reach of aircraft.

U-boat construction had kept well ahead of losses[1] enabling the 'wolf packs' to keep up intensive attacks on the North Atlantic convoys by day and by night for four months. At the same time many escort vessels suitable for service in the Atlantic were required for the main Allied offensive in Africa. The shipping losses were appalling, reaching their peak in November 1942 when 117 ships[2] of over 700,000 tons were sunk by U-boats in all areas.

In this black month, Max Horton took upon his broad shoulders the responsibility for 'the protection of trade, the routeing and control of all convoys and measures to combat any attack on convoy by U-boats or hostile aircraft within his Command.'[3]

He lost no time in getting in touch with the leaders of the shipping industry. One of them says that he found him uncongenial, but all agree that he gave them confidence and 'undoubtedly achieved the mastery over the U-boats which saved the war for us.'

The extent of his Command was both general and specific. His responsibility ranged from the ice in the north to Portugal in the south; Iceland–Britain–Biscay in the east; and a line down the middle of the Atlantic in the west. By general assent, however, he later controlled operations on both sides of the 'chop' line.[4] There was no question of any other supreme commander while Horton was at Derby House.

It was his business to ensure not only that the people of Britain should be fed, but also that a constant flow of troops and military supplies should be brought in safety to the British Isles, which were now the advanced base for offensive operations against Germany. Military convoys and fast troopships were controlled by the Admiralty and frequently escorted by warships of the Home Fleet.

Horton was not dismayed by the situation as he found it. He had already made up his mind that there could be no improvement until the initiative could be wrested from the enemy. Doenitz had found the soft spots in the Allied defence. Horton, as a sub-

[1] At the end of 1942 over 400 Axis U-boats were in service.
[2] Forty-five merchant ships were not in convoy.
[3] Admiralty Order.
[4] Line of demarcation between British and Canadian control.

mariner, knew where to look for them in the U-boat attack. The 'wolf pack' technique, 'Die Rudeltactik' as the Germans called it, could be employed successfully without air reconnaissance, but it was vulnerable to air attack. Unfortunately for the British Commander-in-Chief, the R.A.F. was concentrating its offensive power on bombing Germany. In consequence, the number of suitable aircraft available for destroying U-boats was quite inadequate. Hence Doenitz had selected for his grand offensive the middle of the Atlantic, where he hoped to be out of reach of British and American long-range aircraft.

He assigned over a hundred U-boats to the task, and having trained them to work as teams, sent them out in groups, widely separated. The submarines in each group were spread over a broad front to make sure of sighting a convoy. Doenitz himself controlled them by radio from Lorient on the French coast. When a U-boat sighted a convoy she became the 'contact keeper,' reporting its position, course and speed to the High Command, who then directed the rest of the group to the quarry, disposing the other groups according to the situation. The submarines detailed for the attack moved at full speed on the surface to join their group leader, usually at night. When the pack was formed he took over the control, and in would go the U-boats like wolves into a flock of sheep. Having selected their victims and fired their torpedoes, they would make their escape, submerging if necessary, and get ready for another attack on the following night.

In the autumn of 1942, Doenitz had so many submarines at his disposal he could afford to allow the U-boats of a pack to attack whenever opportunity offered, either submerged by day or on the surface at night.

The weakness of the 'wolf pack' technique is plain to see. The submarines on reconnaissance had to report the sighting of a convoy by W/T, and their signals could be intercepted by High Frequency Direction Finding. The 'wolf packs' could be formed only on the surface, hence the U-boats could be detected by escort vessels if enough could be spared from the close escort to range round the convoy. The collection of large numbers of submarines in a comparatively small area simplified the task of locating them, even if submerged.

Back in December 1941, during the homeward passage of a convoy from Gibraltar, Commander F. J. Walker, R.N., in the sloop *Stork* with a highly trained Escort Group including the escort carrier *Audacity*, found that if he took immediate offensive measures, the initiative was wrested from the enemy and given into his own hands. In the course of a battle, which lasted a week, Walker was supported by destroyers from Gibraltar and Plymouth. While agreeing that the safety of the convoy was his real aim, he showed that it paid to go out with his group and hunt a U-boat to exhaustion and death at some distance from the convoy. On this occasion it happened he had sufficient force to do it. As a result, four U-boats were destroyed and others damaged, while thirty out of thirty-two merchant ships arrived home safely. The *Audacity* and the destroyer *Stanley* were lost in the battle.

At about the same time a Canadian Escort Commander, J. D. Prentice, who had been a cattle rancher, applied cowboy practice to the defence of convoys. When he knew that his convoy was being shadowed he would direct some of his meagre escort to 'ride' close the the 'herd,' while the others 'rode' round the boundary to keep the U-boats at a distance. 'Keep 'em well stirred up,' said Prentice. Although these tactics were prompted by the offensive spirit and met with some success, experience showed that it does not always pay to stir up trouble without the strength to cope with it.

Up to the end of 1941 no special tactics had been prescribed for the use of escort vessels when in company with a convoy, but each Escort Commander was free to devise any manœuvre he wished for his own group. In those early days, when escort vessels were few and far between, and none could be spared to leave the convoy, the question uppermost in the minds of their Commanders was 'What do you do when a ship of your convoy is torpedoed at night?' The general answer was 'What *can* you do except keep a good look-out?' This may seem an odd state of affairs, but the escort vessels, mostly corvettes, were thinly spread about six miles apart round the convoy. The speed of these little ships was less than that of the U-boats on the surface. If rockets went up in the night, with their tragic tidings, it was usually impossible for a corvette to reach the scene of the disaster before the enemy had made his escape.

New ideas, however, were taking shape, and all agreed that it was better to do something than nothing. Commander Walker produced the first offensive manœuvre to. be executed simultaneously by all ships of the Escort Group. On receipt of the code word 'Buttercup,' all escorts made an outward pounce for a few minutes, firing star shells to illuminate the waters round the convoy; the idea being to make the U-boat submerge, thus reducing its mobility and facilitating its destruction by depth charges.

By March 1942 a universal type of counter-attack had been devised to suit the unheralded torpedoing of a ship in the dark, and it bore the name of 'Raspberry.' After experience at sea and further investigation on the tactical table, other offensive tactics were introduced as conditions altered, each with the code name of a fruit. They were designed to catch the average U-boat (not a Prien[1]), and had to be simple so that the Officer of the Watch could act immediately without waiting for the Captain to come on the bridge.

Admiral Noble was well aware that the best way to defend a convoy was to allow freedom of action for a part of the escort to go out and kill the U-boat, or, at any rate, force her to submerge at some distance from the convoy. Owing to shortage of escort vessels it was seldom possible for an Escort Commander to detach more than one or two warships from a close Escort Group for any length of time without grave risk to the convoy. For example— if eight warships formed the escort, two might be spared for the counter-attack. At this time, however, the normal escort never exceeded six. As soon as reinforcements became available, it was Noble's intention to create independent striking forces with freedom to take the offensive without responsibility for the close defence of the convoy. Horton saw at once the need for organising and training the naval and air forces within his Command to give full effect to these aggressive tactics. He agreed with Noble that self-contained 'Support Groups' would have to be formed at once to act in support of the convoy escorts, thus relieving the Escort

[1] Kapitän Leutnant Gunther Prien, the famous U-boat Commander.

Commander of his dilemma: 'Can I spare warships to hunt U-boats, while retaining sufficient numbers for the close escort of my convoy?'

The way was clear, but the means were lacking. The new frigates and the best escort vessels had been allocated to convoys taking troops and supplies to North Africa, and most of the destroyers in the Western Approaches had been replaced by corvettes. 'Very long range' aircraft, however, were coming into service and their radius of action had been further extended by the use of airfields in Newfoundland, Iceland and Northern Ireland. Nevertheless, there was still a wide space in mid-Atlantic known as the 'Gap' which only a few 'very long range' Liberators could reach. The Germans called it the 'Black Pit,' and it was just there that Doenitz was reaping his richest harvest. Selected merchant vessels on both sides of the Atlantic were being rapidly converted to aircraft carriers which would provide air cover and reconnaissance all along the convoy route. A few of these had been allocated to 'Operation Torch'[1] and the remainder would not be ready for service for some months. Radar was being fitted to key units to supplement High Frequency Direction Finding, so that U-boats on the surface near the convoy could be located at any time.

At the end of 1942 the oil stocks in Great Britain had fallen dangerously low and the tanker fleet had suffered severe losses in the Caribbean. Mr. Churchill and Mr. Roosevelt had directed that the full strength of the Allies must be brought to bear on the Axis in the Mediterranean where it was already beginning to crumble. All the ships, aeroplanes, tanks and vehicles taking part in 'Torch' would come to a dead stop if the oil failed to get through. So it was agreed that the tankers must sail direct from the Caribbean to North Africa, the fast ships independently and the slow ones in convoy, mostly under United States protection. In order to find the escorts for these convoys on southern routes the number of convoys on the North Atlantic routes had to be reduced.

On the whole the system was successful. Most of the tanker convoys got through without loss, but in January 1943 a convoy

[1] North African landings.

of nine tankers, weakly escorted by one destroyer and three corvettes, fell in with a pack of U-boats, probably by chance. Seven out of the nine were sunk.

In December and January there was a marked easement in the assault on the North Atlantic routes. Doenitz, having learnt that an Allied offensive in Africa was pending, and thinking that Dakar would be the principal landing place, re-disposed his U-boats too far south to catch the troop convoys. Consequently the Allied armies were able to land at Casablanca, Oran and Algiers without the loss of a single man on passage, while the hard-pressed Atlantic convoys benefited for a short while by the diversion.

The outlook was promising in the Mediterranean but it was a critical time in the Atlantic. The U-boats were at their maximum strength and at the peak of success. The escort situation was acute, and our commitments exceeded our resources. The question was, could the enemy be prevented from disrupting the Allied supply lines before adequate counter-measures were ready? Horton lost no time in representing the situation as he saw it to the Admiralty. On 19th November 1942 (the day he assumed command) he wrote:

'I consider it essential to inform their Lordships fully of the escort situation in my Command.

'. . . Experience over the last three years shows that depletion of escort strength may be expected in the winter. Even before the gales have had time to play havoc with the escorts the situation is grave, since there is no reserve in my Command from which replacements can be drawn. . . . In a recent case two destroyers of an Escort Group, *Fame* and *Viscount*, were out of action, having rammed and sunk U-boats on the homeward voyage. A third (ex-U.S.A.) developed serious defects and there was none to take their place. . . . It can be assumed that further losses will be sustained in the North African operations. . . . Only vessels of long fuel endurance are of any use for escorting ocean trade convoys. . . . The urgent need for 'Support Groups' to reinforce convoy escorts has been stressed by my predecessor . . . unless a reasonable number of long-endurance destroyers and long-range aircraft come shortly a very serious situation will develop on the Atlantic lifeline.'

Horton was certain that the only way to defeat the U-boat was to attack in strength with aircraft and warships trained together in the aggressive tactics which Captain Walker, with limited resources, had employed so successfully. But it was impossible to organise and train 'Support Groups' without a surplus of fast escort vessels, preferably destroyers. Existing Escort Groups, being mainly composed of corvettes, were too slow for the purpose.

He appreciated the degrees of importance of our commitments in the Atlantic, the Mediterranean, North Russia and elsewhere, and knew very well that risks would have to be taken to meet the needs of his Command. With true strategic insight he saw that the only course of action was to strike, and strike hard, in mid-Atlantic where the U-boats were massing. But he must have the right force to do it.

He wrote almost daily to the Admiralty stressing the urgent need for such a force. Escort Groups and Support Groups could not be interchangeable. It was the business of the Escort Groups to protect the convoys, and they worked on a programme arranged for months ahead. As an example of their clockwork regularity a staff officer says: 'Peter Gretton, who commanded an Escort Group, told me in February that he wanted to be married in May. I named the day for him and he was married on that day.' The Support Groups on the other hand were to be formed and trained solely for the purpose of destroying U-boats. Each group had to be homogenous and speedy. The ideal composition would be six frigates or six destroyers, and they must carry enough fuel to take them to mid-Atlantic in support of any threatened convoy.

The Admiralty could see no way of providing enough ships to meet these requirements until American-built escort vessels materialised in the course of the year. Horton, with his experience of the Reserve Fleet, knew that the steaming range of a few old destroyers of the V class had been increased by taking out a boiler and substituting extra fuel tanks. The remaining two boilers were found to be sufficient to give the necessary performance. He urged most strongly that all the destroyers of this class should be converted at once. A staff officer writes:

'As soon as Max arrived he took the matter up and pushed it through. Incidentally, I was having a "pure English" campaign against the Admiralty at about that time, and coined the word "duo-boilerisation" for this structural operation, hoping to awake some protest. To my horror the Admiralty adopted the word, and I realised that it never pays to be funny with My Lords.'

On 25th November 1942, Horton attended a meeting at the Admiralty and took the opportunity to reiterate the urgent demands of his predecessor for 'very long range' aircraft. He was happy to learn that two squadrons of converted Halifax type were to be used against the U-boats at once, two more were soon to follow and three squadrons of Liberators with fuel endurance for 2,300 miles were to be ready by March. The number of Liberators would be kept up to full strength by the U.S.A. Although the number fell short of his requirements this was good news, for it meant that the mid-Atlantic gap in air cover would soon be bridged, and also that U-boats in transit to and from their bases in the Bay of Biscay would be constantly attacked.

Accordingly, he arranged with Coastal Command of the Royal Air Force that the seven new squadrons were to be disposed as follows:

1 very long range—N. Ireland.
1 very long range—Iceland.
1 very long range—Newfoundland.
2 long range   —Biscay offensive.
1 long range   —Biscay convoys and reconnaissance.
1 long range   —Western Approaches.

Encouraged by the news of this important reinforcement Horton 'followed through' on 5th December 1942 with a strong paper to the Admiralty on the need for training of the Escort Groups and keeping each of them together as a team:

'The Escort Group System [established by Admiral Noble] has proved itself to be beyond all doubt the basic principle of successful anti-submarine operations. There are many examples of well trained and equipped groups, resolutely led, beating off determined U-boat attacks. There are also examples of convoys suffering disastrous losses when escorted by a collection of ships strange to one another, untrained as a team and led by an officer inexperienced in convoy protection. Until each group is led and manned by competent officers, and until it has attained a high degree of group efficiency and is completely equipped with the latest devices, heavy losses will continue. The immediate object must therefore be: to raise the standard of the less efficient groups to the level of the most efficient ones.'

Horton then examines the problem in its relation to personnel and training. Having pointed out that the protection of convoys against U-boats is a highly specialised form of warfare, not included in normal naval training, he urges that the commanding officers of Escort Groups should be carefully selected and retained within the anti-U-boat organisation:

'Experienced Group Commanders should not be removed from their groups on promotion, since their loss must entail a falling off of efficiency which may well be measured in many thousand tons of shipping sunk . . . These officers and those in command of individual escort vessels are frequently faced with situations demanding the highest standard of decision, resource, and initiative in the most rigorous conditions of the Atlantic winter. . . . If we are to grapple successfully with the increasing number of U-boats now operating, all groups must be highly trained as teams, and changes in their composition must be avoided. No stone must be left unturned to provide the necessary facilities for such training. The training of groups at the moment is the responsibility of the Group Commanders who are in turn responsible for the efficiency of their groups to their respective Captains of flotillas.[1] This system suffers from the inherent weakness that none of these Captains is able to give adequate personal attention to the problem in addition to his routine duties at each of the three base ports. I am firmly convinced that a very carefully selected officer of Captain's rank with the necessary Western Approaches experience should be appointed to my staff whose sole responsibility will be to organise, co-ordinate and direct escort training throughout the Command. The principal training base of the Command would continue to be at Londonderry—developed as necessary.'

He then makes constructive proposals as to how the training should be carried out, emphasising that sufficient time in harbour between convoy sailings must be allowed for rest, boiler cleaning, and repairs.

Horton held the view that it was damaging to morale and detrimental to efficiency to rush ships out to sea again, before they had time to recover from the ravages of tempest and the strain of watching for an unseen enemy.

The initial training of newly commissioned escort vessels had been going on at Tobermory for over two years. Only a fortnight

[1] There were several groups in each flotilla administered by a Captain, R.N.

was allowed for this and he felt that the time could well be extended. 'A new corvette manned by very raw types cannot be turned into a warship in two weeks.'

Time was the vital factor in Horton's scheme. If escort vessels were to spend more time under training, more ships would be required to take their place on the convoy routes. Horton had not overlooked this. His proposals included a scheme for running slightly larger convoys at longer intervals, thus increasing the time allowed for training the Escort Groups and also releasing warships to form Support Groups.

The Admiralty, while agreeing in principle with Horton's views on offensive tactics and the need for training, differed as to the means of finding additional escort vessels for the Support Groups.

Any change in convoy cycles would necessitate a corresponding change in organisation of the ports and internal transport services. Britain, the United States, and Canada were all concerned, and the problem was further complicated by the needs of the combined forces engaged in the North African campaign.

As there had been a big fall in shipping losses in December and January the Admiralty suggested that very large convoys might now be run at longer intervals. Horton opposed the idea of increasing the size of the convoys beyond sixty ships. 'It is appreciated that convoys of 90 and 100 ships have been run in the past with an escort of similar size as at present. This was in 1941 when only 25 to 30 U-boats were operating. . . . The present conditions of 90 to 100 U-boats working in packs of 20 is very different.' Although it may seem that Horton was being inconsistent he was not misled by the lull in mid-Atlantic which, he reminded the Admiralty, was due to U-boats having been diverted by events in North Africa.

Meanwhile, with the arrival of air reinforcements, Horton put forward another scheme to release escort vessels for offensive action. The U-boats had selected for their main attack an area in mid-Atlantic which they knew to be outside the reach of long-range aircraft. In Horton's opinion they would continue to concentrate in this gap in ever increasing numbers. He argued that since the convoys could have air cover up to the limits of aircraft range, the surface escorts could be reduced in strength during this part of the voyage. It was only while crossing the 'Gap' that a full measure of protection was needed. He suggested that the proper way to reinforce the escorts in this dangerous area would be to have at hand highly trained and speedy Support Groups with freedom of action to destroy U-boats near any threatened convoy. He knew that the day was not far distant when very long range aircraft would be able to cover the 'Gap,' and with this ultimate prospect in view he said: 'I feel strongly that the solution of the German U-boat menace will be found only by the development of highly trained Support Groups working in co-operation with an adequate number of very long range aircraft.'

Horton's proposal was no mere stratagem to get more warships. It was a classic example of the correct application of the old principles of war: concentration in the decisive area, offensive action, co-operation and economy of force.

One day in early February 1943, while the matter was being considered on the highest level, the Commodore, Londonderry happened to visit Derby House. A signal came in reporting heavy losses to a convoy. The Commander-in-Chief said to him 'Although this is very terrible, it is all lending weight to my arguments, and I believe I shall get Cabinet approval for forming Support Groups. Higher authority feels doubtful of my ability to place Support Groups in contact with U-boats, but I feel confident that I shall be able to do so *near the convoys* in mid-Atlantic where the U-boats are thickest. It is, of course, a gamble that I must be sure will succeed, because to weaken the close escorts without gaining a dividend would be a fatal blunder.'

As a result of Horton's representations each convoy escort was reduced by one vessel, thus releasing about sixteen warships which were organised in four Support Groups.

CHAPTER ELEVEN

November 1942–February 1943

THE BATTLE OF THE ATLANTIC

'These were the men,
who were her salvation
who conquered the waters and the underwaters,
who,
in storm and calm,
taught England to live anew,
and fed her children.'

*Canada's contribution. Green sailors. Horton's school of battle
and training scheme. Visit of Sir Stafford Cripps. Air co-operation. Tracking the U-boats. The Scientists and the Weapons.*

WHILE awaiting approval for his proposals, the Commander-
in-Chief did not allow the grass to grow under his feet.
Training was the paramount requirement. In the words of one of the
most successful escort leaders: 'the turn in the tide to victory came
only with the improvement in training brought about in 1942 and
1943. Tactics and training are complementary and inseparable.'

The Mercantile Convoy Instructions was the text book on
which the system had been organised. It was based on the
experience of the 1914–18 War, when towards the end, a group
of eight to twelve escort vessels would protect a convoy of twenty
ships. 'Pack' tactics by U-boats at night had not been thought of,
and air co-operation between warships and aircraft was in its
infancy. In 1939 the book proved to be of great value in establishing the system of control, organising the convoys and escorts,
and providing equipment. The tactical instructions, however,
in this and other official publications were, as might be expected,

out of date. Very little had been done outside the Anti-Submarine School at Portland to carry out experiments on a practical scale at sea and to develop new methods.

Commenting on these instructions Captain G. H. Roberts, who commanded the Western Approaches Tactical Unit from 1942 to 1945, said in a lecture at Trinity College, Cambridge:[1]

'The "object" which is the mandate of the Escort Commander, was stated in the Instructions as follows:

"The safe and timely arrival of the convoy at its destination is the primary object, and nothing releases the Escort Commander of his responsibility in this respect.

"At the same time, it must be borne in mind, that, if enemy forces are reported or encountered, the escort shares with all other fighting units the duty of destroying enemy ships, provided that this duty can be undertaken without undue prejudice to the safety of the convoy."

'To analyse this mandate, let us suppose that a U-boat has been encountered near the convoy. Does the Escort Commander detail a part of his Escort Group to detach and kill this U-boat? It may take an hour or two to do so, and the escort will be reduced until the detached warships can overtake the convoy. On the one hand, the death of the U-boat will mean that it cannot attack another convoy later on, but on the other hand, what happens if a second U-boat is encountered while the detached escorts are absent? The second U-boat would have a very much easier task in attacking the convoy and may even attack unopposed.

'An immediate and correct decision on such a problem, which is only one of very many, can only be made by a highly skilled and experienced Escort Commander. But it is unfortunately true that, in 1939, the glamour of the Fleet and the attraction of the Destroyer Flotillas, the cruisers and carriers, and the traditional paraphernalia of Fleet life meant· that few of "the quality" were left over for commands in the escort forces. It was not easy to correct this at first, and when some of our very best were appointed to command ships and groups in the Western Approaches they looked on it as a back-water. They did not realise that the care of half a million tons of shipping on a 3,000-mile trip through nearly every known hazard, to be repeated every five or six weeks, is a task very worthy of a Commander in the Royal Navy, and he must be a very good one too.'

One of the few exceptions was Captain F. J. Walker, R.N. 'The glamour of the Fleet' meant nothing to him. He had devoted his naval life to the study of anti-submarine warfare, and between the wars very nearly missed his promotion, possibly

[1] Lees-Knowles Lectures 1951—Captain G. H. Roberts, C.B.E., R.N.

because his branch of the Service was thought to be a 'bit of a backwater.' As a senior Lt.-Commander he was appointed Anti-Submarine Officer on the staff of the Commander-in-Chief Home Fleet, where he found, strangely enough, that the staff duties required of him were negligible. At his own request he carried out ship duties in addition to his other work. His high qualities as a leader immediately shone, and he received a well deserved but tardy promotion. Yet he was passed over as a Commander, and it was not until the war came that he was able to put into practice as an Escort Commander the results of many years of study and training. He was a strong advocate of offensive tactics for convoy escorts, and, during the war, he destroyed over thirty U-boats with the two groups he commanded. In 1942 when their Lordships realised that they had allowed an officer with the fighting qualities of Nelson to pass through the promotion zone, they made honourable amends and gave Walker his promotion to Captain with two years additional seniority. He was a King's Medallist at Dartmouth, and held the C.B. and four D.S.O.s. He died from illness in 1944. A grievous loss to the country.

The officers and men of the escort forces were almost wholly recruited from civil life; seventy per cent. of the Canadians had never seen salt water until they joined the Royal Canadian Naval Volunteer Reserve. There is a story told of two Canadian corvettes meeting by chance in mid-Atlantic. Each was commanded by a Lieutenant R.C.N.V.R. One asked 'What do you make of our position?' and the other replied 'I don't know, I'm a stranger here myself!'

The rapid growth of the Royal Canadian Navy revealed the latent power of the nation. At the start of the war the strength of Canadian naval personnel was 3,843 officers and men, including reserves. At the end it had expanded to over 90,000, of whom about three per cent. were Regulars. In the same time her small pre-war permanent force of six destroyers grew to a fleet of 400 warships.

In Britain and the Dominions, ships and men for trade protection had to be 'mass produced.' Peace-time training for all would have been impossible, but there was great need for an adequate nucleus of experienced officers and petty officers to indoctrinate the mass. It is to the everlasting credit of British and Canadian manhood that they responded so nobly to the call, and so quickly learnt the rudiments of the naval profession in conditions of appalling danger and dreadful discomfort. Men came from every walk of life. Black coat and rolled umbrella, cloth cap and overall were thrown aside, and all looked with simple faith for leadership and guidance, which came to them in the end. But it took a little time, because few regular officers were available with experience of convoy work. The commanding officers of the British and Canadian destroyers (when able to be present) set a magnificent example of skill in seamanship and resolution in action. This has been justly acknowledged by post-war writers who had served with the R.N.V.R. in the escorts.[1]

The need for preliminary training was obvious from the start, and small units for Asdic and weapon training sprang up like mushrooms at various ports. Officers and ratings were instructed in the latest products of science whenever they could be spared and wherever they happened to be. The weapon training was 'ad hoc' and the tactical training was by 'trial and error,' usually in the face of the enemy at sea. Such a state of affairs might seem to be incredible, but it was the inevitable result of complacency between the wars and lack of funds to provide for contingencies that nobody outside the Services wished to think about. The blame cannot be fixed wholly on the Admiralty who, after all, are the servants of Democracy.

The wolf was at the door and the packs were not far distant. Under this threat Democracy grew benevolent. Provision was made in July 1940 for a training centre at Tobermory where newly commissioned corvettes and sloops could receive initial training in seamanship and weapons away from the hurly-burly of battle. Vice-Admiral Gilbert Stephenson was appointed to command. There could not have been a better choice. He had himself served as Commodore of Convoys, and treated with sympathetic understanding the callow young men who were so soon to take upon their shoulders the heavy responsibilities of escort duty in the tempestuous Atlantic.

[1] Q.v. *The Cruel Sea,* by N. Monsarrat.

'Puggy' Stephenson, combined drive with tact, basing his teaching on the best traditions of the Royal Navy, thus instilling a sense of discipline and pride of ship which brought the crews together and later sustained them in many a tight corner. Stephenson believed in keeping the new ship's companies 'on their toes,' and would pay them surprise visits to test their readiness. On one occasion he crept up the side of a frigate and when he alighted on deck was promptly attacked by a fierce Alsatian dog. This demonstration of vigilance so impressed him that he retired to his barge with dignity, but without the seat of his pants. Various versions of the story went round the Command, and by way of embellishment the Captain of the frigate is reported to have said that his dog didn't like pugs!

Another time, while inspecting a Dominion corvette, the Admiral threw his cap on the deck and said: 'That's an unexploded bomb. Take action quick!' Whereupon a young rating broke from the gaping crew and kicked it over the side. Showing no surprise, the Admiral commended the lad on his presence of mind, and pointing to the semi-submerged cap, said 'That's a survivor—jump in and save him!' It was November.

In January 1942 the Western Approaches Tactical Unit was established at Liverpool on the top floor of the Exchange Building, close to Derby House. Here, officers were trained in the tactics to be employed against U-boats, and new problems were investigated. The course lasted six days and by the end of the war over 5,000 Allied officers, from Admirals to Midshipmen, had passed through it.

It was usually referred to as 'the Game,' and when at sea, officers would discuss problems which had faced them in 'the Game,' thus subconsciously preparing themselves against surprise, should a similar situation arise in grim reality. In this way a common doctrine was established, enabling them to act as the Commander-in-Chief would wish them to act without signals.

In the tactical school the sea was represented by a vast lino-covered floor; on that make-believe ocean Wrens would move miniature convoys, model warships, and escort carriers as directed by the officers taking part in the exercise. Only the staff and the operators were permitted a bird's-eye view. The U-boat 'killers' (commanding officers of escort vessels and aircraft), working on their charts behind screens, were allowed only occasional peeps through slits adjusted to represent the limits of their vision at sea; in simulated darkness or fog they could see nothing. In reality, the commanding officer would be getting all his information from his signalman and Asdic rating. In 'the Game' this was provided by a Wren officer who moved gracefully yet purposefully from table to table. 'Star shell fired here' she would tell one. 'Destroyer (code name) calling you on W/T' she would tell another, then probably a colleague would flit across to an officer already distracted, and give him all 'the works'—'ship torpedoed here'—'Asdic contact there'—'survivors in ship's boats here'—'gun flashes over there'—'R/T from senior officer: "Blow the breeches off him" ' and so it went on. But it was all very carefully planned, and every movement was plotted according to the decisions taken by the young officers. Afterwards at the 'post-mortem' they would be treated to a 'bird's-eye view,' where they could see the tracks of the U-boats in green chalk and their own tracks in white chalk, and learn from the umpires if they had achieved a kill. More often than not they would make ghastly mistakes, and would thank God it was only a game, but the lessons had been driven home; their fore-knowledge would put them on their guard and give them confidence when they took their ships to sea on the morrow.

On the day that Horton became Commander-in-Chief he visited the Tactical School. On meeting the Captain he said: 'What do you *think* you do?' Roberts, with a touch of heat, told him why he was there and what he was *trying* to do. After this hot reply the Admiral, with a merry twinkle in his eye, said mildly: 'If you are right I will help you.' At 9 a.m. on the following morning he arrived, unattended, at the school and went through the course.

Afterwards, he visited the school frequently to study tactical problems. Sometimes in discussion, if he disagreed with the Captain, he would raise his eyebrows and say: 'You think so?' The Captain, having learnt the 'form', would reply: 'Yes, I do!' So they got on very well.

On one occasion Roberts offered to show him a demonstration of a foolproof search for a U-boat sighted by an escort vessel in daylight. The Admiral said he would like to work the U-boat himself. So he was curtained off at the tactical table with the same restricted view of the escort vessel that he would have in practice. Horton dived his U-boat and moved away as only a submariner knows how. After being caught three times he gave in, saying: 'That's all very fine, but you can all see what my U-boat is doing.' He disliked being 'sunk,' even as a tiny wooden model. Nobody dared tell him that the escort vessel which had hunted him so successfully, according to plan, had been moved by a woman, a Third Officer Wren in another room!

Ancillary schools for 'refresher' tactical courses were also established at Londonderry, Greenock, Birkenhead (for trawlers), Bombay, St. John's, Newfoundland, Freetown, and Sydney, N.S.W. They were attended by officers of the Escort Groups under their own Commanders, who welcomed the opportunity to examine problems which had faced them on the voyage.

Horton, while appreciating the value of academic study, felt that it should be followed by practical instruction at sea. In the Submarine Service they have their tactical tables and attack teachers, but graduation is not complete until officers and men have been trained in 'dummy' attacks at sea against target ships. With this experience in mind, Horton reversed the process by creating a unit for exercising escort vessels in the art of sinking U-boats. Early in February 1943 H.M.S. *Philante* [1] and one or two submarines (to act as targets) were allocated to him for this important duty. The flotilla was based at Larne in Northern Ireland under Captain A. J. Baker-Cresswell, and later, Captain L. F. Durnford-Slater, R.N., as Training Captain. It was arranged that each Escort Group, before joining its convoy, should spend at least two days at sea with the *Philante* acting as a ship of a convoy. Exercises would then take place, in co-operation with Coastal Command aircraft, against the submarines representing U-boats.

The Commander-in-Chief took a keen interest in this 'school

[1] *Philante*, 1,600 tons, had been built in 1937 as a luxury yacht for Mr. Tom Sopwith, and is now the Norwegian Royal Yacht *Norge*.

of battle' and would go to sea himself in the *Philante* for important tactical experiments.

The close co-operation between the Naval and R.A.F. Commands at Derby House enabled arrangements to be made for the aircraft of Coastal Command to undergo tactical training hand-in-hand with the Escort Groups. All learnt to work with the same signal code and to make reports of enemy positions on a synchronised navigational basis.

As a result shore-based aircraft could, when necessary, become part of the escort force, and under the direction of the Escort Commander, they could carry out planned circuits and searches, using positions relative to the convoy when making their reports. If an escort vessel obtained a bearing of a U-boat by Direction Finding Wireless, the Escort Commander could have his aircraft swooping down on that bearing in a few seconds.

Two new escort carriers were expected to join the Western Approaches Command in March 1943. These were converted merchant ships, specially designed to carry fighters and anti-submarine aircraft for the protection of convoys throughout the voyage. Many more were to follow, and it was highly important that air crews trained in sea warfare should be ready to embark with their machines as soon as the carriers arrived. This was the responsibility of the Flag Officer Carrier Training, Vice-Admiral Sir Lumley Lyster, who had led the British aircraft carriers in their successful attack on the Italian Fleet at Taranto. The speed at which he trained these newcomers to the Battle of the Atlantic enabled the Commander-in-Chief, a month later, to spring a surprise on the Germans. The standard achieved was evident from the skill displayed by the Fleet Air Arm pilots in landing their aircraft in all weathers on the restricted flying decks of these relatively small ships. Their imminent arrival raised new problems for Horton. Were they to work with the supporting force or in company with the convoy? They were vulnerable to U-boat attack, especially during flying operations, and the loss of the carrier would mean the loss of her aircraft. These problems were investigated on the tactical table and various solutions tried out at sea. The Captains and officers of the Fleet Air Arm designated for the escort carriers were present during the investigations, and later operated their ships with the *Philante's* training group. Whatever plan was finally adopted it was obvious that the carrier must have its own escort, and since speed was essential, two destroyers were the most suitable ships for this duty. If these were not available the only alternative would be for the ship to hide herself in the centre of the convoy, sharing the protection of its escort. Such an idea was anathema to Horton, who regarded the carrier as a means of increasing the offensive power of his Support Groups. In his opinion the best way to defend the convoy was to destroy the U-boats, and his tactics were framed accordingly.

The problem of close air escort was solved later in the year by the introduction of merchant aircraft carriers (M.A.C. ships). These ships carried cargoes but could operate a few aircraft while in convoy.

Horton was not deceived by the slackening of U-boat activity in December 1942 and January 1943. He was quite certain that they would soon return to mid-Atlantic in greater numbers than ever. He pressed on with his training scheme, so that all his escort forces, including reinforcements, would be ready for the counter offensive he had planned.

Although there had been no change in the convoy cycles,[1] he had obtained approval, as we have seen, to reduce the strength of the close escorts slightly, and to use the warships thus released to build up his Support Groups. He was aided in this by improved air cover from the Canadians and Americans in the Western Atlantic, and the Royal Air Force at the eastern end of the convoy routes. Further economy in escort vessels was soon to be achieved by oiling at sea from tankers with special floating hose equipment while steaming with the convoys.[2]

---

[1] Time intervals between round voyages from start to return.

[2] Practically no escort vessels had the fuel capacity to enable them to cross the Atlantic and carry out anti-submarine operations on the way. The escorts, therefore, worked on a system of relays, fuelling in Iceland and Newfoundland. The first trials of oiling at sea with synthetic rubber hoses were ordered by Admiral Noble and directed by Engineer Rear-Admiral Wildish in February 1942. It was not until the early spring of 1943 that the practice became general in the Atlantic convoys.

THE BATTLE OF THE ATLANTIC

The Prime Minister, although well satisfied with the progress being made by the Allied armies in North Africa, had not lost sight of the peril behind their backs in the Atlantic. He knew Horton's needs, and through the medium of the Anti-U-boat Committee hastened the delivery of frigates and very long range aircraft.

In January 1943 Sir Stafford Cripps, Minister of Aircraft Production and a member of the Anti-U-boat Committee, paid two visits to Derby House. Here is an account of the meetings as recorded by Max:

'The first visit was paid at 9.45 p.m. on Saturday, 9th January, on the occasion of his returning his daughter, who is a Wren at Derby House. In response to my invitation if he would care to come up, he did, and remained for an hour. He inquired about the convoy situation at the moment, and I told him of the U.S.A.-Gibraltar tanker convoy that was in serious trouble. Subsequently he referred to the serious state of our shipping situation, giving me certain facts to the effect that ten million tons were required for our commitments in the latter half of the year and that only eight and a half were likely to be available.

'He said that even if the U.S.A. replacements of merchant ships arrive up to schedule, it seems likely that our imports will so bunch in the second half of this year that the ports may have some difficulty in dealing with them.

'He said that the V.L.R.[1] aircraft was the true solution to the U-boat menace and I agreed very heartily. He referred to his action in arranging for thirty-nine of such aircraft to be made available for the Western Approaches Command very shortly, whereat I said I had hoped for far more. He replied that provision of such aircraft depended on U.S.A. keeping their promises which in actual fact were delayed in fulfilment and that thirty-nine V.L.R.s were all that were in sight. He had, however, arranged for sixteen Halifaxes from Bomber Command to be equipped with extra fuel tanks which would give them equivalent endurance to V.L.R.s. He said that U.S.A. was fully alive to the serious threat to our communications owing to the U-boats, and was proving very amenable to the provision of suitable aircraft; and so also was the Prime Minister.

'He said that the Admiralty had never made a clear and detailed case for their need for V.L.R. aircraft. They had simply asked for more aircraft for Coastal Command without giving detailed reasons, and it was mainly owing to their not making out a clear and definite

---

[1] Very Long Range.

case that the Navy had not done better in the past in regard to its suitable aircraft. He reiterated again that V.L.R. had never been asked for before he suggested it.[1] I said that the change of attitude on the part of the highest authorities in regard to the supply of suitable aircraft to Coastal Command and the Navy, was, I presume, more due to their getting frightened in regard to the situation than to any arguments put upon paper. Further, I suggested that Coastal Command knew just as well as Admiralty the number and type of machines necessary to guard the convoys and kill the U-boats that were attacking them, and could have put their case through the Admiralty in the jargon that would prove convincing to the Air Ministry. Sir Stafford Cripps partially agreed to this. I said it was ludicrous that Admiralty should have to prove the use and need of every single sortie to obtain each separate aircraft—it was like a layman with no knowledge of medical technical terms trying to convince the British Medical Council to a course of treatment which the Council had already decided should not be given. I suggested we ought to have a barrister state our case for us. He said we had one now, and laughed.

'He referred to the spare part troubles which had so handicapped our operational aircraft in this country and told me what he was doing to rectify it. He referred to certain aircraft firms whose organisation was in a bad state. He also referred to the peculiarities in the Barracuda design [naval aircraft], which made quick construction so difficult.

'Turning to operational matters, he referred to the geographical importance of Greenland as a base for V.L.R. aircraft and said that he hoped to be able to get the Americans to develop a base there. It is likely to prove of the greatest help to the security of our North Atlantic convoys, as that area is so difficult to reach from Iceland, Ireland or Canada. I expressed cordial agreement to this proposal and told him that a U.S.A. Captain of the American Air Service was on the spot here. He knew the ground, having been to Greenland, and considered the project was feasible for a few Liberators; I arranged for Sir Stafford to see him the following forenoon.

Sir Stafford suggested that perhaps greater security in the convoys themselves would be obtained by instruction of the masters by naval officers in regard to station-keeping, manœuvring, necessity to show no lights, etc. He referred to Lawrence Holt who was keen on this and said that suggestions to this end were put up before the Admiralty. I told him that British masters of merchant ships knew their job pretty well at this state of the war and hardly required instruction in first

[1] This statement is incorrect: in February 1942 the Admiralty asked specifically for thirty-six Liberators and fifty-four Fortresses for 'very long range' and 'long range' work. In May 1942 the air situation was re-examined by the Admiralty and their requirements clearly stated. In June 1942 the Admiralty again pressed for maritime aircraft of all types.

THE BATTLE OF THE ATLANTIC

A Swordfish aircraft of the Fleet Air Arm over a convoy

THE CRUEL SEA
A job for rescue

A CORVETTE 'TAKES IT GREEN'

principles. In fact I suggested they would rather resent it. Cautions with regard to all these matters were given them before every convoy sailed.

'Sir Stafford then left, and visited Derby House again at 11.0 a.m. on Sunday 10th. On his arrival I produced Captain Baker, U.S.A., the officer who knew the Greenland air bases, together with A.O.C. A discussion took place and Captain Baker made it clear that from the point of view of aircraft, the Greenland base was much easier to get away from than to find. He felt it was definitely practicable to maintain a small number of V.L.R. aircraft at the Southern Greenland base. Although the base would be closed for many days during winter on account of the weather, yet there were periods increasing in proportion as winter waned when this force could operate successfully to the assistance of our convoys. It would often be necessary for them, of course, to land either in Iceland or Canada; to await suitable weather for their return to Greenland. He also made it clear that it would not be advisable to make use of this base by pilots who had not previous experience of it; that is to say, we should not count on aircraft starting from Iceland or Canada being able to put into Greenland to refuel or re-bomb. Its use, in the first instance, should be confined to a small striking force based there.

'After these officers had left, Sir Stafford asked me if I received the minutes of the Anti-U-boat Committee, and whether I attended any of their meetings. I replied in the negative. He said he thought it would be desirable and would take action to that end.' [This was arranged.]

Although inclined to be suspicious of new acquaintances and sceptical about their efficiency, Horton took to the Minister at once. This is not surprising, for Sir Stafford was neither a crank, as some people believed, nor did he suffer from the more common limitations of a legal mind. He was deeply sincere and intensely patriotic. He inspired frankness in those he met, and got at the truth more by charm than by cross-examination. He had a puckish sense of humour and above all a brilliant and well-balanced mind. The Commander-in-Chief was encouraged by his visits for he knew that the claims of the Western Approaches would be justly represented to the Cabinet.

Many interesting visitors came to Derby House, among whom was General Sir W. G. Dobbie, who, as Governor of Malta, had sustained the people of the island in their time of trial by his strong religious beliefs. He and Sir Max had much in common. In a letter dated 26th January 1943 to a friend in Malta, Max says:

'In Malta you must be feeling rather a reaction; after being poised on the edge of a precipice for so long. I saw Dobbie up here last week—was able to be of use to him in a small way and having attended his first seance at a local hall on the Monday he came to dinner here afterwards—the seance was well attended and I nearly had to read a Psalm—anyway sang several hymns and listened to his talk on Malta and God—his sincerity alleviated much.

'Other interesting visitors have been Norman Birkett who came to collect material for another broadcast—he stayed two days—such a charming man—I wished he could have stayed longer. Then Stafford Cripps came for an hour or two—very interesting and he has been very helpful to us about the air—certainly we need help in that direction—more and more and more.'

In order to understand the nature of the battle against the U-boats the reader should have some slight knowledge of equipment and weapons used on both sides. The greatest asset of the submarine is its ability to approach its prey unseen and to vanish after delivering its attack. The most important counter-measure developed by the British between the wars was the Asdic, a listening device which gave by echo the bearing of a submerged submarine and its range up to about a mile, but not its depth. Owing to extreme secrecy the limitations of the Asdic were not fully appreciated outside British professional circles. Some American naval officers thought that, in the event of a submarine being located, a destroyer would steam to the spot, 'squirt a couple of "ash cans" ' (depth charges) and that would be the end of the U-boat. It was not generally known that the submarine herself was aware when she was being contacted, and furthermore that the hunting destroyer lost contact when within a hundred yards of her prey. In the early days of the war most escort vessels dropped their depth charges down a slide (like an ash chute) over the stern. Hence, by the time the destroyer could get her stern over the target the U-boat had either dived deep or nipped out of the danger area. To obviate this difficulty, 'depth-charge throwers' were provided. Later on, escort vessels were fitted with multiple projectors called 'Hedgehogs,' which could throw streamlined bombs in a pattern over the target before Asdic contact was lost. The German submarines then tried to mislead the Asdic operators by firing canisters which exuded bubbles giving back false echoes. These 'Pillenwerfer,' however, did not deceive highly trained Asdic operators who knew by experience the true echo of the U-boat. It is obvious that the chances of achieving a 'kill' are better when several escort vessels, not too few and not too many, can join in the hunt. In this form of warfare Nelsonic leadership and patient training are essential, so that officers and men of the attacking group will act correctly without direction when the great moment comes.

By the end of 1942, the construction of U-boats had far out-paced the building of escort vessels. Hence, the German packs, operating on the surface at night, had inflicted heavy losses against weakly escorted convoys. The hastily built corvettes were really improvised whalers, thrown into the battle because it was thought that catching whales and killing U-boats had something in common. They were originally intended for coastal work, but sheer necessity caused them to be used as ocean escorts.

Although too slow and of little value from an offensive point of view, they filled the gap in convoy defence for over two years, while at the same time providing experience in a very tough school for hastily trained personnel. Officers and men who had served in corvettes came to man the new frigates well acquainted with 'the dangers of the sea and the violence of the enemy.' No better crews could have been found for Horton's Escort Groups and Support Groups. In this respect the British and Canadians had the advantage over the Germans, for many experienced U-boat crews had been lost and the new crews were over-diluted by rapid expansion.

The movements of U-boats on the surface could be detected by radar up to a distance of twenty miles, and their wireless signals, while concentrating to attack a convoy, could be intercepted by High Frequency Direction Finding stations on both sides of the Atlantic. This valuable intelligence was a great help to the British tracking organisation, not only for guiding striking forces to the area of enemy concentration, but also for enabling convoys to avoid it.

The head of the tracking organisation at the Admiralty was Captain C. R. N. Winn, R.N.V.R. A barrister by profession, he was well qualified for the task which depended for success on rapid and accurate sifting of evidence. ' . . . his knowledge of the U-boats, their Commanders, and almost what they were thinking about was uncanny . . . his prescience was amazing.' [1]

In the early days of the war, Winn confided to Horton that he felt he ought to learn, at least, something about the potential performances of submarines and how they could be manœuvred by skilled Captains. Max said he would be delighted to teach him, so it was arranged that Winn should go to Northways regularly during the Admiralty dinner hour and fire questions at him. In this friendly atmosphere Winn imbibed much knowledge and a moderate quota of Max's gin. Both were gifted with prescience to a remarkable degree, Winn basing his forecasts on cold fact, while Max relied on instinct born of knowledge and experience. When Horton became Commander-in-Chief, it was his duty to take appropriate action on Winn's conclusions, and this led very occasionally to differences of opinion. One day, in a moment of heat, on the telephone, Horton reminded Winn that since he knew so little about submarines he had better go to sea in one, and learn something. Winn replied that nothing would please him more, so in due course he found himself booked for a passage in a submarine about to sail for the 'Biscay Patrol.' At this stage, the Director of Naval Intelligence intervened, and put a veto on the whole project. No objection was seen, however, to Winn spending ten days of his much-needed leave in one of the target submarines attached to the *Philante*. This was arranged, and he combined business with pleasure in the picturesque waters of the West of Scotland.

Shortly afterwards, Horton and Winn had another sharp difference on a matter of principle. Max complained that he should be given more information about the methods and reasoning from which Winn drew his inferences about enemy movements. Winn politely suggested that, if the Commander-in-Chief could spare the time, he would be pleased to welcome him as a temporary member of his team. Horton accepted with alacrity, and on arrival found himself confronted with a mass of contradictory information. 'It's all yours, Sir!' said Winn. 'And your Chief of Staff at Liverpool is waiting for the answer.' Max, showing neither surprise nor resentment, immediately got down to it, but after

[1] *A Sailor's Odyssey*, p. 579, by Admiral of the Fleet Viscount Cunningham.

spending half a day on the work he confessed that most of it was outside his province. With the old familiar smile, which some called 'catlike' and others 'benign', he held out his hand and said 'Goodbye, Rodger—I leave it to you.' And thereafter he did.

The battle of the scientists was going on all the time. The U-boats had a radar set, but it gave poor results, so they were supplied with an instrument which told them (as in the case of the Asdic) that they were being held by our radar, thus warning them when it was time to dive. The British scientists soon produced a radar set which the enemy could not detect. This worried the Germans who, thinking that we were using some magic infra-red eye, tried experiments with special anti-infra-red paint. In U-boat circles there was intense gloom and general distrust, and the German scientists suffered much criticism.[1]

Two U-boats went to sea, each with a top-ranking scientist. Within a week both were sunk. One scientist was saved, but his disclosures (if any) are outside the scope of this biography.

Speaking of scientists, Max said in a private letter:

'We found in giving effect to our scientists' efforts that there were not sufficient skilled and trained men at sea to keep the instruments at concert pitch. Another job of the backroom boys is to achieve such simplicity, both in working and maintenance, as will enable the men who are to work the instruments at sea to get the best possible results.'

Nevertheless, Horton would be the first to acclaim the work of British scientists in the war. In fact on several occasions he called for the views of Professor P. M. S. Blackett, the Chief of Operational Research, on problems which normally would be regarded as being exclusively within the orbit of the naval officer. The scientists worked in close co-operation with all three Services, and responded with enthusiasm to every call. It was quite amazing how quickly they could initiate new weapons and devices whilst at the same time producing counters to Hitler's 'secret weapons.' If, as Max suggests, the results of their efforts were sometimes beyond the capabilities of the users, the blame lay more with

---

[1] Doenitz admits in his essays that the superiority of British radar was one of the chief causes of his defeat.

the professional officers who passed the instruments into service than with those who conceived them.

An interesting German innovation which helped, for a time, to turn the scale of battle in favour of the U-boats was the celebrated 'milch cow,' a large fat submarine of seemingly infinite fuel capacity. She went about the ocean suckling her infamous brood at pre-arranged rendezvous, and in addition to the fact that she could travel 25,000 miles, she could eke out many tons of fuel to gasping U-boats. Several beasts of this first-class dairy herd were at sea in the spring of 1943. Later they were hunted down by British and U.S. Support Groups working with aircraft carriers.

The question of re-arming the U-boats after they had fired all their torpedoes was not so easy, and up till the end of the war they were obliged to replenish at their bases. In order to conserve these weapons they would use the gun, whenever they got the chance, against undefended merchant ships. The Germans found the electric torpedo to be the best type for their purpose, because it took up less room than the older types and after discharge left no track. The enemy hoped to achieve devastating results with the acoustic torpedo (the 'gnat'), one of Hitler's secret weapons designed to 'home' on to its target attracted by the noise of the ship's propellers. It could be lured away by noise-making devices towed at a safe distance, and proved to be more a nuisance than a menace, yet it could never be ignored. It was not introduced, as we shall see, until the autumn of 1943, when it accounted for several escort vessels.

Mines were used in narrow waters by both sides throughout the war; as a rule the counter-measures employed by the Allies kept them under control, but the constant competition between new mine mechanism and new remedy was keen and arduous. Good results were obtained with mines against U-boats in areas where Allied aircraft and warships could prevent sweeping operations.

Whatever the weapon and whatever the counter, training was the keystone of Horton's regime.

An Escort Commander writes:

'He [Horton] insisted that without training, a collection of ships was useless and co-operation with aircraft impossible.

'He drove and drove and drove at training; shore training at their bases, sea training with *Philante*, and sea and air training all the time, even when with the convoys. His personal interest in training was so intense that he almost defeated his own—and absolutely correct— object. Those responsible for training became so frightened of his insatiable enquiries that they were more interested in sending in satisfactory returns than in preparing the ships to fight the enemy. However, when this was pointed out to him, he was—after an extremely tense period—a big enough man to recognise the situation and put it right.'

CHAPTER TWELVE

February–June 1943

THE BATTLE OF THE ATLANTIC

'A war of groping and drowning, of ambuscade and stratagem, of Science and Seamanship.'—WINSTON S. CHURCHILL.

Influence of air power. The Support Groups go into action. A surprise is sprung. Combined effort turns the scale. Decisive victory.

THE winter of 1942–43 was a wild one in the Atlantic. Although the gales hindered slightly the pack tactics of the U-boats, the weakly powered merchant ships could not hold their stations in convoy against the stormy winds and heavy seas. The dawn would find the wallowing ships scattered far and wide, and the Escort Commanders faced with the threefold task of guarding the main body, collecting the stragglers and dealing with U-boats in visibility often less than a mile. A lull between gales brought no respite, for there were so many U-boats in mid-Atlantic it was impossible for the convoys to evade them, and no escort vessels could be spared to hunt them down at any distance from the convoy.

At this critical time air power came vividly into the picture. Very long range aircraft, fitted with radar and armed with a new type of powerful streamlined depth charge, could locate the U-boats, and either sink them or restrict their mobility by forcing them to submerge. Furthermore, they could break up the packs and prevent them from overtaking a convoy, while at the same time warning the Escort Commander of the whereabouts of the enemy. At night, guided by radar, they could switch on newly devised searchlights as they swooped to attack. The 'Gap', however, was still at the limit of their reach, and it was here, as Horton had expected, that the U-boats were operating in overwhelming strength.

In February 1943, sixty-three merchant ships were sent to the bottom, mostly in the North Atlantic. In March, Doenitz increased the pressure with over a hundred U-boats and came near to doubling the score by sinking 103 vessels totalling 627,000 tons. This was the crisis of the battle, and although the situation from the Allies' point of view seemed desperate, there were grounds for optimism. Owing to improved methods and modern equipment, no less than twenty-three U-boats had been sunk in all areas in February and fifteen in March. One-half of these successes had been achieved by long-range aircraft and the other by escort vessels.

Doenitz, thinking he had victory in his grasp, sent more and more U-boats to the 'Gap.' This was the obvious thing for him to do, but he had no idea of the strength and character of the sea and air forces that Horton was holding in leash.

It was Horton's intention to surprise the enemy in mid-Atlantic with a co-ordinated counter-attack by several Support Groups and carrier-borne aircraft, working in co-operation with very long range aircraft. Each convoy escort while in the 'Gap' was to be reinforced by a Support Group and whenever possible by aircraft. The U-boats had grown accustomed to being counter-attacked by escort vessels from the direction of the convoy, and had framed their tactics accordingly. Horton as an old submariner knew very well that the sudden appearance of his Support Groups, attacking from an unexpected direction, would upset their preconceived plans and probably disturb their morale. He knew, also, and so did everybody else, that the presence of Allied aircraft near the convoys would prevent the U-boats from cruising happily on the surface while taking up their positions for attack.

He besought the Admiralty to hasten delivery of the long-promised escort carriers (two of which were already operating with the North African convoys) for they would ensure continuous air cover for the Atlantic convoys. At the same time he urged that each carrier should have an escort of two destroyers. He foresaw that it would be asking too much to saddle a Support Group Commander with the responsibility of protecting the carrier while his highly trained escort vessels were hot on the scent of a U-boat. On 13th March 1943 he wrote:

'Much depends on the successful employment of these carriers especially the first two . . . it would be a severe setback to lose them prematurely . . . if new "Swordfish" [naval aircraft] prove successful, a *shrewd blow with all the elements of surprise* will be struck at the enemy in the Battle of the Atlantic. . . . The Support Groups have much to learn tactically before they can reach maximum killing efficiency, and it would confuse them to add the protection of a carrier as a call on their energies whilst developing purely offensive activities. . . . It is quite impossible to provide these escorts from Western Approaches, and I request therefore that three destroyers of long fuel endurance may be obtained from some other source.'

The Atlantic gales had played havoc with the existing escort forces, and the maintenance bases were working at full pressure to get the damaged ships back into service. On 3rd March Horton wrote:

'The whole war situation depends upon the number of escorts available to protect convoys . . . calls on escorts will soon be heavier than anticipated . . . numbers operating in spring and summer must be kept at the maximum, and vessels kept at highest state of efficiency. I urge most strongly that the highest priority be given to refitting and no departure be made from this policy.'

Horton was determined that his ships should have the best equipment, and, above all, that they should go to sea in a fit material state. A breakdown requiring a spare, at short notice, from some remote distributing centre was his special delight. Fur flew in the staff, and aeroplanes also flew to make certain that the defect was remedied immediately. Wildish, himself an Engineer, says: 'He would have made a first-class Engineer. Often he would come on board a ship with me to satisfy himself on some technical point. He would say: "You see, Wildish, people don't expect me to know these things first hand, and it puts me in such a strong position when I am talking to them." He had no use for anyone who half knew a subject.' And, it might be added—no use for half-measures.

He was anxious that the Support Groups which he had formed and had trained to work with aircraft for the counter-attack should not be disturbed:

'No further commitments can be undertaken by my Command

without sacrificing *Support Groups which are absolutely essential to victory in the Atlantic in the coming months.'*

Horton's difficulties were increased by the general strategic situation. The United States wished to withdraw naval and air forces from the Atlantic for service in the Far East. Plans were going ahead for the invasion of Italy via Sicily, and both Allied countries were committed to sending seaborne supplies to Russia by the Arctic route.

In March 1943 an Atlantic Convoy Conference was sitting in Washington under the chairmanship of Admiral King, Commander-in-Chief of the United States Fleet. The First Sea Lord fully appreciated Horton's point of view, which was ably represented by the British delegate, Admiral Noble. The Admiralty based their case on the decision previously taken on the highest level at Casablanca, where it was agreed that 'the defeat of the U-boat must remain a first charge on the resources of the United Nations.'

The Convoy Conference recommended better arrangements for pooling British, Canadian and American naval and air resources, including more V.L.R. aircraft and escort carriers to cover the gap in the Atlantic. It was also agreed that American 'hunter-killer' groups would work in their own strategic zone, but the Canadian Support Groups would operate under Horton's orders either side of the 'chop' line. Mutual understanding of the air problem was evident; recommendations were made for a redistribution of available aircraft and for priority to convert a quota of bombers for anti-U-boat duties. If a decision to this effect could have been taken a year earlier, many ships with their priceless cargoes would have been saved.

The conference, however, could not make bricks without straw. New construction was behind requirements, and there were not enough properly designed escort vessels and aircraft to go round. After much juggling it was found possible to spare a few destroyers and sloops from certain theatres by replacing them with corvettes.

Horton himself had succeeded in getting the loan of a flotilla of Home Fleet destroyers to augment his Support Groups and to provide escorts for the aircraft carriers. So by the end of March he had under his command five Support Groups and the escort carrier *Biter* fully trained and ready for battle. They were organised as follows:

1ST SUPPORT GROUP.[1]—The sloop *Pelican* (Captain G. N. Brewer, R.N., Senior Officer), U.S. Coastguard cutter *Sennen*, the frigates *Rother*, *Spey*, *Wear* and *Jed*.

2ND SUPPORT GROUP.—The sloops *Starling* (Captain F. J. Walker, R.N., Senior Officer), *Cygnet*, *Wren*, *Kite*, *Whimbrel*, *Wild Goose* and *Woodpecker*.

3RD SUPPORT GROUP.—The destroyers *Offa* (Captain J. W. McCoy, R.N., Senior Officer), *Obedient*, *Oribi*, *Orwell*, *Onslaught* and *Icarus*.

4TH SUPPORT GROUP.—The destroyers *Milne* (Captain A. C. Scott-Moncrieff, R.N., Senior Officer), *Matchless*, *Eclipse*, *Impulsive* and *Fury*.

5TH SUPPORT GROUP.—The escort carrier *Biter* (Captain E. M. C. Abel-Smith, R.N., Senior Officer) and the destroyers *Inglefield* and *Obdurate*.

The escort carriers *Bogue* (U.S.A.), *Dasher* and *Archer* were expected to join the Western Approaches Command during the month and more were on the way. The merchant aircraft carriers, later to become an integral part of every Atlantic convoy, did not come into service until May 1943.

On 23rd March 1943, Horton wrote to Admiral Darke:

'This job has been pretty sombre up to date, because one hadn't the means to do those very simple things for which numbers are essential, and which could quash the menace definitely in a reasonable time; but in the last few days things are much brighter and we are to be reinforced, and I really have hopes now that we can turn from the defensive to another and better role—killing them.

'The real trouble has been basic—too few ships, all too hard worked with no time for training and all that that entails. The Air, of course, is a tremendous factor, and it is only recently that the many promises that have been made show signs of fulfilment, so far as shore-based stuff is concerned, after $3\frac{1}{2}$ years of war. The Air carried afloat is now turning up to an extent which may be almost embarrassing in the next few months, if they are to be properly protected. As usual there has not been much foresight shown in the provision of all those dull things which are necessary if a flock of carriers are to be properly mothered and trained. All these things are coming to a head just now, and although the last week has been one of the blackest on the sea, so far as this job is concerned, I am really hopeful. . . .'

[1] Escort Groups selected for support duty are styled Support Groups in the narrative.

Meanwhile, Coastal Command was increasing its strength. The converted very long range Fortresses and Liberators were killing U-boats far out in the Atlantic, while the Wellingtons, Halifaxes, Hudsons and Catalinas kept up their offensive in the Bay of Biscay. At the same time American and Canadian aircraft operating from Iceland and Newfoundland were closing the Atlantic gap from the north and west. The 'Gap' could be reached by very long range aircraft, but could not be wholly covered.

The Bay of Biscay being well within the range of air squadrons operating from the United Kingdom, Horton regarded air attacks on U-boats near their bases in the Bay as a most important ancillary to his main offensive. Even if they escaped destruction, they would be forced to submerge and consequently delayed while going out and coming back. As a submariner, he knew that the morale of the tired crews of homeward-bound U-boats would suffer if they could be subjected to heavy air attack while joyfully anticipating rest and relaxation. And better still, if the R.A.F. bombers could carry on administering the dose after the submarine crews had reached the haven that their jangled nerves so ardently craved.

All this would be fitting retribution for the crime of leaving men, women and children to drown in mid-Atlantic and for the torture suffered by the crews of tankers, whom the U-boats had left with the choice of being roasted alive in a white-hot hulk or leaping into an inferno of burning oil. Sailors and airmen of the escort forces and Support Groups, inspired by Max Horton, and led by men like F. J. Walker, A. A. Tait, P. W. Gretton, G. N. Brewer, M. J. Evans, P. W. Burnett, D. G. F. Macintyre, C. Gwinner and other experienced Commanders had but one aim —'Attack and kill.' Their intent was murderous not merely for retribution, but to save their country from slow strangulation.

So the combined plan took shape:

A main offensive by naval and air striking forces to destroy the U-boats clustering round the convoys in mid-Atlantic.

A subsidiary offensive by shore-based air forces to destroy U-boats in the Bay of Biscay, to delay them in transit, to attack them in their bases, and to destroy their morale.

In giving effect to this plan, Horton was most particular that the Support Groups should not waste time searching for their prey in the wide waters of the 'Gap.' It was no use 'chasing a hornet all round the farm.' The place to find the U-boats was near the convoys. Accordingly, on 24th March 1943 he directed that each Support Group, on entering the area of operations, was to get into visual touch at daylight with the senior officer of any convoy escort requiring reinforcement. Thus, the Support Group Commander would get all the latest news of the whereabouts of the enemy. Having learnt the state of affairs, he would then carry out searching operations by day in the vicinity of the convoy, but out of sight. He would be assisted in this by very long range aircraft or carrier-borne aircraft, if available. Whoever sighted a U-boat first would immediately report and attack, at the same time guiding warships and aircraft to the spot. The senior officer would then re-arrange 'the field,' allocating just enough escort vessels to do the killing, and the remainder to search for more U-boats, reinforcing the close escort if required.

The night was the most dangerous time for the convoy, so the ships of Support Groups unless otherwise occupied, would close in at dusk, taking up positions in the deep field around the convoy. As a result of these tactics the U-boats were forced to submerge at some distance from the convoy and became cautious in their approach. The most hopeful time for killing U-boats was after a night attack, when some might be damaged and others would want to come to the surface to re-charge batteries. If the attacking pack was held off till morning, the Support Group would leave the convoy and drop back among the U-boats, rejoining the convoy before dark. It was a fine plan requiring intensive team training at sea and in the air.

During April, the Allied sea and air offensive grew in strength. More escort vessels were made available by the temporary suspension of the Arctic convoys and by readjusting the Atlantic convoy cycles. More escort carriers and M.A.C. ships were joining his Command and more very long range aircraft were covering the 'Gap.' Horton however refused to rush them into battle until they had been trained to work with the escorts and Support Groups. In April he wrote to the Admiralty:

'Great benefit has been derived by the Fleet Air Arm squadrons

THE BATTLE OF THE ATLANTIC

from escort carriers and M.A.C. ships doing a ten-day course at Ballykelly aerodrome resulting in improved liaison and understanding between the officers of the surface escorts, Fleet Air Arm and R.A.F.

'In my view many advantages would be gained by setting up a Combined Services Anti-Submarine Warfare Training Centre in Northern Ireland. . . . I want the surface escorts to take every opportunity of exercising with the aircraft. . . . I see no reason why full-scale exercises could not be arranged with convoys on passage in the vicinity of the North Channel.

'Ultimately I should like to see U.S.A. and Canadian officers associated in the Training Centre. When the organisation has proved itself, or perhaps before, I am sure Canadian and U.S.A. authorities will want to open similar centres in their own countries with Allied staffs. With the free interchange of experience in tactics and weapons we may reasonably look forward to a big concerted advance in U-boat killing efficiency.'[1]

As a result of Horton's training policy there was a marked improvement in the co-operation between warships and aircraft, and also between the close escorts and the Support Groups. All knew what to do when a U-boat was detected, and their action was swift and sure. As an example, one Support Group spent twenty-seven consecutive days at sea mostly in gale conditions, joined and supported five separate convoys (none of which suffered loss despite heavy attack), fuelled at sea six times, and sank four U-boats.

There was, however, strong opposition. An Escort Group left Newfoundland in April 1943 with convoy HX 231 which was attacked by seventeen U-boats for four days in foul weather. With the assistance of a Support Group and very long range aircraft, four U-boats were sunk for a small loss of merchant tonnage.

On their next trip the same Escort Group took the slow convoy ONS 5 westward from the United Kingdom and after eight days of gales, during which no fewer than thirty-nine U-boats attacked the convoy, six U-boats were sunk for the loss of twelve merchantmen. Two Support Groups were with this convoy for the last and most critical phase of the battle.

[1] This training centre was established afterwards at Maydown, N. Ireland. Officers of Coastal Command went through the course together with Canadian, American, French, Polish, Dutch and other Allied nationalities.

The same group then brought convoy SC 130 safely home from the west, sinking three out of the twenty-odd U-boats which attacked over a four-day period, there being no loss to the convoy ships. V.L.R. aircraft were particularly successful on this voyage.

Towards the end of April 1943, Horton and his colleague, Air Marshal Slatter, became certain that the tide of battle was turning in their favour. Not because an abnormal number of U-boats had been destroyed, for this was no greater than the previous month, but because the monthly shipping loss had fallen by over fifty per cent. In the middle of May Horton made a bold decision. Disregarding the instructions for evasive routeing, he ordered certain convoys to steam directly through the area where the enemy concentration was known to be strongest. The convoys suffered no loss and ten U-boats were destroyed. In a private letter to a Sea Lord he said:

'The shy tactics of the U-boat demands that the bait should be put right under its nose before it will take risks, and so give us the chance to make kills.'

The enemy had been repulsed, but not defeated. The waters round the convoys were so closely watched by aircraft and Support Groups, and the close Escort Groups were so efficient, he dare not show his head. Gone were the days when the U-boats could mass at will and prowl round the convoys, eagerly awaiting the grim command 'Attack when darkness falls.' In the short space of a month the enemy had learnt what would be coming to him if he drew near a convoy, and he lost his nerve.

Now was the time for Max to strike. The U-boats, although weakened in morale, were still there. It was simply a question of locating and destroying them. Every warship and aircraft of the Western Approaches Command and every aeroplane of Coastal Command was needed for the knock-out blow.

He asked the Admiralty to open the intervals between convoy sailings still more, and so release more escort vessels for offensive action. He asked also for the air offensive in the Bay of Biscay to be stepped up and for intensive bombing of the French ports. Finally he asked all officers and men of his Command for a supreme effort, even to the extent of undergoing training while

THE BATTLE OF THE ATLANTIC

n escort vessel attacks with depth charges

A LETTER OF THANKS

THE BATTLE OF THE ATLANTIC
Precision bombing by an aircraft of Coastal Command R.A.F.

THE BATTLE OF THE ATLANTIC

The end of a U-boat. Captain F. J. Walker deals the death blow from the
bridge of the *Starling*

RETURN OF THE VICTOR SHIP

THE BATTLE OF THE ATLANTIC
'Was it a "kill"'

their ships were boiler-cleaning. Needless to say they responded with a good heart. In a signal to them he said:

'I congratulate the officers and men of the Western Approaches Escort Force and of the U.S.A. and R.C.N. groups and ships working with us, on the splendid work they have so successfully carried out in guarding and maintaining our all-important sea communications during this the most violent and tempestuous winter experienced for many years. With the extra escorts and aircraft, together with improved training facilities, it will only be necessary for each ship to reach the 100 per cent. killing standard for the situation in the Atlantic to turn radically in our favour. Nothing will dishearten the Hun more than to realise that the Battle of the Atlantic has been lost and with it his last hope of defeating Britain.'

No extra effort was required of the men of the Merchant Navy, for they were already giving their all. With traditional tenacity they had kept the trade flowing for nearly four years in the face of appalling danger. Yet never a ship had failed to sail for want of a crew. Led by retired Admirals of the Royal Navy and senior officers of the Royal Naval Reserve, the convoys sailed doggedly on while the battle raged around them, and probably few of these indomitable sailors realised how great was the part they played at the moment of crisis. For them it was all in the day's work.

While Horton was disposing his forces and supervising their operations, he kept his finger on training and paid close attention to the development of new weapons. A staff officer of the Fleet Air Arm (Commander R. A. B. Phillimore, R.N.) writes:

'He was that *rara avis* among Admirals, a technician who had completely mastered the scientific discoveries and devices brought in to aid the ships and aircraft engaged in the battle against the U-boats, an ever-changing battle of tactics and weapons and science.
'With his technical ability he was a man of immense drive who refused to accept frustrations, delays and objections to any scheme on which he had made up his mind. He had heard of a new idea to fire rocket projectiles from aircraft, and wondered if it would be suitable for use on the Swordfish aircraft which were just starting to operate from escort carriers in the Battle of the Atlantic. Trials were taking place at Boscombe Down. I was sent down there in the Admiral's aircraft to report on the progress of the trials and to give an opinion if the R.P. [rocket projectile] was likely to be of value as a weapon against U-boats. At Boscombe Down all were enthusiastic

about it, and although the Admiralty were not in favour of it being used before a new sight had been developed, I was able to give a favourable report to Admiral Horton the next day. This was immediately before he went to one of the fortnightly meetings of the Stafford Cripps Committee which met to deal with the problems of the anti-U-boat war. An immediate decision was taken to introduce it, and the absence of a special sight in the aircraft was overcome by standardising the angle of dive of the aircraft. After some vicissitudes and much hard work H.M.S. *Archer* [escort carrier] sailed six weeks later to support North Atlantic convoys and had three aircraft fitted with R.P. Two of these aircraft were badly damaged in landings in rough weather, but the last of the three succeeded in attacking and sinking a U-boat (on 23rd May 1943) on the eastward passage. It seems incredible, but it is true, that only eight weeks elapsed to introduce a new weapon, get aircraft fitted with it, crews trained in its use, and get a kill with it in mid-Atlantic. Max Horton was the only man in the country who could have done this. Far from being deterred by the difficulties, he met each argument with increased determination and drive.'

The rocket projectile was originated as an anti-tank weapon for the Tactical Air Force, yet through Horton's enterprise it was first used in battle against a submarine! The projectile had a solid head which pierced the pressure hull and prevented her from diving. In the incident described above, the U-boat tried to fight it out on the surface with her gun, but the Swordfish who had dealt the blow called up a Martlet fighter from the *Archer*. The submarine's crew, overcome by machine-gun fire, sank their boat and leapt into the sea.

Reporting on this particular convoy the commanding officer of the escort, Commander M. J. Evans, wrote:

'Air coverage by shore-based aircraft was excellent from both sides of the Atlantic. . . . H.M.S. *Archer* more than filled the thirty-six-hour gap between the departure of the last aircraft from Newfoundland and the arrival of the first home-based aircraft.'

The long experience and hard training of the British and Canadian warships and aircraft were beginning to tell. They all talked the same language and each Service understood the limitations of the other. Above all, they knew that they had mastered the U-boats and that a mighty combined effort would sweep them from the seas. Confidence was increased by improved weapons and equipment. Technical advance in radio enabled offensive action to be taken as soon as a U-boat broke wireless silence. Improved radar had been fitted to all key units and aircraft. Depth charges and other weapons were more accurate and powerful. Constant practice had made intercommunication between ships and aircraft reliable and efficient. V.L.R. aircraft had learnt to 'pass the ball' instead of sitting on it; indeed their accurate reports of the range and bearing of U-boats at some distance from the convoy were invaluable to the Escort Commander in bringing about the destruction of the enemy and also in keeping the convoy clear of trouble.

A full chronicle of the many gallant actions which, in the sum of their results, brought victory in the Atlantic must be left to the historian. For the purpose of this biography one episode at the time of crisis will be sufficient to show the high standard of efficiency attained by all sea and air units operating under Horton's command.

On the 11th May 1943, thirty-seven merchant ships of all shapes and sizes, having an average speed of about six knots, sailed in a slow convoy for England from Halifax, Nova Scotia. They were formed in ten columns and escorted by eight vessels of B 7 Escort Group commanded by Commander P. W. Gretton, R.N., in the destroyer *Duncan*. Air cover was provided by the Royal Canadian Air Force based on Newfoundland up to the limit of their fuel endurance, and for the first six days of the voyage all was quiet. On the evening of the seventh day, while the convoy was well inside the 'Gap' there were indications that it was being shadowed by at least four U-boats. No ships were lost in the night, but just before dawn Gretton turned the convoy a full ninety degrees away from the shadowers. This manoeuvre placed the U-boats dead astern of the convoy, compelling them to come to the surface to gain the necessary distance to place themselves in a good attacking position. At this moment, by the grace of God, a very long range Liberator from Iceland arrived on the scene right over the exasperated U-boats. The aeroplane immediately attacked and destroyed one. A few minutes afterwards, this same Liberator sighted five more U-boats obviously trying to close the ring round the convoy. They submerged immediately, and an escort vessel went out to the attack. From the point of view of the crew of the Liberator (No. 120 Squadron, R.A.F.) it was indeed a crowded hour of glorious life. For months and months these young airmen had kept their weary vigil over the wind-swept waves of the Atlantic with perhaps never the sight of a U-boat, and now, at the very limit of their fuel endurance, the sea seemed to be full of them. With great reluctance they returned to base, leaving the escort vessels to deal with the submerged submarines, one of which was sunk by the *Duncan* and *Snowflake*. At 11.20 a.m. another Liberator reported four more U-boats as she went in to the attack. Thanks to the accurate reports of the aircraft and their previous combined training with surface ships, Gretton had a complete picture of the scene of operations, and was thus able to direct the convoy clear of danger. It was not only Gretton who benefited by the results of Horton's policy. Commander G. N. Brewer with the 1st Support Group had received all the signals and was approaching at full speed from the west. A fortnight previously he had taken part in a convoy battle south-west of Greenland which he described as the 'Trafalgar' of the war when six U-boats were sunk and four damaged. It was music in his ears therefore when he heard again on his radio telephone such signals as 'four U-boats position so and so'—'two more here'—'five more there'—'am attacking'—'oil on the surface'—'oil and wreckage coming to the surface'— 'have run out of depth charges'—'U-boat surfaced, am engaging with gunfire'—'have rammed U-boat'—'convoy alter course to so and so.' All this was thrilling for Brewer and his Support Group, but the most heartening thing of all was that he had not received a single distress signal from the convoy. Brewer approached from astern, for he knew from experience that U-boats suffering from depth-charge attack or wishing to readjust their positions might come to the surface after the convoy had passed. He was soon rewarded. At noon, when fifteen miles from the convoy, two U-boats broke surface close to his group. They had barely time to submerge before the frigates *Jed* and *Sennen* were on top of them, plastering the area with depth charges. Oil and wreckage came to the surface, and another U-boat was accounted for.

In the afternoon more Liberators appeared. Fuel capacity

restricted their time on patrol to the space of an hour, but air cover was maintained by a system of reliefs until dark. As a result four U-boats were destroyed, the honours being shared equally by the aircraft and warships. During the night, the 1st Support Group kept near to the convoy which carried out some evasive alterations of course. These measures discouraged the enemy, who made only one more attempt to attack the merchant ships, and this was beaten off. From the next day (the ninth of the voyage) onwards, air cover increased in strength. Fourteen U-boats were sighted, all at some distance away, and it soon became clear that this large pack was breaking up and had no intention of continuing its operation against the convoy. The happy and effective co-operation of the two Escort Commanders, the Commodore of the convoy, and each individual aircraft was the principal factor in bringing about this satisfactory result. Careful study on the tactical table, training at sea and at the combined sea and air centre, together with battle experience, had all contributed to a common doctrine without which true co-operation is impossible. The vital importance of good station keeping and attention to signals was fully appreciated by the ship masters in the convoy. 'No fewer than twenty emergency turns were made during the forty-eight hours that the U-boats were trailing the convoy, and the thirty-seven merchant ships in ten columns carried out these complicated manœuvres, as Commander Gretton wrote, "with the precision of a battle fleet." '[1]

The passage of this slow convoy will ever be remembered by the crews of the merchant ships, for they saw, for the first time, sure signs that the U-boats had been mastered. In the beginning, it seemed like any previous voyage with its usual alarms and grim tidings that U-boats were in contact. Then, as the days passed, while bombs and depth charges exploded around them, it seemed that the battle was being fought farther away than usual, and they noted with relief that no torpedo had found its mark in the convoy. Yet there were many U-boats about, and this motley collection of old-fashioned ships, carrying out parade-like movements at little over walking pace, should have been an easy target for them.

[1] *Battle of the Atlantic*—Official Account, page 63. H.M.S.O.

After ten days, when it became known that several U-boats had been destroyed and that more friendly warships and aircraft were on the horizon, these sorely tried men realised for the first time in their long experience that the enemy was being held at some distance from the convoy. They did not immediately appreciate that the enemy assault in the Atlantic had been decisively repulsed. This revelation came, however, to all convoys crossing the Atlantic in the last two weeks of May, and it was no miracle. It was the result of cold calculated planning and the strategy of a master mind.

The following statistics,[1] give a true picture of the magnitude of the Allied effort and the part played by the Western Approaches Command in the decisive phase of the Battle of the Atlantic. During the four weeks 27th April to 24th May 1943 a daily average of 108 U-boats operated in or near the 'Gap.' In that time twenty-four convoys totalling 894 ships passed through the area homeward or outward bound. Twenty-seven merchant ships including five stragglers were lost in the convoys, and five more while sailing independently. In terms of gross tonnage the total loss was 165,068 tons, eighty-eight per cent. being in convoy, including the five stragglers. But there was a marked decline in losses during the last fortnight; in fact, after 17th May no ship was lost north of Lat. 45 N.

In the four weeks under review, six Support Groups, all British, operated in the area, over and above the close escorts with the convoys. Three groups each had an escort carrier with them. One carrier was American and the other two were British. Thirty-nine V.L.R. aircraft from Newfoundland, Iceland, and Great Britain co-operated with the convoys and Support Groups.

In these four weeks ten U-boats were sunk by aircraft near the convoys, eleven by escort vessels, and three by escort vessels and aircraft working together. Eight more U-boats were destroyed by air patrols in the transit areas.

The brunt of the battle was borne by British and Canadian sea and air forces under Horton's command, and these accounted for twenty-four U-boats out of a total of thirty-two destroyed.

[1] Admiralty Records.

THE BATTLE OF THE ATLANTIC

Towards the end of May, Doenitz started to withdraw his U-boats from the 'Black Pit.' (the 'Gap'). On 24th May 1943 he wrote in his War Diary:

'We have to accept the heavy losses, provided that the amount of enemy shipping sunk is proportionate. In May, however, the ratio was one U-boat to 10,000 gross tonnage of enemy shipping, whereas a short time ago it was one U-boat to 100,000 tons of shipping. U-boat losses in May therefore reached unbearable heights.'

This was the moment of victory for the Allies in the long-drawn-out Battle of the Atlantic. 'The great contenders had arrived at one of those periods so familiar in history; long months and years of war had dragged ponderously upward to a pinnacle of time on which one supreme effort would decide all.'[1] It was obvious to everyone on the British side that the strength of the German offensive was ebbing fast, not merely because the shipping losses had fallen and the enemy losses had gone up, but far more because the U-boats now failed to press home their attacks.

They feared the combined onslaught of sea and air forces and could not stand up to their numbers, equipment, endurance and skill. The spirit of the enemy was broken by the steadfast resistance of the crews of the merchant ships which outshone in courage and tenacity any siege in history.

The cornerstone of the whole fabric was the convoy system, and this had stood firm while Admiral Horton built up and sustained his forces for his well-timed counter-stroke.

At the end of May he sent this message to the British, Canadian, and American naval and air forces under his command:

'The Battle of the Atlantic has taken a definite turn in our favour during the past two months, and the returns show an ever-increasing toll of U-boats and decreasing losses of merchant ships in convoy. All Escort Groups, Support Groups, escort carriers and their aircraft, and aircraft of the various Air Commands, have contributed to this great achievement, which is the outcome of hard work, hard training, and determination on the part of all officers and men of the surface forces and air units involved. Quite apart from the spectacular kills which have been achieved by the Escort Groups and Support Groups, many notable victories have been achieved by the safe and timely arrival of a number of convoys in the face of heavy enemy attacks. . . .

[1] *The Far Distant Ships*, Canadian Official Account, by Joseph Schull.

'... The tide of the battle has been checked, if not turned, and the enemy is showing signs of strain in the face of the heavy attacks by our sea and air forces. Now is the time to strike and strike hard, bearing in mind always that the secret of success is trained efficiency and immediate readiness for every conceivable emergency.'

Among the many congratulatory messages he received from his colleagues in Britain, Canada, and the United States, he prized the following from Admiral Darke:

FORT BLOCKHOUSE,

6th June 1943.

My dear Horton,

Just a line to congratulate you on the remarkable success achieved during May—the working organisation and drive of the master hand showing concrete results in the shortest possible time. Now it remains to show this is no flash in the pan, but only a sample of what is to come—their morale must be badly shaken. No one knows better than we submariners what sudden heavy losses mean. The master hand will know how to rub it in and thus leave them impotent and squealing.

Yours ever,

(Signed) R. B. DARKE.

On 15th June 1943 Max replied:

It is nice when one's friends appreciate some success or bit of luck. It is a profound change in the Atlantic—nothing sunk since 17th May —about thirty-four certainties in the shape of U-boats sunk in May alone, and quite a few since. The Support Groups inaugurated the change, when we got reinforcements from the Home Fleet late in March—then came our own Support Groups and the escort carriers (very well trained too)—then new weapons and increased V.L.R. aircraft of Coastal Command. The combination was too much for the Hun. His morale and determination obviously weakened early in May, and although he continued pack tactics till third–fourth week in May, his last attacks brought him no success at all and caused him heavy losses. Since then he must be scratching his head and stern hard— anyway he is comparatively clear of my special area—I expect he'll come back, but our plans are sufficiently flexible to compete.

The great point to me is that *we know now* what strength and composition of forces (properly trained) is necessary to deal with the U-boat menace against convoys. He may wriggle as much as he likes, but the inherent disabilities of a submarine if properly exploited will reduce our losses in convoy to a reasonably small factor.

Yours ever,

MAX HORTON.

Thus spoke the Master Submariner.

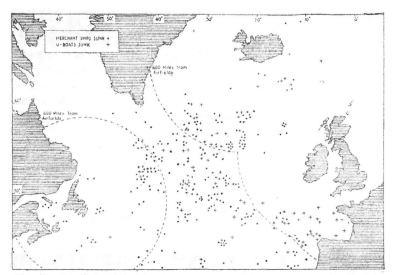

The Battle of the Atlantic: August 1942 to May 1943—months of trial.

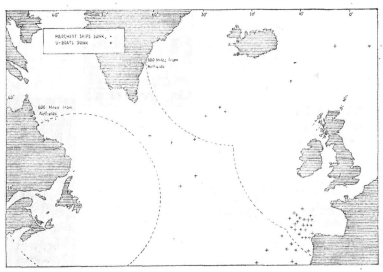

The Battle of the Atlantic: June 1943 to August 1943—victory achieved.

Reproduced from official publication *The Battle of the Atlantic* by permission
of the Controller of H.M. Stationery Office.

Plans were compiled from contemporary records and do not exactly conform to
the total sinkings finally assessed. They show correctly the trend of the battle
in the North Atlantic leading to the defeat of the U-boats.

CHAPTER THIRTEEN

June 1943 – May 1945

THE BATTLE OF THE ATLANTIC

'From fearful trip the victor ship
comes in with object won.'—WALT WHITMAN.

*Peace in the Atlantic. Combined offensive in the Bay. Doenitz
comes back with the acoustic torpedo. Horton's reply. Walker's
triumph and death. The ' Schnorkel.' Inshore fighting. D-Day.
Victory in Europe.*

FOR the rest of the summer the convoys, practically unmolested, carried their precious cargoes across the North
Atlantic. Opportunity was taken to exploit the victory by running
bigger convoys and also by sailing some of the faster ships
independently. By this means, the volume of imports and strength
of reinforcements could be increased, thus helping to consolidate
the Allied gains in the Mediterranean and accelerate the preparations for the Normandy landings.

The grand conception for the liberation of Europe might never
have materialised if the U-boat had not been mastered in the
North Atlantic. The battle of the 'Black Pit' therefore may justly
be regarded as one of the decisive battles of the war.

On the other hand, Horton, while feeling confident that he
could ward off any further assault on the main supply line, took
a guarded view of the extent of his victory. He rejoiced because
he had wrested the initiative from his antagonist. This he intended
to keep, but there were many good U-boats still afloat and many
bad Germans still alive. He knew very well that Doenitz had
withdrawn his U-boats because, for the moment, their morale had

cracked, and he felt reasonably sure that they would be sent to sunny climes where they might find another 'paradise' far away from troublesome Escort Groups and aircraft. By this move, Doenitz would hope to tempt Horton to split up his redoubtable sea-air striking forces in a vain attempt to 'chase the hornet.' Doenitz might also expect that a prolonged absence of U-boats from the North Atlantic would tempt the Admiralty to relax the convoy system. Max concluded therefore that it was highly probable that the U-boats would come back again to the North Atlantic when their morale was restored and they had had time to lick their wounds.

On 16th June 1943 he addressed this message to his staff at Derby House:

'When considered in relation to the very heavy losses inflicted on the U-boat fleet in the last two and a half months, the relative peace that now prevails and has prevailed in the Western Approaches area over the last month, during which no ship in convoy has been sunk, marks in no uncertain manner a clear-cut victory over the U-boat.

'No claim is made that the victory is final in this or any other area. Far from it, for the Hun is probably searching now for softer spots and, after an interval, will probably come back to his old hunting ground; *this last does not worry us unduly.*

'The precise magnitude of the victory and its effect on the war effort generally we can leave to history, but, besides seriously disheartening the enemy, it is immediately beneficial to the people of this country by increasing our stocks and reserves.

'Everyone in the Headquarters who has been engaged in Operations, or in work connected with the Battle—and that covers you all—is legitimately entitled to feel very proud indeed.'

The Admiralty, while agreeing with Horton's appreciation of the enemy's intentions, told him that all U-boats now returning for rest and refit were being equipped with a strong anti-aircraft armament and improved radar. By this means, it was hoped to keep aircraft at a reasonable height while the U-boats moved on the surface to favourable positions for submerged attacks on the convoys. This was wishful thinking on the part of the Germans. Horton's highly trained combined forces were well prepared, and would welcome such an attack.

Many U-boats had already been sunk by aircraft in the Bay of Biscay and in the North Atlantic. In some of these combats the U-boats had preferred to fight it out on the surface with their existing armament, rather than risk being destroyed by depth charges. The airmen, however, were not deterred from pressing home their attacks, so the U-boats formed themselves into little flotillas for mutual support while running the gauntlet in the Bay of Biscay. The heavy volume of fire and better look-out of several boats in company, supplemented by shore-based fighters, began to take toll of the gallant squadrons of Coastal Command.

Although air casualties were likely to increase when the strongly armed U-boats came to sea, the Air Officer Commanding-in-Chief, Air Marshal Sir J. C. Slessor, was determined that his aircraft should not be forced by anti-aircraft fire to attack from too great a height. Both he and Horton saw in the new situation a golden opportunity for a combined offensive by sea and air forces. The U-boats dare not remain for long on the surface if warships were within call, so a few 'crack' support groups were rushed to the Bay.

The hard school of war was bringing home to sailors and airmen alike the simple truth that neither could exist without the other. Aircraft had proved to be indispensable to the Navy in defeating the submarine assault on the Atlantic convoys; now the ships were coming to the Bay to support the aircraft in their offensive against the U-boats.

In an attempt to keep outside air supervision for as long as possible, the U-boats in transit approached and left the Bay via the north coast of Spain. Horton therefore sent Walker with his famous Support Group to see what he could find off Cape Ortegal, and on 24th June they sank two U-boats in seven hours. In the first encounter Walker in the *Starling* blew the U-boat to the surface with depth charges, then rammed and rode over her.

On 30th July, a Liberator sighted three U-boats in company on the surface some ninety miles north-west of Cape Ortegal. Nine aircraft converged on the spot and pressed home their attacks in spite of concentrated anti-aircraft fire. Walker's group, having been called to the scene, arrived to find that two large supply submarines ('milch cows') had been sunk by the aircraft, who by that time had reached their 'prudent limit of fuel endurance.' The third U-boat had dived. This was Walker's bird, so the departing airmen wished him 'good hunting.' The scene of the action was conveniently marked by five collapsible dinghies full of Germans, and Walker immediately got an Asdic contact. Paying no heed to the dinghies he smothered the place with/ depth charges and desisted only when the terrified Germans, bobbing about in the swirling waters, screamed that he was bombarding their own sunken submarine. Walker then spread his group to search for the surviving U-boat, which soon fell a victim to his skilful tactics and devastating attack. The loss of the 'milch cows' was a serious embarrassment to the far-flung German flotillas now operating off the coasts of Brazil and West Africa. The U-boats in the sunny climes were not having the 'piece of cake' they had hoped to enjoy. In July, three were sunk by United States forces in Brazilian waters, one by Catalinas south of Madagascar, four by United States aircraft off the Azores and one by a British Escort Group off the Canaries. But the greatest Allied triumph was in the Bay of Biscay. Here in the same month, nineteen U-boats were sent to the bottom within three hundred miles of Cape Finisterre. All but one of these had been sunk by British, Australian, and American aircraft operating under the direction of Coastal Command.

On 3rd August 1943, Horton sent this message to their Commander-in-Chief, Sir John Slessor:

'Western Approaches offer their sincerest congratulations to Coastal Command on their remarkable and continually growing scale of success against the U-boat. We are filled with admiration for the gallantry with which attacks are pressed home in the face of fierce opposition. That the standard of accuracy of attacks under these conditions should not only be maintained but continually improved, is an achievement of which officers and men of Coastal Command must indeed be proud.'

At the same time the Admiralty summed up the position in a signal to Western Approaches, Coastal Command, and United States authorities concerned:

'In May the U-boats suffered a severe defeat in their endeavour to attack the North Atlantic convoys. Their losses were so heavy that they were forced to withdraw from this route to others which they knew must be less productive, but which they hoped would be less dangerous. At the same time efforts were made to re-arm the U-boats with A/A weapons, with which to drive off our aircraft.

'During June our shipping losses were almost the lowest on record, but the U-boat sinkings, though substantial, were also considerably reduced.

'Allied counter-measures to enemy strategy have borne fruit in July, and the Admiralty congratulate all concerned on the heavy punishment inflicted on the U-boats. Particular credit is due to Coastal Command and to Allied aircraft from the Gibraltar area for the vigour of the offensive against U-boats on passage, and for the determination and gallantry shown by Captains of aircraft and their crews against the powerful armament of the U-boats.

'The effective A/S measures in the Mediterranean have greatly contributed to the success of amphibious operations and are highly creditable to the Commands concerned and to the surface and air forces.

'All in the United Kingdom concerned with the conduct of the U-boat war have noted with admiration the results obtained by the carrier-borne aircraft of the U.S. Fleet, and the successful manner in which U.S. forces have taken the offensive against U-boats operating in American waters.'

The Admiralty, with some justice, were anxious to take advantage of the quiet spell in the North Atlantic by cutting down the intervals between the convoy sailings.

This would have meant the provision of more escorts and a consequent reduction in their 'lay over' periods.

Horton was quite certain that the U-boats would return in strength to the North Atlantic, so he stoutly resisted any proposal which would reduce the time for rest, repairs and training of his escort vessels. Weapon efficiency and skill were uppermost in his thoughts. He argued that the need to keep up the high standard already attained was all the more urgent at a time when there was no fighting.

On 23rd July 1943, in a letter to the Admiralty, he said:

'The recent successes achieved by air and surface forces co-operating in U-boat warfare have been due to improved training for which time and facilities must be allowed. It is highly important that the standard of convoy protection and U-boat killing should be maintained. A period of seven days' training at sea is the absolute minimum when opportunities are so infrequent.'

He also urged that target submarines and gunnery targets should be made available for exercises on the western side of the Atlantic. A staff officer who went with Horton to a conference at the

Admiralty on this question says that Sir Max finally won the day by thumping on the table and spitting out the words: 'Buy your experience in training, and not when fighting the enemy.' The same staff officer remarks:

'Although he drove ships and crews damned hard, he had a very clear mind about the need for rest and repairs. He knew that men had limits just as much as machines, and there was never any occasion when escort vessels, having just arrived in harbour after a long trip, would be ordered to fuel and go straight out again.'

Max drew on his own experiences as a submariner in resisting all attempts to reduce the 'lay over' periods for his escort groups. Fourteen days for rest and repairs and seven days for training (at sea) was the minimum period he would accept in a convoy cycle of 100 days.

On 19th September 1943, Doenitz, with startling suddenness, staged his expected comeback in mid-Atlantic with new tactics and new weapons. He chose a moment, perhaps fortuitously, when two outward-bound convoys were within ninety miles of each other at the extreme range of V.L.R. aircraft. In the late afternoon, Liberators from Iceland observed large packs of U-boats concentrating on both convoys, and immediately called a Support Group to the scene. Just before dawn on 20th September the stern of the frigate *Lagan* was blown off by a torpedo (she did not sink and was towed safely home). A few hours later two merchant ships were sunk. The sea was calm and their crews were saved by the rescue ship *Rathlin*. At about noon the senior officer of the escorts, Commander M. J. Evans, R.N., decided it would be prudent to bring the two convoys together and combine their escorts. This rather complicated manœuvre was effected before dark, with the result that sixty-six merchant ships came under the protection of seventeen warships. During the night the Support Group was constantly in action. All attacks on the convoy were detected and beaten off, but two more escort vessels, the Canadian destroyer *St. Croix* and the British corvette *Polyanthus*, were sunk.

Next morning fog came down, persisting throughout the day. Some of the ships in convoy lost touch with one another, but in spite of the difficult conditions, a Swordfish aircraft of the Fleet Air Arm flew off in a clear patch from the M.A.C. ship *Macalpine*, and by a miracle was able to 'land on' in dense fog. At least fifteen U-boats continued to track the convoy, and during the night when the fog had dispersed, tried to pierce the escort screen. Evans, in the destroyer *Keppel*, sank one by ramming, while two others were put out of action by depth charges and gunfire. No merchant ships were sunk.

At dawn on 22nd September, fog came down again, but did not prevent the escorts continuing their Asdic hunt astern of the convoy. In the afternoon the weather cleared, disclosing the scattered merchant ships vulnerably disposed over a wide area. At the same time Canadian Liberators from Newfoundland appeared over the convoy and these, together with the Swordfish from the *Macalpine* and the naval escorts, joined in a combined attack on the U-boats. The battle went on all through the night and the following day. Three U-boats were sunk and many damaged. In the circumstances it was not possible to prevent some of their attacks from getting home, and in the course of a hundred hours' fighting six merchant ships were sunk. At midnight the frigate *Itchen* sighted a U-boat ahead on the surface. The ship switched on her searchlights and opened fire. Almost immediately she was torpedoed and blew up. By tragic coincidence the *Itchen* carried on board the survivors from the *St. Croix* and *Polyanthus*, and only three men were rescued from the three ships' companies. On the 25th September two fresh escort groups took over the convoy, which reached its destination without further interference.

The torpedoing of four escort vessels on one voyage was significant, for it indicated that the enemy was shifting his target from the merchant ships to the warships. Hitherto Doenitz had left the escort vessels severely alone; now it seemed he was singling them out for attack. This did not surprise Horton, who had often stated officially that a constant flow of imports depended more on the strength of escorts than on the ships that carried the cargoes. But he was worried by the effectiveness of the attacks. Normally an efficient escort vessel should be able to hold her own against torpedo attack, but here they were falling down like nine-pins before they could grapple with the enemy. Horton lost no time. Suspecting a new weapon, he telephoned the

HORTON AND HIS FLAG
LIEUTENANT

LISAHALLY, 14TH MAY 1945

'ALL QUIET IN THE WESTERN APPROACHES'
A corner of the Operations Room at Derby House, Liverpool, just after VE Day

EXPLANATION

A Weather symbol.

B Clock.

C Convoy, Canada to Liverpool.

D Convoy, United Kingdom to Far East.

E Convoy, United Kingdom to Gibraltar.

F Ditto.

G Board showing current situation at sea.

H Submarine Tracking Officer.

I Key to symbols used on the plot.

J Light conditions and tides at Liverpool.

K The Convoy Control Officer.

L Subsidiary plot for Irish Sea and local convoys.

M Wren Plotting Officer moving convoy.

N Wren Rating reading out information on which M works.

O Wren Signal Traffic Officer.

P Files of signals to and from ships at sea.

Q R.A.F. (Coastal Command) Meteorological Officer.

R Navigator checking and resetting the board.

S R.A.F. (Coastal Command) Signal table.

T Files of weather signals.

U Coastal Convoy off Portugal.

V Surrendered U-boat under escort.

Admiralty, who confirmed that an acoustic torpedo (the 'gnat') was being used. He immediately warned his commanding officers, informing them also that the enemy had adopted an anti-escort policy. He told them that counter-measures were being produced on the highest priority and directed that, for the moment, escorts were to take certain tactical precautions while attacking U-boats. These manœuvres, when correctly done, subsequently proved to be an adequate safeguard.

Horton, however, did not remain long on the defensive. The material antidote, already mentioned,[1] which the Germans called the 'singing saw' was soon produced by the scientists. This, together with new tactics, enabled the Support Groups to continue their pressure. More V.L.R. aircraft could now be operated from the Azores, thus increasing air coverage in the Atlantic. In consequence the U-boats, although still working in packs, remained submerged by day, approaching the convoys cautiously on the surface at night. Their attacks were half-hearted and seldom pressed home, so the shipping losses were low. On the other hand the U-boats were more difficult to locate, and there were fewer opportunities to destroy them. In November Admiral Horton signalled to his Command that it was only at night that U-boats 'may surely be found on the surface' and therefore escort carriers and M.A.C. ships were to seek every opportunity for night flying experience. He directed that 'carriers should leave the convoys for night flying training when conditions appeared to be favourable.' He also arranged for night flying exercises to be included in the training programme of the *Philante*'s group.

In the early morning of Trafalgar Day 1943, Admiral of the Fleet Sir Dudley Pound died in harness as a result of overwork and strain. Horton paid this tribute to him in a public speech:

'*There* was in truth, a fine man. He died from strain and overwork at the moment when, owing to his efforts and planning, the tide of war at sea against Germany had definitely turned in our favour.

'I can never forget my feelings when, prior to taking over Western Approaches Command in November 1942, the First Sea Lord of that time, Sir Dudley Pound, sent for me.

[1] A noise-making device to attract the torpedo away from the target, q.v. page 182.

'He said that unless the menace and depredations of the U-boat fleet—then rapidly increasing in numbers—were checked and reduced, the mounting of a Second Front in Europe would be impossible and the outcome of the war itself would be doubtful.

'On the issue of the Battle of the Atlantic hung the fate of the Empire, and indeed of the world.

'He explained how our material deficiencies in ships and equipment and in long-range aircraft were being gradually overcome.

'He told me that every proposal and request from me would have top priority, and would be met so far as the resources he could command permitted—and how he kept his word!

'Indeed the subsequent support, both moral and practical, I received from him passes words to relate.

'From *him*, I was always certain of a sympathetic reception, and whole-hearted backing, whatever happened—and how that helps one in times of strain and stress!

'How tragic it was, that this man who had borne the heat and burden of the day for close on four years, at the most vital period of our history, should not have lived to see the complete victory he had done so much to achieve. . . .'

It is said that he had suggested Horton should be his successor as First Sea Lord and judging from letters received by Max at this time, many people thought he might be given the post. Admiral Gilbert Stephenson wrote with mixed feelings:

'I am from a personal point of view most thankful that you are remaining. And I daresay that you also are not sorry, having directed this great organisation you must wish to see it through to victory.

'The political jobs are always a questionable satisfaction, whereas in your present Command you have an instrument you have trained and tested and found 100 per cent. efficient—the only instrument which can win or lose us the war. Without you to inspire them, they would be lost. The greatest Command the British Navy has ever had!'

In a letter dated 7th October 1943 an ex-submarine officer employed at Vickers-Armstrongs said:

'I am writing *now* to tell you from the depths of my heart how sorry I am you were not made our First Sea Lord. Your angle will no doubt differ from mine, but that cannot influence my private feelings.

'I realise fully the enormous responsibility of your present post; that success or failure influences the whole course of the war; the great difficulty in finding a successor; and the salient feature of your now having the U-boat beaten. Yet with it all, I am sad and disappointed because always I felt sure that should war occur you would in due course run the Royal Navy.

'Please do not laugh at me and do *not* be annoyed, I cannot help feeling as I do, and to say the least I am honest *and*—I am sure, dead sure—I echo the sentiments of all submariners. I heard a fellow say: "I was hoping Our Admiral would get the job." "Our Admiral," those words meant worlds to me; the Submarine Service still feels you are part of it.'

Horton himself told a friend 'Even if the post had been offered to me officially I should have refused—I have got Doenitz where I want him, and I intend to keep him there till the war is won!'

Towards the end of the year the U-boat offensive in the Atlantic dwindled. The enemy had some minor successes in regions as far distant as Penang, but the Atlantic convoys went on inexorably. More and more munitions were piling up in the United Kingdom spelling the doom of Hitler, and there was nothing he could do to stop it. Statistics showing the satisfactory position have been quoted in many publications, and it would be wearisome to repeat them. Broadly speaking, the new construction of merchant ships had far exceeded losses. Hitler's new weapon and new tactics so far had been countered, and more U-boats were being destroyed than the enemy could replace. Above all, Max Horton had put fear into the hearts of most U-boats' crews and made them cautious in their outlook. On 17th January 1944 he wrote to Darke:

'It *is* a game, this U-boat struggle—the "gnat" is a nasty snag and delays the approach—all ships hit to date have not completely carried out instructions [careful approach to the U-boat], but in the heat of the moment the offensive spirit of the escort vessels takes charge, and it is hard to blame them severely.'

In January 1944 Doenitz in an apologia to the Fuhrer said: 'The enemy has succeeded in gaining the advantage in submarine defence.' He might have added: 'by taking the offensive against us' which he knew only too well, but in the true spirit of the flamboyant Nazi he went on to say: 'The day will come when I shall offer Churchill a first-class submarine war. The submarine weapon has not been broken by the setback of 1943. On the contrary it has become stronger. In 1944, which will be a successful but a hard year, we shall smash Britain's supply with a new submarine weapon.' He had at the back of his mind the 'Schnorkel,' a hollow folding mast designed to keep a current of fresh air blowing through a submarine at periscope depth, enabling the Diesel engines to be run and batteries to be charged without coming to the surface. The 'schnorkel' intake tube showing above the surface was not much bigger than the periscope. From the air it looked like a dustbin and was difficult to detect except in a calm sea.

Horton was not perturbed by this new device. The speed of U-boats when 'schnorkelling,' would not be much more than five knots, and although they might not be seen from the air, it would take them a long time to reach the convoy routes. Even when they had arrived, they would have to come to the surface if they wished to use speed to gain suitable positions for delivering their attacks. In these conditions he felt confident that his well trained Support Groups and aircraft could deal with them.

Doenitz apparently thought the same, for the boats fitted with 'schnorkels' never ventured far into the Atlantic. They were usually found operating singly in focal areas near landfalls off Northern Ireland, in the southern Irish Sea and in the Bristol Channel.

Doenitz however had another card up his sleeve. In 1944 some details of a new Atlantic U-boat were filtering through. These disturbed Horton considerably. Whispers were heard of underwater speeds of twenty-five knots, colossal armaments and inexhaustible endurance. The actual performance of these allegedly phenomenal craft was not known to him, but Intelligence confirmed that sections of U-boats, embodying the results of war experience, were being prefabricated in factories all over Germany. The destruction of these plants was a task for Bomber Command, and was duly assigned to them. The only way Horton could meet the threat was to destroy as many as possible of the existing U-boats, thus preventing experienced officers and men from manning the new types. He also hoped to damp their enthusiasm by continuously hammering at morale. But much hammering also had to be done to get the Government to keep on supplying the tools.

The activities of the U-boats having become more widespread, more trained Support Groups were needed to deal with them. Horton, as we have seen, refused to allow his Atlantic groups to be drawn away by the diversion, but at the same time he wanted adequate force to strike at the U-boats wherever they appeared. The Admiralty agreed, and the construction of new frigates and escort carriers was accelerated.

On 20th January 1944 Air Chief Marshal Sir W. Sholto Douglas became Commander-in-Chief Coastal Command in succession to Sir John Slessor, who said in a farewell letter to Admiral Horton:

'What a great year we have had in the Atlantic! I hope it will not be long before you get a few more Support Groups. . . . I feel we have made real progress in the technique of co-operation this last year.'

Early in 1944 Doenitz moved his main concentration of U-boats to an area 200 to 400 miles south-west of Ireland. He hoped to be aided, to some extent, by his own V.L.R. aircraft in attacking convoys bound for the Mediterranean and Atlantic convoys which at that time of year were routed well to the south. Horton was fully aware of the danger and had Support Groups at hand. It was here in February that Captain Walker, with the sloops *Starling*, *Wild Goose*, *Woodpecker*, *Magpie* and *Wren*, destroyed six U-boats in one trip, and captured the entire crew of one of them. No merchant ships or transports were sunk in this area. The *Woodpecker* had her stern blown off by an acoustic torpedo. She remained afloat for a time but later capsized while being towed home in a gale. Fortunately, with consummate seamanship, the crew had been taken off beforehand.

Meanwhile the Commander-in-Chief had arranged that Walker and his group should be cheered into harbour on their return to Liverpool. Captain G. N. Brewer, a friendly rival of Walker's in U-boat killing, was to lead the cheers.

Here is a description of the scene as witnessed by Commander D. E. G. Wemyss of the. *Wild Goose* as they approached the jetty to the merry strains of 'A-hunting we will go.'

'And what a welcome they gave us. We steamed up the Channel into the Mersey in line ahead and turned left in succession to enter the lock leading into Gladstone Dock, and there was the crowd. Rows and rows of our comrades from the escort ships were there, together with the Captain and ship's company of the battleship *King George V*, which was in dock nearby, masses of Wrens (who were making as much noise as the rest put together), merchant sailors, crews from Allied ships and dock workers. To lead the cheer party stood Captain G. N. Brewer on a dais, himself not long returned from a career of violence at sea that included one of the longest and most savage battles fought round a convoy in the course of the whole war. He had strung up a hoist of flags which read: "Johnny Walker Still Going Strong."

'My personal impressions of the proceedings, however, were over-shadowed by the anxiety of having, in the midst of all this hubbub, to steer the ship to her berth in the lock without hitting either the quay or the *Starling*, where the Boss [Walker] was receiving his wife and daughter.

'Later, when we were all berthed in the dock and had landed our prisoners, Sir Max Horton came to welcome us, bringing with him the First Lord, Mr. A. V. Alexander, who was on a visit to Liverpool and who made us a rousing speech. The proceedings came to an end with that ever-popular wind up to a day of emotional strain, a "splicing of the mainbrace," which, needless to say, was duly noted on our banner, and then the lucky ones among us went on a few days leave.'[1]

It was Walker's custom to make the signal 'splice the main-brace' when a ship had either shared or achieved a definite kill. This meant that an extra rum ration was to be issued. Commander Wemyss, having joyfully complied with the order on several occasions, designed a banner to be worn by the *Wild Goose* when entering harbour. The idea is best described in his own words:

'Our Commander-in-Chief, Sir Max Horton, when he was in command of a submarine in the last war, used to fly a black flag when returning to harbour from a successful patrol. This flag was orna-mented with the skull and crossbones and bore strange devices to commemorate exploits of which the crew was proud. The custom was widely followed in the Submarine Service, but, so far as we knew, had not spread to other ships. We could see no reason why it shouldn't, and if so, what class of ship could more logically adopt it than an anti-submarine vessel. Slavish copying was not called for, but some-thing dignified as befitting to our ship's size and appearance was what we needed, and the outcome was a really handsome banner. It was dark blue in colour, with the ship's crest [a wild goose] in white on a light blue ground in the middle, and the devices were white.'

[1] *Walker's Groups in the Western Approaches*, by Commander D. E. G. Wemyss, D.S.O., D.S.C., R.N.

The 'devices,' needless to say, represented jars of rum—one jar for each kill.

The destruction of U-boats went on relentlessly through 1944 at an average rate of twenty a month (excluding Japanese) and since the enemy preferred to remain submerged rather than risk being sighted by aircraft, shipping losses gave no cause for anxiety. Enemy aircraft were troublesome for a while to convoys in the Far North, but were soon countered by escort carriers. One day, Swordfish from the carriers *Tracker* and *Activity*, working with a convoy escort, shot down six aircraft, and on another occasion Swordfish from the *Chaser* destroyed three U-boats with the new rockets.

On 7th March 1944, the First Lord, Mr. A. V. Alexander, speaking in the House of Commons, summed up the position in North Atlantic and coastal convoys:

'In 1941 one ship was lost out of every 181 which sailed; in 1942 one out of every 233; in 1943 one out of every 344. The losses in these convoys during the second half of last year were less than one in every 1,000. . . . The reduction in the loss of tonnage has been happily reflected in the Merchant Navy casualties, and in 1943 I am glad to say the number of officers and men lost was roughly only half of that in 1942. The Admiralty . . . has been able to increase substantially the number of special rescue ships [strongly advocated by Horton]. . . . Each carries a naval doctor and a hospital staff, and they are now an integral part of the convoy system.'[1]

In the same speech the First Lord, while giving full credit to the Western Approaches Command for the results achieved, said that the Battle of the Atlantic was fundamental to the fortunes of the country. He reminded the House that the Navy could be relied upon to hold what it had won, and not spare itself in supporting the armies and air forces in the large operations yet to come.

In preparation for the Normandy landings Horton reduced, at considerable risk, the escorts of the Atlantic convoys in order to build up striking forces for a grand offensive against the U-boats on 'D-day.' He took immense pains to train his Support Groups for the inshore battle against every kind of enemy who might be expected to attack the invasion convoys. At this time

---

[1] *Hansard*, 7th March 1944.

there was some apprehension as to what might happen when the 'schnorkels' really got going. Max took a hand in the training, and devised dummy 'snorts'[1] for target submarines, and also 'snort' buoys to enable ships and aircraft to practice locating them by radar. In addition to the Support Groups, over 200 warships from the Western Approaches were required for the close escort of invasion convoys. These were given intensive training, closely watched by Horton in the *Philante*. The high standard of efficiency in maintenance is evident from the following signal made by Horton to the responsible commanding officers and engineer officers:

'On the eve of impending operations, it is a great satisfaction to me that out of 295 escort vessels either in or recently in my administration, 286 are at this moment fully fit for sea service. I know that during the last two months not only have all these ships been kept efficient and ready for service, but an immense amount of special armament and equipment has been added. All this reflects the greatest credit on those responsible for their preparation and fitting out. Please convey my appreciation to all those concerned.'

By the end of May, Doenitz had concentrated over seventy U-boats in Biscay ports for a massed counter-attack against the expected invasion. He had hoped to have more available, but six were sunk and others damaged by Coastal Command in the north while on passage from Norway. A week before 'D-day,' Horton had five Support Groups, including escort carriers, patrolling an area to the westward of the approaches to the English Channel. Their duty was to prevent the enemy taking up preliminary positions for attacking the invasion forces. Meanwhile British, Canadian, Australian and American aircraft under the direction of Coastal Command kept a close watch on the French ports. On 'D-day' (6th June 1944) the whole area from the south of Ireland to Lorient was swamped with aircraft. Every U-boat that showed itself was immediately attacked, and those that tried to get through submerged were hunted mercilessly by the escort vessels. As a result the huge volume of invasion traffic achieved its purpose completely unmolested by U-boats. For this 'outstanding contribution' to the success of the landing Horton received special commendation from the Admiralty.

[1] Naval slang for Schnorkel.

THE BATTLE OF THE ATLANTIC

From now until the end of the war the enemy in home waters made increasing use of the schnorkel, crawling submerged along the coast to reach their patrol positions, thus enjoying comparative immunity from air and surface radar. They would sit quietly on the bottom by day, and come to periscope depth at night, using the 'schnorkel' to get fresh air while topping up their batteries. Merchant ship losses were few indeed, but it was very difficult to catch a U-boat, especially in shallow waters where Asdic echoes became confused with rocky ledges, tidal swirls and sunken wrecks.

Horton was perplexed, but according to his Training Captain (M. J. Evans):

'He breathed determination and a complete refusal to accept defeat. In the later stages of the war when the U-boats with the aid of "snorts" were once again working with complete immunity in the shallow waters of the Irish Sea and West Coast channels I happened to visit him. I told him that in spite of intense efforts I had failed to find a solution to this problem and could see no chance of the situation improving. "You are never to say such a thing outside the office," he said, "we will beat them yet by better and better training."

'A few weeks later—for no reason that I have yet discovered—we suddenly started to find and kill them in these waters and once again Sir Max was proved right.'

It was not long before escort vessels, fitted with the latest navigational instruments, and aided by Asdic and echo-sounders, had charted and buoyed most of the snags in coastal waters. When this was done, quite a number of U-boats were found and duly dispatched. Great skill however was required on the part of the Asdic operators to distinguish by ear between an echo from a submarine (sub-echo) and that from a rock, wreck, shoal of fish, or other object (non sub-echo). Good results could be obtained by trained ears and long practice, but it was more of an art than a science. The real experts had to have talent as well, and some of the best of them came from symphony orchestras.

The dangers of inshore navigation in all weathers put a heavy strain on the commanding officers of the hunting craft. They had the additional anxiety of keeping their ships off the rocks while seeking out dormant U-boats. An Asdic contact every half-hour over a period of three weeks was not uncommon, and it became necessary to appoint a separate Captain for the senior officer's ship so that the Group Commander could conduct operations without having to worry about the safety of his own ship.

Many officers have spoken of Horton's genuine concern if he felt that he had imposed too great a strain upon them. Nobody could be harder if he suspected negligence or even stupidity, but an error of judgment in a difficult situation or a frank confession of fault usually won his sympathy. On the other hand his 'post mortems' and cross-examinations were often more disturbing to the victim than the incident itself. There was the time when a young commanding officer, having damaged his ship while hunting U-boats close inshore, was recalled by the Commander-in-Chief. The young man had been on the bridge for many days and nights and had reached that stage of tiredness where he did not care whether he answered Horton's questions correctly or not. So he entered the office with an exaggerated air of self-assurance. Horton was not deceived. Having taken one look at him and seeing that he was completely worn out, he led him to his own bedroom. Pointing to the bed, Max said 'Turn straight in—I will look after your ship!' He slept for eighteen hours.

On 9th July 1944 Capt. F. J. Walker, R.N., died as the result of a stroke brought on by heavy strain. The funeral service was held in Liverpool Cathedral where Admiral Horton read a solemn acknowledgment. Afterwards Captain Walker's body was taken on board the destroyer *Hesperus* for burial at sea. As if arranged by Providence, an unusually large number of merchant ships had collected in the River Mersey, one convoy having just arrived while another was about to sail. All the crews of these undefeated ships stood bareheaded and motionless as the *Hesperus*, with her colours at half mast, passed by. They knew how much they owed to him.

In a foreword to a book[1] chronicling the achievements of Walker and his groups, Max Horton said:

'He trained and welded his own group into a splendidly efficient Band of Brothers who finally became so imbued with his methods and

[1] *Walker's Groups in the Western Approaches*, by Commander D. E. G. Wemyss.

doctrine that they could, and did, carry out his wishes in the face of the enemy with the barest minimum of signals and use of radio telegraphy.

'The spirit of emulation is a wonderful incentive and all my groups benefited from his example and methods.

'What this battle at sea meant to our country and Allies is best expressed by our great Prime Minister, Winston Churchill, when he said in 1944: "We who dwell in the British Isles must celebrate with joy and thankfulness our deliverance from the mortal U-boat peril, which deliverance lighteth the year which has ended. When I look back upon the fifty-five months of this hard and obstinate war, which makes ever more exacting demands upon our life's springs of energy and contrivance, I still rate *highest* among the dangers we have overcome the U-boat attack on our shipping, without which we cannot live or even receive the help which our Dominions and our grand and generous American ally have sent us."

'In my opinion no single officer at sea did more than Frederick John Walker to win this battle, the hardest and longest drawn out of the war.

'In conclusion let me quote again a part of the epitaph I was proud to deliver at Captain Walker's impressive funeral service in Liverpool Cathedral[1]: ". . . Not dust nor the light weight of a stone, but all the sea of the Western Approaches shall be his tomb. His spirit returns unto God who gave it." '

Walker was at his best as a lone hunter, blazing a trail which others, inspired by Horton, were quick to follow. Several Escort Commanders attained the same high standard, and the tributes already paid to Walker apply equally to them. Some names have been mentioned where their achievements fit in with the narrative, but there were many more, and for these we must look to official records.

It is fitting here to mention one more incident to show how Allied ships in the Western Approaches Command came up to the standard expected by the Commander-in-Chief. B 3 Escort Group had seen most of the fighting, and was a particular favourite of Horton's. It was an Anglo-French-Polish team commanded first by Commander A. A. Tait, R.N., and later by Commander M. J. Evans, R.N.

In the middle of a night in March 1943, Tait's ship, the *Harvester*, rammed a U-boat at twenty-seven knots. The force of the impact caused the U-boat to become jammed under the

[1] For complete quotation see Epilogue.

destroyer's stern. After about ten minutes she slid clear, and tried to escape on the surface at slow speed, but Lieut. de Vaisseau J. M. Levasseur,[1] in the French corvette *Aconit*, was too quick for her. Holding the U-boat in the beam of his searchlight he rammed her, and finished her off with depth charges. *Harvester* had been severely damaged in the first encounter. Levasseur wanted to stand by, but Tait ordered him to rejoin the convoy. In the morning, another U-boat at periscope depth found the *Harvester* drifting helplessly, and sank her with two torpedoes. The gallant Tait and most of his crew went down with their ship, but their loss was quickly avenged by the faithful *Aconit* who returned to the scene, and destroyed the second U-boat.

Max was very fond of his Allied helpers. French, Dutch, Polish and Norwegian officers were constantly seen at Derby House and in the Tactical School. Every Wednesday he would ask two or three of them to lunch, and required a list to be submitted to him during the forenoon. One day, the name of Commander Lichodziezjewski appeared on the lunch list. Horton telephoned the Tactical School for confirmation, and got the reply: 'We call him "George" here, Sir!' The Admiral, pretending he was not amused, directed that, in future, a list was to be prepared in three columns:

(1) Name as spelt.

(2) Name as phonetically pronounced.

(3) Nickname used.

This attention to detail and obvious desire to make them feel at home made a favourable impression on the foreign officers under his command.

The advance of the Allied armies caused a migration of U-boats from French ports to Germany and Norway for rest and re-equipment. As there had been no attacks on the Atlantic convoys for some time, it was evident that the enemy, for the present, intended to confine his activities to coastal waters. Horton felt therefore that the escort forces in the Atlantic could be reduced

[1] Lieutenant Levasseur of the Free French Navy was awarded the D.S.O. for his achievements. He was killed after the war in a gun accident on board a French Cadet training ship.

in strength and the convoys increased in size. In August 1944 a convoy of 167 ships came across safely with an escort of one frigate and six corvettes of the Royal Canadian Navy. The construction of new escort vessels was now in line with requirements, and although many of them were destined for service in the Far East all passed through the Western Approaches Command for initial training.

On 20th November 1944 the Commodore Western Isles, Admiral Stephenson, signalled: 'H.M.S. *Clover* the thousandth vessel to be worked up at Tobermory sailed at 2200 today.' Horton replied: 'Hearty congratulations on the thousandth vessel. The unique methods of training employed and high standards you have set have been of the utmost value in defeating the U-boat and preserving the old traditions. Helen of Troy's historic achievement was no greater, although possibly gained with considerably less effort.' Stephenson expressed his gratitude in a further signal: ' . . . your reference to Helen of Troy. May I say that you are the first of my friends to appreciate my face value.'

Max loved a joke, and although he may have been feared by some as a grim Commander-in-Chief he was still a boy to those who knew him well. Indeed the following letter to a friend in Malta dated 20th April 1945 might have been written when he was at school:

'Thanks a thousand for the most wonderful oranges. The last consignment (big ones, Oh!) arrived yesterday. They were the most luscious of all—have never tasted such wonderful specimens and thanks for the ones before with the chocolate nuts—much appreciated.

' . . . A fortnight ago we had a very pleasant visit from the King and Queen—they lunched in my flat (top floor, Derby House) and visited ships, etc.—all went very well I think, as usual the Queen with her enormous charm and naturalness made everything easy for everyone.

'Our special job continues to be very busy, not that the Hun is achieving much, but they are always there. I do not work so late as before and take things a bit easier. The staff now are so well trained that they relieve me of much I had to do myself before. . . . I have some golfing friends staying—the St. Johns. It is nice to be able to put people up. Do you know Gordon Ramsey, the "Ocean Swell" [Vice-Admiral Sir C. G. Ramsey, K.C.B., Commodore of Convoy]? He has been staying here prior to his next trip. For a wedding present he asked for a very loud check cap I bought some years ago and hadn't ever worn—it suited him perfectly and he's taken it over to U.S.A.

'War should be over, even the pockets, in six weeks or two months. Everyone who speaks true is very nervous of the *peace*!'

Horton's main task was to destroy U-boats and with this object in view, and an eye to the new brew which Doenitz was preparing, he allocated the thirty Support Groups he now had available to the following areas: Cape Wrath, Moray Firth, N.W. Approaches, S.W. Approaches, English Channel, Atlantic, and North Russia.

The strength of the force in each area varied according to U-boat activities, and at least four groups were kept handy to reinforce the Atlantic convoys if required. Apart from these dispositions, other groups trained in Horton's methods were operating in the Mediterranean and on distant stations under their respective Commanders-in-Chief.

Coastal Command, having been partially frustrated by the 'schnorkel,' carried the war into enemy waters, while Bomber Command and the United States Air Force bombed building yards and factories. Even the Home Fleet took part in the anti-U-boat offensive, supporting the escort carriers *Searcher*, *Queen* and *Trumpeter*, while their aircraft sank a depot ship with U-boats alongside at Harstad in Norway.

Under the weight of this continuous offensive the rate of destroying U-boats kept well ahead of merchant ship losses, and in 1945 it rose steadily month by month reaching its peak in April, when fifty-seven U-boats (exclusive of Japanese) were destroyed. This was the highest monthly total of the war. Thirty-three of these were sunk at sea. But over 200 U-boats were known to be available. Thus even at the eleventh hour, when the doom of Germany was apparent to all, there were many U-boats still afloat with crews ready to man the new types which Doenitz had promised would revolutionise submarine warfare.

After Germany capitulated, it was found that two of these craft were actually at sea, fifty-five were in commission and sixty-eight were partly completed. Most of the crews had recovered from their setback in the 'Black Pit.' After the surrender, when on their parade ground at Kiel, they carried themselves with the pride of undefeated men: and this, after they had lost 781 U-boats out of a grand total of 1,173, and 30,000 men out of 38,000. Doenitz had had grounds for his optimism and Horton's anxiety had been justified.

It was the Allied armies who prevented the threat materialising, so to them must be given the credit for striking the final blow in the Battle of the Atlantic. On the other hand they would never have conquered if the sailors and airmen had failed to keep the seaways open.

Almost to the end, the enemy considered the U-boat offensive to be his best hope of averting defeat at the hands of a nation which lives by seaborne supplies. 'This is a highly important fact which will, I trust, never be forgotten by future First Lords, future Boards of Admiralty or future Governments, or by the people of this country.' [1]

The Battle of the Atlantic embraced nearly every branch of human activity and in truth was won by the war effort of the Allied people, but through it all, the front line was held by the men of the Merchant Navy. For sixty-eight months these trusty 'non-combatants' bore the brunt of vicious submarine attack, while the Allied navies and air forces struggled to remove the tentacles closing round the throats of the British people. There was nothing spectacular about it. Unlike the fall of bombs, the slow process of strangulation was neither seen nor felt by the masses. Yet it was infinitely more deadly, and the call was close.

Victory at sea came suddenly to the Allies, but it would have gone the other way if there had been no convoy system to ensure that the right force could be sent to the right place at the right time.

It can be said with certainty that Horton's success in the Battle of the Atlantic will live in history as a classic example of the correct application and complete vindication of the ancient principles of war.

By hard training and relentless drive, Horton achieved perfect co-operation between the warships and aircraft in his Command whose task it was to preserve the merchant ships and kill the U-boats. Thus he created the right force.

By attacking the U-boats near their objective, when they were

[1] Mr. A. V. Alexander in the House of Commons, February 1945

partly pre-occupied with trying to close the convoy, he chose the right place.

By refusing to be diverted by Doenitz or anybody else before the right force was properly trained, he fell upon the enemy at the right time, and the weight and suddenness of the blow came as a surprise to them.

His object was to destroy U-boats, and from this he never wavered, yet he did not neglect the security of the convoys and insisted that the efficiency of the close escorts should be of the same high standard as that of the Support Groups. He sustained the morale and health of all ships' companies by arranging that the interval between trips should allow time for rest, recreation, and repairs.

Horton believed in the old principles of war, applying them at times with a degree of cunning born of countless battles at cards and other forms of contest. He studied history and read widely. In his motor tours between the wars he had visited many of the battlegrounds of the past, and even went to Quiberon Bay to see for himself the conditions in which Hawke had won his victory in shoal waters on a lee shore in a westerly gale.

CHAPTER FOURTEEN

1945

VICTORY

'Thus
all that had been won and lost again
between the Wars
was returned
"by blood and sweat and tears"
and the U-boat host
shepherded as sheep
trailed to the pen
in England's harbours.'

Surrender of the U-boats. Attitude of the crews. Horton visits Germany. American appreciation. Lessons of the Battle. Personal tributes.

A T noon on 8th May 1945, the Admiralty directed the German High Command to give surrender orders to all U-boats at sea. They were to come to the surface, hoist black flags, report their positions, and proceed to certain ports. Some of them were operating in distant seas, so it was not until September that the lists could be analysed with any degree of finality. It was then found that 156 German U-boats had surrendered and another 221 had been destroyed or scuttled by their crews.

Admiral Sir Max Horton formally took the surrender of a token force of eight U-boats at 2 p.m. on 14th May at Lisahally, near Londonderry.

The day turned out to be foul with a south-westerly gale, low visibility and a cloud base of about 200 feet. However, he took off from Liverpool in his Dominie aircraft. The pilot said that he had a most objectionable journey, and had to do a steep banking turn to avoid the cliffs at Larne. After arrival, the weather improved to a 'pleasant afternoon.'

The U-boats had been escorted from Loch Alsh where their torpedoes and two-thirds of their crews had been removed. As the sinister black forms crept slowly up the Foyle, a surge of emotion swept through the crowds who lined the banks. Some cheered and some wept. The people of Londonderry, that vital outpost of the Western Approaches, had reason to know the portent of the great event, and their hearts went out to the men of the Allied navies who had brought it about. The White Ensign flew triumphantly in each boat, and they were led by the British destroyer *Hesperus*, Commander R. A. Currie, D.S.C., R.N. The Canadian frigate *Thetford Mines* and the U.S.S. *Paine* assisted them to their berths. On the jetty the Prime Minister of Northern Ireland stood beside the Commander-in-Chief in front of a parade of seamen of the Londonderry Command, most of whom were seeing for the first time the faces of the men they had mercilessly hunted in the grim years of war. The German crews were mostly very young men. Some were sullen and many were arrogant. Simpson was struck by the length of their hair which in some cases, he says, was like a female 'bob.' An officer on Horton's staff says that the morale of the commanding officers was unbroken. They were convinced that Hitler had died in action, and their first question was 'When do we start fighting the Russians?' One or two of them firmly believed that war with Russia was imminent, and had retained their confidential books and secret equipment to be ready to continue the war facing east.

Simpson describes the scene:

'On returning to the jetty Admiral Horton said he would like to interview for a few moments the German commanding officers, because he wished to see the type of men then in command. The difficulty was that we had no German interpreter; however, one German commanding officer spoke quite good English, and Horton said: "I do not wish any officer to answer a question that he objects to." He then asked a few simple questions regarding ports from which they had sailed; how long at sea, how much had they used their "snort," etc. His questions were answered promptly. The interpreter was very forthcoming; he said that he had used his "schnorkel" throughout the sixty-eight-day patrol, and had practically never come to the surface. This may not have been true, but he did not seem to have much offensive left in him. Horton then said: "Tell me—are you a Regular officer or a reservist?" to which he replied: "Neither, Sir. I am a conscript from the Luftwaffe." On further questioning it appeared that just before the war Goering had persuaded Hitler to transfer considerable numbers of junior naval officers and cadets from the Naval Academy to become pilots in the Luftwaffe, and he was one of them. In 1943 dilution in U-boats became so severe that a number of airmen were sent back to the U-boat arm of the Kriegsmarine. This officer, on return to the Navy, had served on two patrols as a First Lieutenant, and had then been given command of a U-boat. Which goes to show that the heavy losses in the middle of 1943 caused serious dilution and consequent lack of experienced U-boat Commanders. Thus the lack of offensive spirit towards the end of the war was the direct outcome of the 1943 battle.'

A British senior officer who was in charge of the party disarming U-boats at Loch Alsh says:

'I think the officers could be divided into three types—the young ex-Hitler super-Nazi type, aged 22–23, who were perfectly bloody; the slightly older, and presumably pre-war Kriegsmarine, who were very "correct" and not very forthcoming; and the ex-reservist type, perhaps from the Merchant Navy, who had knocked about the world a bit. These latter were quite pleasant.

'To sum up, I don't think that the U-boat morale had been crushed, and they certainly did not feel that they had been defeated. I think that these men, manning the new U-boats, types XXI and XXVI, would have given us the most awful headaches had the war continued. In the end, however, I am certain that Sir Max would have beaten them.'

When Horton got back to his office at Derby House he hardly mentioned the surrender. He thought of it more as a comma on the page of history than a terminal point. There was plenty of work for him to do, unwinding the convoy system and his vast Command. In any case, Great Britain was still at war with Japan, and he was anxious to find out as soon as possible all there was to know about the German Submarine Service. He wished to analyse the information in the light of his own experience. So he sent a strong team, including Captains G. H. Roberts, R.N., P. W. Gretton, R.N., and Group-Captain Gates, R.A.F., Coastal Command, to join an Allied Mission of Inspection in Germany. On their return, Max asked but one question, 'Did you find out anything I did not know?' The reply was 'No, Sir!'

A few months later Horton visited Germany to see for himself, and afterwards said in a public speech:

'The last and greatest effort of the Germans to get ahead of us in the bitter struggle was the prefabricated U-boat, the Mark XXI. It had an underwater speed of sixteen or seventeen knots to overtake any convoy; and by getting underneath an eight- or ten-knot convoy it hoped to maintain itself there relatively safely while firing, re-loading, and firing its full outfit, which amounted to no fewer than twenty-five torpedoes.

'In any case, we were prepared for them as soon as we heard their boasts in the autumn of 1944. We stripped and adapted several of our own submarines to give them a very high speed, and trained all our Escort Groups to compete with the special problems it entailed. In addition, we issued tactical orders which would have done much to eliminate the threat. . . .

'The yards at Wilhemshaven, Bremen, Hamburg and Kiel were cluttered up with sections of this new type of U-boat—literally scores and scores of them. I have little doubt that it was on the U-boat mainly, boosted up subsequently by the secret V-weapons, that Hitler based all his hopes of victory after Stalingrad.'

On another occasion, speaking of the future, he said:

'We must be prepared for a definite increase in underwater speed with a new type of self-contained submerged propulsion. Due to the type of fuel used, the air inside the boat need not become foul, and the U-boat virtually need never surface. But hand in hand with high underwater speed goes an increase in underwater noise. Hence, if the future U-boat decides to use speed at an inopportune moment, it may well give away her presence at a considerable distance. It may, therefore, be deduced that if such high speed is to be available, it will be used mainly for withdrawal from being attacked by an escort vessel or withdrawal to safety after firing torpedoes. I believe that the actual method of attack in the future will still be slow, stealthy, and silent.

'This new propulsion may also affect torpedo design, and we may find long-range fast torpedoes fired at convoys from outside the screen. Yet I believe that the skilled torpedoman will prefer to get to short range in order to obtain maximum hits. This again implies close range and stealthy infiltration of the screen by the U-boat.

'New tactics for attacking the fast U-boat must be devised, new types of faster escort vessels, and new types of weapons are very early and pressing requirements.'

It was fitting that the surrender of the U-boats should have been taken by Max Horton at Lisahally, for it was here in 1941 that American technicians had created, in record time, a naval base for their warships employed on convoy duty.

In those dark days President Roosevelt, lest we forget, had undertaken to give every assistance to Great Britain, short of war. In accordance with this policy the United States Fleet gave protection to all and sundry in the Atlantic convoys for part of the voyage; and it will be remembered he also provided fifty old destroyers to fill the gaps in the sadly depleted British escort forces.

It is true that the United States Navy was slow to learn from British war experience, and was ill-prepared to meet the U-boat offensive in the Caribbean. Like anybody who lends anyone anything, they sadly missed their antiquated 'four pipers,' [1] which would probably have been more effective in the placid waters of the Caribbean than breaking down in mid-Atlantic. Nevertheless, Lisahally stands as a monument to a great American effort given to us with a 'good hand' at a time of dire peril.

Horton had always impressed American officers who came his way because he was a 'go-getter.' It is unlikely however that he would have got very far with Admiral 'Ernie' King, the United States Commander-in-Chief, for their personalities clashed on first acquaintance when Horton took him to Portsmouth to see a demonstration of a 'chariot.' King thought the idea was crazy, and it is said that the atmosphere was tense in the car going back to London. Max usually got what he wanted through Admiral Noble at Washington and the American Admiral in London, 'Betty' Stark. King had other anxieties and Stark was pro-British.

The United States Navy had reason to be grateful for the part played by the Western Approaches Command in the Battle of the Atlantic. The British victory relieved them of all anxiety for the security of the American supply lines to Europe, thus enabling them to direct their maximum naval strength against Japan.

After the war, when the facts were known, the United States with characteristic magnanimity awarded Admiral Horton their most coveted honour in its highest degree for 'outstanding services to the Government of the United States.' The citation is quoted here in full because, apart from being a tribute to Horton, it

---

[1] A distinctive feature of these old destroyers was their four thin funnels or 'smoke stacks.' Hence in the U.S. Navy they were commonly called 'four pipers' or 'four stackers.'

shows that the Navy Department fully appreciated the significance of his victory.

THE SECRETARY OF THE NAVY,

WASHINGTON.

LEGION OF MERIT, DEGREE OF CHIEF COMMANDER
awarded to
ADMIRAL SIR MAX HORTON, G.C.B., D.S.O.

For exceptionally meritorious conduct in the performance of outstanding services to the Government of the United States as Commander-in-Chief Western Approaches from 19th November 1942. Assuming his important Command at the peak of the German submarine menace, Admiral Sir Max Horton brilliantly directed the control and protection of all convoys in the approaches to the United Kingdom, devising and effecting superb measures to safeguard Allied shipping in British waters. With the enemy underseas craft threatening our control of vital sea lanes in the Atlantic, he skilfully employed all available escorts and facilities, developed special training programs and services to insure the dissemination of the latest information concerning anti-submarine tactics and hostile activity, and formulated effective plans for the co-ordination of operations to provide maximum safety for Allied shipping during arrivals, departures and periods at sea within his Command. By his inspiring leadership, extraordinary professional ability and comprehensive understanding of the overall Allied strategy in this area, together with his unswerving devotion to duty, Admiral Sir Max Horton contributed immeasurably to the success of our combined naval operations against the common enemy and the maintenance of a steady flow of supplies, equipment and personnel to the European Theater of War.

Commenting on this, a friend in the British Delegation at Washington wrote:

'I'm delighted that at long last your services in connection with the Battle of the Atlantic have been recognised. Must confess that I was greatly surprised this has not been done before. Were they waiting to see if you would make a mess of the last round? If so I could have told them the answer myself.

'Anyway the award will give very great satisfaction on both sides of the Atlantic. We have a great struggle at Washington to make the Americans appreciate the British war effort, and get very little help on this side to put our case properly. As it is, the U.S. published *their* side of the U-boat war and suggested by inference that we just helped a bit. But the Navy Dept. of course have the facts and I'm sure they'll all be delighted that your work has been recognised.'

The total number of German U-boats sunk at sea in all areas by naval and air forces controlled by Great Britain was 505, and the corresponding figure for the United States was 132. Of this total, the 'kills' were shared equally by ships and aircraft. Further statistics bring the grand total to 783[1] destroyed by all causes. But it took a long, long time. The Allied counter-measures did not become really effective until after three and a half years of war. If adequate provision had been made between the wars, the U-boat threat to our national existence would never have become acute.

Horton has earned his place in history, not only for the conspicuous part he played in the Atlantic victory but also as the leader who, perhaps more than any other, achieved perfect unity of sea and air forces in naval operations. He has given full credit to Coastal Command of the Royal Air Force and its distinguished Commanders for their part in the struggle. And they would agree that the burden of training naval and air forces to work together and of directing their operations when fighting together fell largely on his shoulders. In the words of Air Chief Marshal Slessor 'no one knows more about the Battle of the Atlantic or played a more critical part in that battle than Admiral Horton . . . the association of the airman and the scientist with the sailor, which stood us in such good stead in the Battle of the Atlantic, must be developed and extended in all forms of air/sea warfare.'[2]

It is satisfactory to know that the teamwork resulting from successful co-operation between naval and air forces, as practised in the Western Approaches Command, has not been lost in the limbo of the past. The joint Sea-Air Anti-Submarine School established by Admiral Horton and Air Marshal Slatter still flourishes at Londonderry. It is attended not only by British naval and air officers but also by those of the N.A.T.O. nations, and is proving invaluable.

Although Horton had defeated Doenitz he was never complacent, and remained unshaken in his belief that the greatest

---

[1] Figures are taken from Cmd. paper 6843 of 1946 plus two ascertained later. See also Appendix VII.
[2] Royal United Service Institute Lecture, February 1947

danger to be faced in a future war would be a large-scale U-boat assault. In his final report he said that he was 'more than ever convinced that there was a pressing need for the appointment of a Chief of Anti-U-boat Warfare . . . analogous to that of Admiral Doenitz.'

The Government, as we know, did not agree, but with deeper consideration the idea might have come to them that a Chief of Sea-Air Co-operation for anti-submarine warfare was just as needful as a Chief of Combined Operations for landing on enemy beaches. True co-operation can be achieved only by a common doctrine in strategy, tactics, equipment and training. It would have been in the country's interest, therefore, if a post could have been established to enable Horton to consolidate in peace-time the unity he had created in the hard school of war, and to ensure that the lessons of the Battle of the Atlantic would not be forgotten. Such a post he probably would have accepted irrespective of the rank it carried.

Everybody knows that the invasion of Europe by land and air forces won the war, but somebody was needed, and is still needed, to remind the people that the defeat of the U-boats by sea and air forces prevented us from losing it.

On 8th May 1945 Admiral Horton made this signal to the Western Approaches Command:

'On V.E. Day, whilst the battle for which the Western Approaches Command was created to fight draws to a victorious close, I send this personal message of gratitude and admiration to all of you who have so faithfully and nobly borne the brunt of the long drawn-out struggle.

'In winter gales of the North Atlantic and every kind of weather, the little ships of this Command have kept continuous close touch and faith with those they had to guard, but this alone was not enough. High technical skill, reached only by intensive training, added to that seaman's eye and judgment which long experience at sea under the hardest conditions gives, produced the polish which earned our great but still unnumbered successes.

'The standard you have set and maintained in anti-submarine warfare is, in my opinion, quite unsurpassed by any of the combatant nations, and your standards in all other respects have been a source of pride and joy to me.

'Your losses have been heavy indeed and our thoughts at this time must constantly turn to our comrades and friends who have paid the price of victory.

'In thanking you for your unfailing loyalty and support and wishing you good luck, remember it is still too early to relax. Utmost vigilance is necessary until the last U-boat is surrendered.'

Amongst many replies, he received the following letter from 'one of my best group leaders' (double D.S.O. and D.S.C.):

'First thank you very much for my share in your grand signal to your Command. Secondly I am writing to try to express my personal appreciation of your leadership.

'The Western Approaches Command, viewed from the sea-going angle, is, I do assure you, the only Command in this war which has shown a grip of the situation from day to day, and the only one wherein an escort felt it was given a fair chance to have a crack at the Hun. I, who have been in the Command since September 1940, have everything for which to thank you.

If I may be allowed, I want to say that, in addition to being my Commander-in-Chief, I have looked to you always as my friend. You have frequently given me the most kindly advice, and have always encouraged me in my endeavours.

'I have had so many good chaps killed under my command, in the four ships lost to this group, that the second paragraph of your signal is most personal to me.

'I shall never forget your sympathy and cheerfulness after I myself had been torpedoed.

'Thank God I have had the satisfaction of destroying an even larger number of the enemy.

'I fear this letter may be an awful breach of etiquette and of Service custom, but I hope you will read it as my most sincere expression of personal loyalty and gratitude to you.

'As a nation, we were lucky enough to have Churchill; as a member of your Command, I feel we were equally fortunate in having *you*!'

Space does not permit publication of the many messages of gratitude and congratulation received by Max from all over the world. The following letter dated 13th May, from Captain G. B. H. Fawkes (then Chief Staff Officer to the Flag Officer Submarines at Northways), cannot be overlooked because it is a heartfelt expression of the esteem in which Horton was held by the whole Submarine Service:

'I feel I must write and tell you what your message on this day of Victory Thanksgiving has meant to us and to me in particular. You must know that the whole Submarine Service realises and will never forget what it owes to you. I can assure you this is handed down to officers and men who have joined since you left us. *You* put us on the map, you gave us our opportunities and all we have done is due to you.

'I shall never forget that instant decision you took at a meeting at the Admiralty (on some totally irrelevant subject) when it slipped out from Admiral Phillips that mines were being laid in Norwegian territorial waters.

'Your orders to send all available S/Ms to sea at once—with orders *to sink at sight.*

'The Norwegian campaign that followed, and which would have sustained such crippling blows at its very inception, had *Sealion*, *Sunfish* and *Triton* had just a shred of luck that was due to them, and had not the German force passed the next night through the positions of three of our submarines in a dense fog.[1]

'Those and many other incidents I remember so well. . . . My turn came as Captain (S) 8 during the N. African campaign, to take some big decisions. The Admiral and Governor of Gibraltar having both told General Clark it was impossible to land his party under the circumstances at Algiers, the latter turned to me and asked my opinion. I thought rapidly to myself, "What would Admiral Horton have done and have me do?" I replied "It can be done and we'll be ready to start in an hour."[2]

'Forgive this outburst, Sir, but I think it is representative of how we all feel.

'We all realise, too, how much the nation and the world owes to the man who won the Battle of the Atlantic, and we are proud that he was previously our leader. You took over that job at a time when, to use your own words "if things go on as they are now, the Navy will very soon blow a whistle and say the war is lost, and neither the other Services nor the Cabinet will realise why, in time." The only whistle you blew was the whistle for victory.

'It is so very fitting that the surrender of the German U-boats is taking place to you.

'If, in the days of peace to come, short-memoried people forget, for a time, what the nation owes to you, the Submarine Service (and I, as one of them), will never cease to remember.

'I am looking forward to the day, Sir, when we can give you a real welcome at Blockhouse, it will be a great event.'

[1] See page 78.
[2] General Mark Clark, U.S.A. see page 120.

234

VICTORY

Horton's reply gives an indication of his feelings at this time of triumph:

COMMANDER-IN-CHIEF,
WESTERN APPROACHES,
LIVERPOOL, 2.
17th May 1945.

My dear Fawkes,

I could not express in words my feelings on reading your letter—it raised thoughts and reactions almost overwhelming—so you see how inadequate it is to say how deeply I appreciate it.

With the end of the German war it is natural to pause a while and recall those days of big and poignant issues, where one happily had done right and where most unhappily done wrong and failed to cut a loss perhaps early enough—these thoughts are inevitable, but the one great consolation and source of joy and strength under every circumstance was the certain knowledge that every man-jack in S/Ms afloat or ashore was putting all his will and strength on the same end of the rope—so universal and strong a spirit I had never experienced before and never shall again, for in my opinion it was unique in any modern navy. As a result, our submarines have gone on from strength to strength, and maintained a standard, despite the prolongation of the war, under the most difficult and arduous conditions which is the envy of the rest of the Service.

I will not say more now, but just thank you again not only for your letter but also for your unfailing help and resource when we worked together. It means much and I have not forgotten.

Yours e.,
MAX HORTON.

CHAPTER FIFTEEN

THE ADMIRAL

'He never courted men in station,
Nor persons held in admiration;
Of no man's greatness was afraid,
Because he sought for no man's aid.'—SWIFT.

ON 14th June 1945, Horton was awarded the G.C.B., but apart from the Freedom of Liverpool no other British honour came to him. Judging him by results many people thought that he deserved a peerage. This is not surprising since his decisive victory over the U-boats was just as vital to the Allied cause as the conquest of North Africa and the defeat of the Luftwaffe. The feeling is frankly expressed in a letter dated 17th June from a Sea Lord who, while congratulating Max on his G.C.B., said:

'I had hoped that the great service you have done for the nation, the Allies and the Empire would have been recognised in a very handsome manner . . . all my colleagues feel likewise.

'It takes a long time for these things to sink in, but when the history of this war is digested, the world will wake up to the fact that without the great Battle of the Atlantic being won under your inspiring leadership, we could never have had a D-Day or any V-Day!

'However I still have hopes that this nation will not prove itself ungrateful.'

Horton had said more than once that war would find him where he was most wanted. With the coming of peace the enemy had vanished, and his work was done. Having fulfilled his destiny firstly with his own submarines and finally against those of the enemy, he told the Admiralty that he wished to retire 'to facilitate the promotion of younger officers.'

Thus for the second time in his career he placed himself out of the running for promotion to Admiral of the Fleet. It is probable that he did not consider himself to be eligible by tradition for the Navy's highest rank, as he had never commanded one of the principal fleets and had refused the appointment when it was offered to him. Yet, at the turning point in the Battle of the Atlantic he had led to victory, in close co-operation with Coastal Command of the Royal Air Force, a naval force unsurpassed in efficiency and numerically larger than any of the main fleets.

In the course of the war the Western Approaches Command expanded enormously. As already mentioned, over a thousand escort vessels passed through the initial training centre at Tobermory. Many of these found their way to other stations, but the average sea-going strength in the last year of the war was about 300 escort vessels manned by 4,000 officers and 40,000 men. There were over 100 naval establishments in the Command (some of which had very little to do with the Battle of the Atlantic), bringing the total strength of personnel to 121,500 officers and men, including 18,000 W.R.N.S. It was so large and widely spread that the only way Horton could cope with the administration was by decentralising drastically on the seven Flag Officers in charge of the principal ports, the Commodore Western Isles, the Commodore Londonderry and the Captains of Flotillas.

The only appointment which could have been offered to Horton was that of First Sea Lord. In wartime he would have filled the position admirably, for his professional knowledge was unmatched and his judgment sound. In the lean post-war years, however, while the strength of the Navy dwindled, political factions would have irritated him. He would brook no opposition, and it is unlikely he would have got his way in the face of disunity and misguided public opinion. He knew what he wanted, and would fight tooth and nail to get it. Once, when he was told that a Minister had said he was 'obstinate as a mule,' Max replied 'Two mules—when I know I am right.'

A distinguished writer and critic says:

'So great, indeed, was my confidence in Horton's genius as a seaman and executive officer, that at the height of the war crisis, when our fortunes were at their lowest ebb, and when I was acting as war commentator and critic to many of the leading newspapers and journals, here and elsewhere, and in B.B.C. broadcasts to the Empire,

I expressed the conviction to a high naval authority that Horton was the proper man for the post of First Sea Lord. I was then told that he had been offered, and had declined, the Command of the Home Fleet, and that in doing so he had revealed a disinclination for supreme responsibility, an alleged reason which, knowing Horton, I personally doubted.'

Admiral Pound, as First Sea Lord, gave him a free hand, possibly because he had already so much on his plate, but more likely because he knew Max Horton. Admiral Cunningham, shortly after he relieved Pound, queried the length of time in harbour Horton allowed his escort vessels for rest, training, and repairs. Max resented this, but when he realised, after sleeping on it, that the ships were needed for the greatest combined operation in history, he said in a letter to the First Sea Lord, dated 2nd January 1944:

'I am very sorry that our telephone conversation on Friday went so badly and if I appeared unforthcoming—I didn't understand what you were driving at, and it seemed that you had just rung up to say that in my Command we were deliberately keeping ships in harbour which ought to be at sea.

'Since then I've learnt that you were searching to see if more Support Groups could be got by any possible means—cutting "lay overs" [intervals for rest and repairs], even training if necessary.

'I have been on a similar search since joining this job; but have got my staff on once again, to see if by any possible means we can make it practicable to bring the convoys across with less groups, and thereby extract a Support Group. Even if it were possible, it takes some time before the actual extraction becomes feasible.

'Anyway a memorandum is being made out to cover all the points you wanted information about, which I hope will show you the situation clearly, and I will bring it up to go through with you on Wednesday or Thursday at any time convenient to you.

'I was very worried after our talk; now even more than ever do I wish to pull on the same end of the rope with no other thought than to help you, who have such a tremendous task in these next few months especially.'

It has been said that Horton was a bad loser at games. This characteristic also made an unfavourable impression in conference at high level, but he was a bad loser for the very good reason that he could not bear to be defeated. No better man therefore could have been found to match the wily Doenitz. He was abnormally sensitive to any reprimand and would misconstrue even a friendly criticism from a senior officer as being a reflection on his efficiency. Lack of recognition of what he knew to be in him hardened him, and this sometimes roused hostility in those who had not perceived his qualities. On the other hand, he encouraged and welcomed criticism from his juniors, for this could be used or discarded according to his own estimate of its value. He alone could be the judge, not only of them, but of himself. If he had made a mistake he would not hesitate to admit it, and for the benefit of his submarine commanders he would draw from his large store of experience to tell them of occasions when his own judgment had been at fault.

It is natural, therefore, that he should have expected the same frankness from them, and when he got it he was sympathetic and tolerant. 'There is always hope,' he said, 'for one who realises his limitations and mistakes; it is a step to improvement. That is why I only worry people who will not cheerfully admit their mistakes.' This, as we have seen, was well understood by his submarine commanders and no less so by his Escort Commanders in the Western Approaches.

In a report to him of a convoy battle Captain P. W. Gretton said: 'I think he [a commanding officer] made an incorrect decision . . . but I would have made it myself.' In another report Captain M. J. Evans said: 'I am convinced that my mistake in allowing the convoys to be formed astern of one another was a fatal one.' The reports of Captain F. J. Walker, the greatest 'killer' of all, were notable for their colour and frankness: 'Most of the time that we were in contact with U-boats, it seemed that things were going off bang in all directions, and it was difficult to sort out which were "gnats" or secret weapons or just U-boats coming to grief.'

In the interests of the Service Horton sought the truth. In war, however, there is usually neither time nor opportunity for meticulous enquiry if things go seriously wrong. Sometimes, when the circumstances were not clear and Horton felt that it was a case of 'the round peg in the square hole,' he would have a commanding officer removed without further ado, rather than give him the benefit of the doubt. 'It is highly dangerous to shield inefficiency,' he said. His judgment in these matters, however, was not infallible.

Although he may have been ruthless and at times inconsiderate in dealing with his staff it had a tonic effect on his sea-going Commanders. Their requests were dealt with at once and he welcomed advice resulting from their experience. Captain M. J. Evans says: 'In his area of Command everything ran on oiled wheels. His orders were clear and practicable, aircraft arrived when expected, call signs were passed in adequate time, and the whole vast organisation inspired confidence.' Rear-Admiral Durnford-Slater says: 'I cannot remember any case of "back seat driving" by Max . . . he was without doubt an outstanding leader . . . . his insistence on the highest standard of training was the major cause of victory in the Atlantic.'

Horton regarded staff officers as an extension of his own brain, expecting them to be ready with the right answers at any time of day or night. Once in May 1944 he said to Captain B. W. Taylor in the middle of the night, 'Have you thought what to do with all the U-boats when they surrender?' Taylor pertly replied, 'Sink them, I hope.' 'Not that,' said Horton. 'Where are they to be taken? They must be berthed in lochs where they can float, but if they scuttle themselves they'll rest on the bottom with their conning towers above water. I should like a paper on the subject with my breakfast.'

He demanded a very high standard of mental and physical endurance from his staff, and every officer who joined it was virtually tested over a probationary period lasting about a month, which to them was purgatory. Only after weathering this test successfully was an officer deemed to be acceptable. The Commander-in-Chief was determined that the staff should be an example to the whole Command and that they should be prepared to give every consideration to all, high or low, who came to his Headquarters. In this respect his Chief of Staff, Commodore I. A. P. Macintyre, set a magnificent example. Having served close to Max at Northways and again at Derby House, none is better qualified than he to give this well-balanced view:

'To me, Sir Max was a very great man possessing perhaps a dual personality, having on the one hand charm and a kindness of heart

'DOES IT WORK?'

Horton characteristically tries out a telescope before presenting it to a Chief
Captain of cadets at Eaton Hall, Cheshire

VICTORY PARADE, 1946

Admiral Horton (left) and Admiral Noble (right) salute the King

INSTALLATION OF KNIGHTS GRAND CROSS OF THE ORDER OF THE BATH, 24TH MAY 1951

Admiral Horton, as Bath King of Arms, stands on the right of His Majesty at the foot of the Altar

not always realised, and on the other hand hardness which could at times be terrifying to even the toughest of men. He was a man of few friends, but no one could be a more charming host than he to those who were privileged to receive his hospitality. In the years I knew him it seemed that two things which were always forward in his mind were the Service and his golf. I have heard much adverse criticism of the fact that even in wartime he seldom missed his daily game. Such criticism can only come from those who fail to appreciate the reason, namely the maintenance of a proper balance, both mental and physical, so essential for efficiency. As his staff, we were thankful indeed that for some part of the day his outstanding drive was applied to a golf ball, for had it not been so, we could not have stayed the course. We shall always owe a debt of gratitude to Duty Staff Officers who in their "days off" had, as part of their duty, to partner him with tact and efficiency. "Relax and play for a period each day if you wish to keep your health and vision clear," he said, "without vision the people perish".'

Horton's passion for golf is reminiscent of Drake and his game of bowls. No threat of enemy or prod of Admiralty could stop him having his daily round at Hoylake or Formby. Golf attracted him because it demanded absolute concentration, compelling him to dismiss from his mind for a few hours the many problems that beset him.

An experienced staff officer dug out from retirement, who had served in the Western Approaches Command throughout the war writes:

'When I went to say goodbye to him in July 1945 I told him that of the seven Admirals I had served he was *facile princeps*. This was no flattery, but the truth. He was a great man, in the tradition of St. Vincent rather than of Nelson. His technical knowledge and genius for detail never obscured his eye for the main issues: he could always see both the wood *and* the trees, and his driving force saw to it that the policies he initiated were carried through.'

His heart went out to the dependants of those lost at sea. One day a docket started by the Ministry of Pensions arrived suggesting that the loss of a certain small submarine might have been due to stress of weather, in which case the 'Lost-in-Action Gratuity' might not be payable. Horton protested violently, engraving his minute so fiercely that the pen went through the paper.

Max presented many contradictions to those with whom he

served. His impatience was disturbing to some sensitive characters. He was no bully, however, and realised that no one can know
everything. At one time it was thought that he was having a
bad effect on a senior staff officer. A nervous breakdown was
feared, so Wildish as the oldest member of the staff tackled
Horton: 'His reaction was extraordinary. He could not believe it,
and he could not thank me enough for telling him.'

On the human side, Captain R. W. Ravenhill remarks:

'He was always most thoughtful for people in trouble, and underneath the formidable exterior was a very warm heart. He would often
make some remark about a person which revealed that he had been
thinking about their misfortunes, when you imagined his mind was
occupied with the problems of war.'

Yet there was the time when another staff officer reported
that a certain cruiser had been lost, and that his son was on board.
Horton instinctively replied, 'Yes—but what happened to the
ship?' Paradoxically enough, Horton was being consistent. His
subconscious reaction was 'first things first'—'the ship—the ship,
what happened to the ship?' The shock of the disaster prevented
him from expressing spontaneously the sorrow which he
undoubtedly felt at the private loss. The good of the country
transcended the individual, and much was at stake.

No one can deny that Horton was efficient, thorough, hardworking, realistic, unaffected, devoid of pomposity, highly
intelligent, intensely patriotic, phenomenally courageous and a
master of his profession. In other words a great Admiral, loved
by some, admired and respected by all, but not universally liked.
He had few, if any, friends in high naval circles. Individualism
was his most pronounced characteristic, and officers who were
closely associated with him in the Navy say he was a lonely
man. He liked to keep sentiment away from his work and his
social life apart from the Navy. In a private letter he said:
' "Friend" is too precious a name to give, except to very few, and
most of those who could really be called such in the Service are
gone. . . . I guess you're right about my enemies not being so
few, but it's a poor creature that is not either disliked or envied
by some.'

THE ADMIRAL

As Commander-in-Chief, Horton's stature was clear enough to everybody. His contemporary Brodie, who was sceptical in the beginning,[1] came under his Command again as a Commodore of Convoys in the last two years of the war. He says:

'The big staff at Derby House were hard driven by Max but consciously a winning team. My slight contact with the escort personnel was enough to show their tails were up, however weary their bodies. . . . The legends about Max and his former economy of praise gave added value to every pat on the back. . . . In March 1945 I saw perhaps more of him than I ever had before and I glimpsed something of the Max who paid a moving tribute to Walker in Liverpool Cathedral, a side of him that was wholly new to me. . . . Horton had that bit extra that makes a good leader into a great one. No wonder that hundreds of his young officers at sea called him Der Fuhrer, and perhaps quoted "Max knows all, Max sees all" and added that "Max will have an ace up his sleeve, if Fritz tries any new trick." '

In a farewell speech, shortly before hauling down his flag, Horton expressed his gratitude to the officers and ratings of the combined naval and air staff at his Headquarters in the following words:

'It has been our privilege to have lived in stirring times—vital years in the history of our country and our Empire. In 1940 we narrowly survived our greatest ordeal, and from that year onwards our strength and hopes began to rise. It was not, however, long after the fall of France that a cloud began to appear on our horizon which was to spread to such dimensions in the course of the next three years that the very existence of our country and the fortunes of the United Nations were again in jeopardy. I refer, of course, to the threat of unrestricted U-boat warfare. The defeat of the U-boats was a vital prelude to the unsurpassed victory over the Germans which we are celebrating today.

'Chief credit for that victory rightly goes to the fighting men in our escort vessels and aircraft and to the steadfastness of our Merchant Navy. Today I particularly wish to thank and pay tribute to you who, year in, year out, by day and by night planned, organised, administered and directed this great battle, surely one worthy of recognition as one of *the decisive battles of the war*. The U-boats were fought on sea and from the air, and success in both elements could only be achieved by the closest co-operation between our two great Services.

[1] Q.v. page 26.

243

'In Derby House we lived together, fed together and worked together; only by these means could we have achieved together the splendid co-ordination of effort on the sea and in the air which spelt the doom of the U-boats. Quite rightly there was friendly rivalry between the two Services, but we never thought of measuring the relative contribution of each Service in our united successes. It is, however, of academic interest, indeed I would say eloquent testimony of our combined effort, to note that of the many hundreds of U-boats sunk, the numbers sunk by aircraft and by surface craft are almost exactly equal.

'This close co-operation could never have been achieved unless it had started from the top, and here I would like to thank Air Vice-Marshal Sir Leonard Slatter for his loyal co-operation and valuable advice to me personally on all questions appertaining to the air. His high standard of efficiency and friendship percolated through every branch of 15 Group R.A.F.

'Two other Services, the W.R.N.S. and the W.A.A.F., have been incorporated in the Western Approaches Headquarters. What a multitude of duties, hitherto considered only to be in the province of men, have been brilliantly performed by the officers and ratings of these two Services. The Navy and the Air Force are justly proud and jealous of the high standard of efficiency of their "sister" Services.

'In dealing with the various departments of Western Approaches I realise that Coastal Command has in each case their counterpart. I would therefore ask the R.A.F. to consider that any remarks I make equally apply to their corresponding departments.

'The Western Approaches Command embraced the largest number of vessels ever assembled under one flag. As hunters of U-boats our ships and aircraft gained renown, but this could never have been achieved had they not been cared for and kept in repair. I cannot adequately express to Engineer Admiral Wildish and his staff the extent of my gratitude for the manner in which they have performed their stupendous task. As with repairs, so with the administration of this vast fleet of ships and aircraft. Those concerned with the administration and secretarial duties have every reason to be proud of a job well done; a job which gets to the very core of the well-being and efficiency of the whole.

'Ships and aircraft cannot operate unless we can talk to each other, and in wartime this is a complicated business. How complicated is best shewn by the magnitude of the communication staff, manned predominantly by women. All of us, I know, would like to testify to the brilliant manner in which they have carried out their duties.

'It is said that an army marches on its stomach. I can only assume that the Navy floats and the Air Force flies on the same part of their anatomy. A special word of thanks is due to those who have administered to our wants—a task so necessary, but one, I fear, without much glamour.

'What an achievement has been that of the R.N.V.R.! To what full use has been put the nautical training of the R.N.R.! Added to these we get a number of retired naval officers, many of whom have suffered grievous disappointments in their experience between the two wars. They have filled posts of the utmost importance. They have given ungrudging service of the highest order to younger active service officers whose lot has been luckier but no more meritorious than theirs.

'The task of Western Approaches is finished. The curtain will soon be rung down and when I survey this concourse in front of me I feel that no words of mine can adequately express my gratitude. I say to all of you: "Hold your heads high by virtue of a double qualification —that of having served in the Navy or Air Force, and that of having taken a part in the Battle of the Atlantic." Goodbye—Thank you— The very best of good luck to you all.'

A year later when Horton received the Honorary Freedom of the City of Liverpool he said that he felt that the honour was 'shared and earned by every man Jack and woman Jill in the Western Approaches Command.'

He reminded the large audience of the difficult conditions that faced his predecessor, Admiral Sir Percy Noble, when 'we never had enough escorts to compete with the duties required . . . and how splendidly he dealt with this adverse state of affairs.'

In a tribute to the citizens of Liverpool for the part they had played in the Battle of the Atlantic, Horton said:

'Looking back on those strenuous days, I can realise now even more than at the time, the warming atmosphere of help and encouragement that surrounded us all at the Combined Headquarters, Derby House.

'From Lord Derby, who was kindness itself, from the Lord Mayor, members of the Emergency Committee, the Mersey Docks and Harbour Board, the shipping companies, the re-fitting firms and their devoted workmen, the Liverpool and Glasgow Salvage Association and the many local institutions that helped and comforted the sailor. Never a call was made without a most heartening response, and I can assure you these calls were frequent.

'Where so many are concerned, it is perhaps invidious to mention names, but certain individuals were, by reason of their jobs, being called upon almost daily. Mr. Hodges,[1] General Manager of the

[1] Now Sir Rex Hodges.

245

Mersey Docks and Harbour Board, was necessarily incessantly in the picture—always unperturbed and helpful. We owe him a deep debt of gratitude. Too little has been heard of the magnificent work done by the Liverpool and Glasgow Salvage Association. Mr. Critchley and his men earned my warm admiration for the way they carried out many difficult and dangerous tasks.

'And there are others I would mention who deal in a different plane and helped in a different way. I refer, in particular, to our Dean of Liverpool Cathedral. What mortal man or priest could do to aid and strengthen us, he did—and I wish publicly to acknowledge the debt I and Western Approaches owe to him.

'The scroll of our dead of the Western Approaches Command, six thousand and eighty-one names of gallant men, was received into the keeping of Liverpool Cathedral by the Archbishop of York and now lies there in all honour.

'Whilst for nearly six years the swaying battle in the North Atlantic went on, the whole population of this city and port of Liverpool were working for victory at the docks, at the yards, or in the factories, warehouses and shops. Liverpool was the principal port of the United Kingdom during the war. The unceasing effort of its inhabitants with their stern resolve to keep going in every adversity was admirable to observe. They set an example which withstood every bitter test the Nazi could provide, besides providing a haven for many Western Approaches ships.

'It is small wonder then that I am very moved today by the great honour your city has thought fit to confer on me. . . . The beautiful casket you have given me with its symbolic design will ever recall great days and highly charged moments together with poignant memories of those gallant men who paid the price of victory.

'I thank you for this day, not only on my own behalf, but on behalf of all who served under me in one of history's longest and most bitterly contested battles at sea—the nerve centre of which was situated in your great city of Liverpool.'

Before he left Liverpool he took the opportunity in public speeches to impress upon the people of the North the vital need for a strong Navy and Air Force. At Blackpool on 18th July 1945 he said:

'We must resolve that never again shall the freedom of this country be put in such jeopardy. . . .

'I have no hesitation in saying that had we possessed a Navy and Air Force in the middle '30s of adequate size in all the essential categories and modernly equipped, neither Hitler nor Mussolini would or could have got away with their initial aggressions or dared to contemplate world domination.

'As one British Minister said at that time: "Tell me how great is the strength of the British Navy and Air Force and I will tell you precisely how loudly my voice will be heard in the European Conference."'

While in command of the Western Approaches, Max took a keen interest in the efforts of the Church to promote the spiritual welfare of the officers and men of the Royal Navy, Merchant Navy and Royal Air Force. Although he was not an habitual churchgoer he, like most sailors, had a firm belief in Almighty God—'In Deo Confido.' One day, Wildish congratulated him on the accuracy of one of his hunches. Max replied with a smile, 'Well, you see, I always pray every night for guidance and foresight. Back your judgment, and if it goes wrong, bow your head to the Almighty and try to do better next time.'

He sincerely believed that no country could exist without Divine inspiration and he attributed the seeming miracle of his victory to a source outside himself. He believed in Democracy, but could see no hope for it without discipline and leadership. In a letter written a few years later he said: 'No politician dare talk order and discipline for fear of being branded a Fascist, yet Communism thrives in the Orient because the people prefer order to chaos. . . . As everyone knows, it is the basis of Communist policy to create chaos before introducing their obnoxious form of discipline.'

Max constantly refers in his post-war letters to the ' downward slide' and more than once expresses the view that the only way to stem it is by increasing the influence of the Church.

His sincerity and genuine desire to support the Church in every way brought him into touch with Dr. F. W. Dwelly, the Dean of Liverpool—'I often take the pulpit; the Dean is so difficult to resist.' They became close friends, and would dine together frequently in Horton's flat on the top floor of Derby House. They would talk late into the night on subjects which the Dean prefers should remain confidential, but we can be sure that Max with his scientific mind was seeking the Truth not only for his own enlightenment but for that of his country. He encouraged the idea that the officers and men should look upon Liverpool Cathedral as the 'Parish Church of the Western Approaches.'

On 18th April 1945 the Dean wrote:

My Dear Admiral,

... And I want once again to thank you for the way you read those passages in the Cathedral—old Lord Derby writes to me: "The reading moved me more than I can ever remember."

It means more than you can imagine that you should take the leading part on these occasions, for well we know that we owe our very life as an island to the unconquerable resolve that you, Sir, have inspired, impelled and compelled. Thank you for allowing your Cathedral to symbolise this without expressing it.

Yours,

(Signed) F. W. D.

Captain Acworth writes:

'My last sight of Max, if I remember rightly, was in the great pulpit of Liverpool Cathedral, from which he read with impressive solemnity the selected passage from the Scriptures. Following him in the pulpit, as preacher, was the Archbishop of York.'

On 9th August 1945 a service of thanksgiving and celebration was held in the Cathedral exclusively for the Western Approaches Command. During the service, Admiral Sir Max Horton read the words of Admiral Lord Nelson and the congregation made response in the words of Admiral Sir Francis Drake:

'Proud of the call which has made us go forth, we will trust in God and English valour;

Response: All of one company.

'In time of danger, or in glorious jumble, or when very miserable, which is very foolish, but such things are, we shall do our best, never fear the event;

Response: All of one company.

'Though nothing is sure, the uncertain position the enemy may be found in, we will fag ourselves to death before any blame shall be at our doors, a powerful fleet, not to be held cheap;

Response: All of one company.

248

'At sea where nobody has entirely his own way, we will not think of little nonsenses too much, but help to form the best disposed fleet of friends;

Response: All of one company.

'Like the Rock of Gibraltar our resolution is fixed, not made to despair, what man can do shall be done;

Response: All of one company.

'God only knows where we shall be, but it shall be our pride to take care that our friends shall not blush for us, and Heaven bless all which we hold dear in this world;

Response: All of one company.'

Admiral Sir Percy Noble read a lesson from Holy Scripture, and at the end of the service 'The Record of the Western Approaches' was placed by Admiral Horton in the Memorial Chapel for safe keeping.

Then the two Admirals ascended to the parapet—'a place high over the city, a look-out to the sea'—where in the presence of the Dean and senior officers, they set their marks 'in like manner as our forefathers knew and in such wise that generations yet unborn may read the same and reading give thanks for the great deliverance wrought by the Royal Navy.'[1]

A few days later Max received this personal letter from the First Lord of the Admiralty:

ADMIRALTY,
WHITEHALL.

10th August 1945.

My Dear Max,

Now that you are giving up the appointment of Commander-in-Chief Western Approaches, I wish first of all to tell you that I think it is typical of your generous spirit to offer to retire in order to help on the prospects of more junior officers. I do so appreciate your attitude in this matter.

No one can ever have given up a Command with a more satisfactory feeling of complete achievement than you do now. You took over in the darkest days, and led and inspired your great Command right through to complete victory over the U-boats.

[1] Extracts from the Order of Service.

I cannot thank you enough for all that you have done, and in particular I want to say how greatly I have always appreciated the close association and accord which has existed between you and me and which has led to complete mutual confidence and frankness between us.

All good luck to you in the future.

Yours v. sincerely,

A. V. ALEXANDER.

Admiral Sir MAX K. HORTON, G.C.B., D.S.O.

This was followed by an official letter of appreciation from the Board of Admiralty. In their reference to Horton's greatest achievement, victory in the Atlantic, it will be seen that their Lordships did not mince their words:

ADMIRALTY, C.W.

27th August 1945.

To Admiral Sir MAX HORTON, G.C.B., D.S.O. and two Bars,
11 Chesham Place, S.W.1.

Sir,

I am commanded by My Lords Commissioners of the Admiralty to convey to you their appreciation of your action in asking to retire to facilitate the promotion of junior officers, and to acquaint you that they have accepted your offer.

My Lords desire me to take this opportunity to express to you their high appreciation of the great services you have rendered during your long and noteworthy career on the Active List of the Royal Navy.

In particular they recall that the Submarine Branch of the Royal Navy owes you a great debt for your inventions, inspiration, and leadership in the many appointments you have held in that branch of the Service—culminating with the period during which you were Flag Officer Submarines from 1940-42. They also recall that during the last war you were awarded the D.S.O. and two Bars for your very gallant conduct and outstanding qualities whilst serving in submarines.

My Lords also wish to place on record that you commanded with distinction the 2nd Battle Squadron from 1934 to 1935 and later the 1st Cruiser Squadron in the Mediterranean at the time of the Spanish Civil War.

Through your tenure of the command of the Reserve Fleet from 1937 to 1939 you were responsible for the high state of its efficiency at the outbreak of the war, when you assumed command of the Northern Patrol in Arctic waters.

My Lords also recall that you assumed command of the Western Approaches in November 1942 at a time when the United Kingdom was subjected to the most grievous maritime attacks in its history —and are sensible of the signal and outstanding services which you rendered as the leader and organiser of the Command during the period of its greatest activity, and fullest development, culminating in complete victory.

Never has this country endured so dangerous a threat to its existence, and with the overcoming of that danger your name and that of the Western Approaches Command will ever be associated. On the successful issue of the Battle of the Atlantic depended the future of this Empire—and indeed the world.

I am commanded to express to you My Lords' profound regret that the time has now come for the transfer of your name from the Active Flag List to the Retired List of the Royal Navy.

I am, Sir,

Your obedient servant,

(Signed) H. V. MARKHAM.

The flag of Admiral Sir Max Horton was struck at sunset on 15th August 1945, and as the Cross of St. George came slowly down, the epic of the Western Approaches passed into history. Under that banner the dragon had been slain, so the victorious warships sailed away leaving the Port of Liverpool to its rightful occupants, the merchant ships of Britain.

Together, in a spirit of comradeship and mutual respect, the men of the Royal Navy and Merchant Navy had sailed from the same docks, faced the same dangers, endured the same hardships and fought the same battles. Again and again they had returned to the friendly port, thankful to see the towers of the Liver Building and the tall Cathedral with its spiritual import. But, nearly always, the joy of homecoming would be marred by vivid memories of stricken ships and fears for the safety of their crews, who might or might not have been picked up in the wide expanse of ocean.

The White Ensign and 'Red Duster' flying side by side in those long years of war was a symbol of hope to many weary citizens, reminding them after a night of bombing that they must get on with their job, for British sea power prevailed. So Liverpool took the Navy to its heart, and the Navy will never forget the hospitality of its people and the heroism of the crews of the merchant ships, while the longest sea battle of all time hung in the balance.

By conferring upon Admiral Horton its honorary freedom and by finding for him a last resting place within its Cathedral, the great city did honour to Max, to itself and to the thousands who died in the Battle of the Atlantic.

'For we
have lived the story too often
have faced the threat without end
yet lulled our senses in days of peace
and trusted the stranger without honour or mercy.
Shall we for ever sleep in trust of waking
for ever forget until we must remember?
Ignore our best in days of ease
and reward the base and ignorant?
Allow
men forgot
ships rusted
weapons lost?' [1]

[1] The above quotation and those heading Chapters XI and XIV are taken from the Solemn Bidding to the Service of Celebration of 9th August 1945 at Liverpool Cathedral.

EPILOGUE

By C. C. MARTINDALE, S.J.

WHEN Admiral Horton hauled down his flag on 15th August 1945 he had not yet completed his full term as Admiral; but he had always decided that he would leave the Navy the day the Western Approaches Command came to an end, saying that even if he were offered the post of First Sea Lord (the only Command he could have had in the Navy), it would be for him an anti-climax, and he wished to be free to live the life he wanted.

The only reason the present writer should have been asked to supply these last few pages is precisely the fact that he is quite ignorant of naval affairs as such, though he entertained a strong affection for the Admiral personally. It will be seen that Horton neither did nor could thus sever all connection with the sea; but the prolonged strain had had a grave effect upon his health, and he was to undergo five major operations in the six years that remained to him. True, he hated any allusion to this, and if he was laid up he would characteristically tell enquirers that he had caught a cold in his head. Still, he was ordered to take a long rest, and immediately after the war went abroad for over six months.

Not that he proposed to remain idle. He had already sent a team of experts to examine the effect of bombing upon enemy ports in Germany, and now, at the invitation of Sir Sholto Douglas (now Lord Douglas of Kirtleside, Marshal of the R.A.F.) with whom he had been closely associated in the Battle of the Atlantic and who was now in charge of the British Zone, he went to see conditions with his own eyes. Directly after this he went to Italy, to Padua where he had first made acquaintance with St. Anthony, and then to Assisi.[1]

[1] It may not be out of place to recall that it was through the story of St. Anthony that he learnt of the small friary of San Francesco del Deserto, near Venice. Max has often been called a 'dual personality' and it is quaint that this man, so devoted to meticulous cleanliness, orderliness and efficiency should

In 1946 he returned to England to take his part in the great Victory March through London, and to receive various civic honours and degrees. He received the Freedom of the City of Liverpool on 18th September 1946, and was made Hon. Doctor of Law at Queen's University of Belfast on 3rd May 1947. He had intended to return to the Continent and live there permanently; but his recurrent illnesses and three grave operations caused him materially to alter this plan though he went abroad as often as he could. Still, he accepted invitations to become a Director of Humphreys Ltd., the Liverpool Exchange Coy. Ltd., and other companies. He became a member of the Executive Council of the London Clinic and a member of the Council of the Victory Club for ex-Servicemen. Mr. A. V. Bridgland, the well-known financier, professed himself astonished that so distinguished a naval officer could grasp so quickly the principles of finance; but this may be but another example of Max's many-sidedness, since few, perhaps, of his naval companions would have guessed how passionately he loved what was beautiful—not only the Italian scenery and skies and even bells, not only the good food and wines and the special mental stimulation that he found in France, but he was a good judge of the theatre, and a devotee of opera, not only hearing every opera he could, but trying to be present also at rehearsals. His theatre friends were numerous alike in England and in France. He was hardly less interested in architecture.

Despite his resolve to turn his back on naval affairs, it would have been impossible for his retentive memory and active mind really to do so, and in fact he was constantly asked for advice in such matters. It has been said in the Preface that it was most unlikely that he would ever have written a full autobiography, to say nothing of a mere record of his personal exploits; but his

so much have loved this place, since these virtues are not, perhaps, immediately noticeable in the older Italian monasteries. Anyhow, one day he saw a friar laboriously paddling the long boat, or barge, in which the friars went to collect their daily food. Max could not quite stand this, and himself embarked and drove the boat along. 'How did you learn to row so well?' asked the friar. Max said he was a sailor and knew about boats. In fact, as a result of this knowledge of the sea, he was able to tell the friars that unless they shored up their friary—built, of course, upon piles—in two years they would have the Adriatic into it. They said 'Tell us how to do it. We do everything with our own hands.' He not only told them, but joined in doing the work.

innumerable notes, his collection of papers official and otherwise, prove that he wanted his strongly held views about the wars in which he had been engaged, and any future war, to find expression, and that past mistakes should be recognised and rectified. It may be worth repeating that one of his main views was that since England by herself could no more maintain the balance of power within Europe, ever closer and more friendly relations with the United States should be fostered. Further, that co-operation between Navy and Air Force should be far more intimate and consistent than it had been at any rate hitherto. Other strongly held views concerned the whole system controlling the dependence of the Services upon Whitehall and the inter-relation of Ministries within Whitehall itself.

For more than one cause he was experiencing some despondency. The Duke of Edinburgh, seeing him at the Victory Club, said he was sorry not to have seen him at a recent naval dinner. Max said it saddened him to mix with the Navy now that he was no more part of it, and related that the Duke said to him: 'Well, you were there in spirit and in history, so why not in person?' This encouraged him to attend such functions rather more frequently. But on 21st July 1950, he wrote of the Royal Navy Club dinner at Greenwich when King George VI was guest:

'A well-run show, but so many (350) that it was impossible to have a yarn with everyone I wanted to. The King in good form—he stayed half an hour after midnight standing in the ante-room for nearly two hours. . . . I found the reunion rather pathetic. The Navy seems to count for so little in the coming struggle, cold or hot. The great gallantry of the personnel in the last scrap has given the rest of the world (in their opinion) no great victories that would make them think of us as ultra-efficient—except for the little ships . . . and now three-quarters of the Navy is ashore. . . .' [1]

It would, then, be false to think that Admiral Horton had become saddened simply because he had been a 'crisis man' and

---

[1] Horton, in his depressed state of mind, seems to have overlooked the British naval victories of the River Plate, Taranto, Matapan, the rounding-up and destruction of the *Bismark* and *Scharnhorst*. Although these battles were not fought on the grand scale of Trafalgar and Jutland, the rest of the naval world must know by now that they were won by experienced leadership, brilliant staff work and an efficient personnel.

had duly been sent for in the two great crises of 1939 and 1942, and that he could foresee no third crisis in which, given his age and increasing illness, he could be of use. The present writer would venture to affirm that—paradoxical as it may seem to some —Max was realist indeed, but essentially a humble-minded man; in fact, the twinkle you could catch in his eye, even when he said rather startling things, made it impossible to suppose he was 'self-sufficient,' for the self-sufficient can hardly have a sense of humour. It may seem barely credible, but so far was he from advertising himself that he had known M. Caillaux well, for two years, before the Minister so much as knew that Max was a sailor; and a well-known playwright whom he had known for ten years seemed (said Max ruefully) much less impressed when he discovered that Max had won the Battle of the Atlantic than by the excellence of his dramatic criticisms. What really depressed him was that while he believed in 'democracy,' it must be disciplined democracy, and that democracy without discipline meant chaos. He experienced a sense of frustration, a feeling that all the sacrifices made in the two great wars had gone for nothing; that there was a general lowering of standards which meant deterioration of civilisation itself. He went up and down the country speaking to this effect in dockyards, factories, and on any 'platform' he might find, insisting always on the 'Nelsonian' ideals of order, discipline, sympathy and comradeship. True, at Belfast he begged that Universities in particular should train more and more men of science in view of the ever-increasing reliance upon science which he foresaw; but he was clear that a multiplication of mere technicians would be worse than useless were they not inspired with that absolute loyalty and spirit of united *service* which he supremely valued.

In June 1945 in the Victory Honours Max Horton was awarded the Grand Cross of the Bath for his war services; and France, Norway, Holland and the U.S.A. gave him their highest decorations. But perhaps the one he prized the most was that of Chief Commander of the Legion of Merit (U.S.A.), for only very few received it.[1]

On 8th January 1946, Max Horton was appointed Bath King of

[1] The actual Citation is printed on page 230.

Arms. This appointment is no sinecure. King George VI, as Sovereign of the Order, ordained that an installation of the Knights Grand Cross should take place in the Chapel of King Henry VII in the Abbey Church of Westminster on 24th May 1951. It is the duty of the Dean and the Secretary of the Order to prepare the Order of Service in accordance with the commands of the Sovereign, and this was in fact the procedure followed in 1951, when a special ceremonial, moreover, had to be added for the installation of the Duke of Gloucester as Grand Master. After the Order had been duly approved by the King, Max Horton rendered most valuable service in the conduct of the rehearsals, especially as the intricate ritual needed to be adjusted so that parts should be performed by the Knights collectively, not one after the other, so that the strain on His Majesty, whose health was already noticeably failing, should be lessened. Several rehearsals were needed, in which the King indomitably took part. So on May 24th, habited in his mantle of white satin lined with crimson silk, wearing the Gold Badge of King of Arms, and, outside his robe, the Collar of a Knight Grand Cross of the Order, Max Horton, carrying in his right hand the White Rod of Bath King of Arms, preceded his Sovereign to the Chapel, where, in the name of all, King George VI dedicated his own sword and passed it to the Dean, who laid it on the Altar. We venture to say that the strain imposed upon Max Horton by the marshalling of this ceremony was even less than that due to his anxiety for the health of the King.

The strain was indeed increased by his having to leave immediately for Rome where he wished to be present at the beatification of Pope Pius X, and where an audience with Pope Pius XII was to be arranged for him. He had already been received by Pius XI in 1937 and had been deeply impressed by the dignified simplicity of the Vatican court and by the character of that forceful Pontiff. He returned in 1950 and took part in the ceremonies of the Holy Year, including the visits to the great Basilicas, and had been still more deeply struck by the indefatigable activity of a Pope seemingly so frail; but those crowded days were clearly not the time when a private audience could be asked for. In 1951 he was in fact present at the beatification of Pius X, a ceremony which

Pius XII suddenly caused to be transferred from morning to evening, and to the vast piazza in front of St. Peter's, since it was evident that even that basilica could not contain more than a fraction of the multitudes. It was about that date that he had his protracted audience with the Pope, for which he had prepared himself by a lengthy study of the great Encyclicals, those, that is, which were concerned with social justice and national or international morality which had been appearing ever since the reign of Leo XIII. We may surmise that the satisfaction he derived from these visits was not due only to the high personal esteem for the two Pontiffs whom he met, but because he encountered a discipline, a firm yet paternal government, and a continuous philosophy both moral and intellectual of which he became increasingly aware and which corresponded, on the spiritual plane, to the social virtues we spoke of above and were prized by him so highly. As for his private religious life, something has been said about it in previous chapters; needless to say that he kept it veiled, though he went to Mass whenever he could; and the mere fact that so long ago as 1919 he was wrestling with the works of St. John of the Cross (which might be regarded as the crown rather than the beginnings of the spiritual life) suffices to indicate how personal and interior was his religion, and by no means an affair of pilgrimages to shrines and so forth. When he died, his own pilgrimage was not completed, and there was much ground to be travelled before he could reach that Franciscan goal towards which he had constantly tended, though few enough could have guessed it.

He left Italy for Malta to stay with friends but very soon fell ill again and was flown home to the London Clinic where he had two further operations. While in bed there his thoughts kept returning to his beloved submarines. They were his first love and his last. He wrote to Admiral Simpson:

'My visit to Malta recalled to my mind so vividly my previous visit to you and your submarines during those very critical war days. I am so terribly pleased and gratified that such a splendid tribute has been paid, by Andrew Cunningham in his book, to the great work of our submarines which decided the battle in North Africa. . . . I am making good progress but one gets very weary of illness.'

EPILOGUE

Any success or loss to Submarines was always to him a *personal* joy or grief, and the loss of the *Affray* still lay heavy on his mind. In fact, on the morning of Monday, 30th July 1951, he sat up and remarked that he was at last beginning to feel well, and asked 'Any news of the *Affray*?'; but this was followed by a collapse, and at 11 o'clock he died of coronary thrombosis.

Admiral Sir Max Horton was accorded (says *The Times* of 10th August 1951) the exceptional honour of a State funeral (9th August). It was right that this should take place at Liverpool, since for three years it was thence—at Derby House, where the King and Queen visited him on several occasions—that he directed the vital phase of the Battle of the Atlantic.

To the salute of guns, with the flags of the City at half mast, the long procession marched with arms reversed.

Naval ratings from various ports of the kingdom mounted guard along the route where thousands of Merseysiders filled the streets.

Beside the gun carriage drawn by sailors marched Admirals, Generals, and Air Marshals, followed by members of the Board of Admiralty, the Army Council and the Council of the R.A.F. Their uniforms and decorations contrasted vividly with the sombreness of the muffled drums of the massed Bands of the Royal Marines.

As the gun carriage approached the Cathedral, the Guard of Honour mounted on the steps presented arms for the last time. For the last time the Boatswains piped their Admiral 'over the side,' as the coffin was borne into the Cathedral precincts.

Within the Cathedral itself were representatives of H.M. the King, H.R.H. the Duke of Gloucester, the Prime Minister, the Governor of Northern Ireland, and the Dominions and Colonies. The Lord Mayor of Liverpool with the City Council and other civic dignitaries joined with high-ranking officers, diplomats and representatives of all the allied governments in paying their tribute.

MAX HORTON AND THE WESTERN APPROACHES

During the ceremony the Dean of Liverpool, Dr. F. W. Dwelly, a close friend of Admiral Horton's, spoke a brief address from the chancel steps. In the course of it he said:

'In the dark days of that war when others were busy in many things, he found time, despite the immeasurable responsibilities he carried, to outline for those in difficulties, for those in trouble, for those who were afraid—ways in which calmness and courage had full sway. Here in Liverpool we grew to serve, as only he could tell us best, to serve the country in her hour of peril. . . . In this spirit we will say our prayers. . . . Nothing could be more fitting as an epitaph for this great man, than the words *he himself wrote* on the death of a brother officer whom he held in deep regard: "In the days when the waters had well-nigh overwhelmed us, our brother here departed, apprehended the creative power in man, set himself to the task of conquering the malice of the enemy. In our hour of need he was our doughty protector of them that sailed the seas on our behalf. His heart and his mind extended and expanded to the utmost tiring of the body, that he might discover and operate means for saving our ships from the treacherous foes. Truly many, very many, were saved because he was not disobedient to his vision. Victory has been won and shall be won by such as he. May there never be wanting in the realm men of like spirit and discipline, imagination and valour, humble and unafraid. . . . His spirit returns to God who gave it." ' [1]

Suddenly the tense silence was rent by the shattering of rifle fire. High up in the Cathedral Tower, Marine buglers sounded the Last Post. As the echoes died, from the distant cloisters came the call of the Reveille. The Royal Navy had paid their highest tribute, and said their last farewell.

The vast congregation slowly dispersed but the grandeur and dignity of that day will live long in the memory.

One felt through each successive moment that not only all ranks of the Services were mourning the death of a great Admiral —but that every person present had come to pay their respects to a man they honoured, and were truly grieved at his passing.

[1] These lines were written between 1 and 2 a.m. after the death of Captain Frederick John Walker, C.B., D.S.O., R.N., in command of the famous 2nd Escort Group of the Western Approaches for whom Admiral Horton had the highest admiration. They made such an impression that several thousands of copies were printed in response to the request for them.

EPILOGUE

On the cover of the Order of Service these words[1] are written:

'Strange is the vigour in a brave man's soul.
The strength of his spirit and his irresistible power,
The greatness of his heart and the height of his
    condition,
His mighty confidence and contempt of dangers,
His true security and repose in himself,
His liberty to dare and to do what he pleaseth,
His alacrity in the midst of fears, his invincible
    temper, are advantages which make him master
        of fortune.
His courage fits him for all attempts,
Makes him serviceable to God and man.
And makes him the bulwark and defence of his being
    and his country.'

---

[1] Thomas Traherne, 17th-century poet.

APPENDIX I

CHRONOLOGICAL RECORD OF SERVICES OF ADMIRAL SIR MAX K. HORTON, G.C.B., D.S.O.**

Born 29th November 1883

Ship	Rank	Period of Service	
		From	*To*
Britannia	Naval Cadet	15 Sept. 1898	14 Jan. 1900
Duke of Wellington	Naval Cadet	15 Jan. 1900	31 Jan. 1900
Majestic	Naval Cadet	1 Feb. 1900	14 Feb. 1900
Majestic	Midshipman	15 Feb. 1900	1 Jan. 1901
Blenheim	Midshipman	2 Jan. 1901	11 Mar. 1901
Hermione	Midshipman	12 Mar. 1901	30 June 1901
Eclipse	Midshipman	1 July 1901	14 Feb. 1903
Goliath	Sub-Lieutenant	15 Feb. 1903	27 Feb. 1903
Duke of Wellington	Sub-Lieutenant	28 Feb. 1903	30 Apr. 1903
Excellent	Sub-Lieutenant	1 May 1903	21 Feb. 1904
Cambridge	Sub-Lieutenant	22 Feb. 1904	27 May 1904
Vivid	Sub-Lieutenant	28 May 1904	30 Sept. 1904
Thames	Sub-Lieutenant	1 Oct. 1904	14 Feb. 1905
Thames for submarine boats and *Mercury*	Lieutenant	15 Feb. 1905	15 June 1907
Bonaventure and *Mercury* for A.1 and C.8	Lieutenant	16 June 1907	17 Jan. 1910
Duke of Edinburgh	Lieutenant	18 Jan. 1910	7 Jan. 1912
Arrogant and *Bonaventure* for Submarines (D.6)	Lieutenant	8 Jan. 1912	14 Oct. 1912
Maidstone for Submarines (D.6)	Lt.-Commander (15 Feb. 1913)	15 Oct. 1912	15 Mar. 1914
Dolphin for Submarines (E.9)	Lt.-Commander	16 Mar. 1914	30 June 1914
Maidstone for E.9	Lt.-Commander	1 July 1914	30 Dec. 1914
Maidstone	Commander	31 Dec. 1914	24 Jan. 1916
Dolphin for J.6	Commander	25 Jan. 1916	15 Aug. 1916
Titania for J.6	Commander	16 Aug. 1916	3 Dec. 1917
Dolphin for K.18 (M.1)	Commander	4 Dec. 1917	15 Sept. 1918
Titania for M.1	Commander	16 Sept. 1918	17 Oct. 1918
Vulcan	Commander	18 Oct. 1918	13 Aug. 1919

APPENDIX I

Ship	Rank	Period of Service	
		From	To
Maidstone	Captain (30 June 1920)	14 Aug. 1919	30 July 1920
Dolphin (for S/Ms and as asst. to R. A. S.)	Captain	31 July 1920	21 July 1921
Dolphin C.S.O.	Captain	22 July 1921	14 Mar. 1922
Conquest in command	Captain	15 Mar. 1922	14 Apr. 1924
Dolphin in command	Captain	15 Apr. 1924	3 Aug. 1925
Victory (leave)	Captain	4 Aug. 1925	7 Aug. 1925
Victory for Course	Captain	17 Aug. 1925	16 Oct. 1925
President (War Course)	Captain	17 Oct. 1925	26 Feb. 1926
Victory (leave)	Captain	27 Feb. 1926	14 Mar. 1926
President (for duty inside Admiralty, Asst. Director of Mobilisation)	Captain	26 Mar. 1926 5 Apr. 1926	4 Apr. 1926 3 Apr. 1928
Victory (C.O.S.)	Captain	20 Apr. 1928	18 Apr. 1930
Victory (Tactl. Course)	Captain	5 May 1930	4 July 1930
Resolution in cd.	Rear-Admiral (17 Oct. 1932)	30 Nov. 1930	25 Oct. 1932
Malaya (2nd Battle Squadron)	Rear-Admiral	12 Dec. 1933	16 Mar. 1934
Barham	Rear-Admiral	17 Mar. 1934	18 July 1935
London R.A. 1st C.S.	Vice-Admiral (19 Aug. 1936)	19 July 1935	1 Nov. 1936
Hawkins (V. A. cdg. Reserve Fleet)	Vice-Admiral	26 July 1937	23 June 1938
Effingham	Vice-Admiral	24 June 1938	17 Sept. 1939
Pyramus (V. A. cdg. Northern Patrol)	Vice-Admiral	18 Sept. 1939	19 Dec. 1939
President (unemployed)	Vice-Admiral	29 Dec. 1939	8 Jan. 1940
Dolphin (Flag Officer Submarines)	Admiral (9 Jan. 1941)	9 Jan. 1940	9 Nov. 1942
Eaglet C.-in-C. Western Approaches	Admiral	17 Nov. 1942	15 Aug. 1945
President	Admiral	16 Aug. 1945	15 Oct. 1945

Placed on Retired List, at own request, to facilitate the promotion of younger officers, 16 October 1945.

Died 30 July 1951.

APPENDIX II

HONOURS AND AWARDS OF
ADMIRAL SIR MAX KENNEDY HORTON, G.C.B., D.S.O.**

Board of Trade Silver Medal for saving life at sea   13.12.11

Mentioned in Despatches for submarine services during the earlier stages of the war   *Gazette* 23.10.14

Order of St. Anne (with swords and diamonds)   March 1915

Allowed to accept Russian decoration in recognition of services in sinking a German destroyer in the Baltic   29.1.15

Order of St. George   .   July 1915

in recognition of services in torpedoing the cruiser *Prince Adalbert*
    Gazette 16.11.15

Chevalier of Legion of Honour   April 1916

for gallantry in attacking enemy warships in the Baltic   *Gazette* 18.4.16

Awarded D.S.O.   *Gazette* 15.4.16

Awarded the Order of St. Vladimir with swords   *Gazette* 7.11.16

Awarded Bar to D.S.O. for long and distinguished service in command of overseas submarines during third period of the war   *Gazette* 2.11.17

Awarded Second Bar to D.S.O. for distinguished services while in command of Third Submarine Flotilla and as S.N.O. Reval   *Gazette* 8.3.20

Good Service Pension   13.2.32

Awarded Medal (not to be worn) and two Diplomas by Hellenic Red Cross Society also Licence to wear Insignia of Commander of the Order of the Redeemer, awarded by Greek Government re Chalcidice earthquake   *Gazette* 26.9.33

Awarded C.B. (Military)   *Gazette* 4.6.34

Awarded K.C.B. (New Year's Honours)   *Gazette* 2.1.39

Mentioned in Despatches   *Gazette* 11.7.40

Awarded Grand Cross of the Order of Orange Nassau conferred by the Queen of the Netherlands   *Gazette* 12.5.42

Awarded G.C.B. (Birthday Honours)   *Gazette* 14.6.45

Bath King of Arms   *Gazette* 8.1.46

Awarded Legion of Merit, Degree of Chief Commander, bestowed by the President of the United States of America (with unrestricted permission to wear) for distinguished service to the Allied cause throughout the war
    Gazette 28.5.46

Granted unrestricted permission to wear the Grand Cross of the Royal Order of St. Olav bestowed by the King of Norway for service to the Royal Norwegian Navy during the war   *Gazette* 13.1.48

APPENDIX II

BEQUESTS

The Admiral had expressed certain wishes, among which were:

That a fund should be created for the benefit of the Submarine Branch of the Royal Navy. A sum has been lodged with the Admiralty for this purpose. It is to be used for providing an annual prize to be known as 'The Admiral Sir Max Horton Prize' for the most efficient officer qualifying in submarine duties in the course of the year.

That a memorial to those who lost their lives in the Battle of the Atlantic should be placed in Liverpool Cathedral. That the awards and mementoes connected with his submarine service should be given to Fort Blockhouse. Here, in the custody of H.M.S. *Dolphin*, are displayed near his portrait the silver-gilt casket of the Freedom of Liverpool; the gold cigarette case with imperial cypher and the Cross of St. Anne with swords and diamonds specially conferred on him by the last Tsar of Russia; the bar carrying his miniature orders and medals; the Log of E.9; a cup presented by Commodore Sir Roger Keyes to commemorate the sinking of the *Hela*; and other trophies.

The Grand Cross of the Bath and his high awards from the United States, Holland, Norway, Greece and France, together with his war medals, are lodged in the National Maritime Museum at Greenwich.

APPENDIX III

REPORT OF PROCEEDINGS OF H.M. SUBMARINE E.9 BETWEEN 13th and 14th SEPTEMBER 1914, INCLUDING DESTRUCTION OF GERMAN CRUISER "HELA," THE FIRST ENEMY WARSHIP TO BE SUNK BY A BRITISH SUBMARINE

12th September

Midnight   Arrived position; rested on bottom 120 feet.

13th September

5.11 a.m.	Rose and proceeded as per chart.
6.30 a.m.	Surface. Weather thick and raining hard, slight swell.
6.32 a.m.	Dived 70 feet.
7.15 a.m.	20 feet; sighted Heligoland, distant 5 miles on port bow, also cruiser [the *Hela*] approximately 1½ to 2 miles off, and wisps of smoke in various directions; attacked cruiser; weather cleared.
7.28 a.m.	Position 600 yards abeam of cruiser (two funnels). Submarine very lively diving. Fired both bow torpedoes at her starboard side at intervals of about 15 seconds.
7.29 a.m.	Heard single loud explosion. Submarine at 70 feet, course parallel to cruiser.
7.32 a.m.	Rose to 22 feet, observed cruiser between waves; appeared to have stopped and to have list to starboard. Splashes from shot on our port side and ahead of cruiser. Turned periscope to see where shots were coming from, but submarine was very deep, and only observed wisps of smoke and mast very close. Dived to 70 feet and picked up trim.
8.35 a.m.	20 feet; sighted trawlers where cruiser had been, 4 or 5 in number in a cluster. Horizon slightly misty, one trawler, one cable on beam. Dived 70 feet.
9.07 a.m.	20 feet; destroyer on beam 100 yards; 70 feet.
9.23 a.m.	Rested on bottom 90 feet.
12.30 p.m.	Heard several destroyers pass over us from southward apparently from Weser River.
3.50 p.m.	Rose to 20 feet; destroyers in sight, patrolling.

APPENDIX III

4.55 p.m.	20 feet; destroyers.
5.05 p.m.	Rested on bottom 100 feet; destroyers passing over us at intervals.
9.26 p.m.	Rose and charged. Horizon clear, loppy swell.
11.10 p.m.	Rested on bottom 110 feet.

14th September

4.45 a.m.	Rose 20 feet. Course as per chart, but observed nothing but trawlers patrolling in the Bight.
6.09 a.m. to 7.18 a.m.	Heligoland well in sight, also outer anchorages all clear of ships except trawlers.
7.18 a.m.	Turned to westward and moved out to endeavour to catch enemy's submarines patrolling. Continued search submerged till dusk, charging on the surface from 11.40 a.m. to 1.25 p.m. Visibility varying from clear to 1 mile. Occasional heavy rain.
6.45 p.m.	Proceeded on surface to westward; sea increasing.
Midnight	Very heavy seas. Bent stanchions and splash plate. Endeavoured to rest on bottom, but disturbance continued to such a depth, i.e. 120 feet, that the submarine, despite 8 tons negative bouyancy, bumped. Rose from bottom and dived at 70 feet during the night.

15th September

5.00 a.m.	Surface. Very heavy seas; unable to remain on bridge, proceeded on gas engine with conning tower closed and ventilator in conning tower open, conning through the periscopes.
1.53 p.m.	Sea abating. Proceeded on surface to port.

(Signed) M. K. HORTON,
Lt.-Commander.

16th September 1914.

APPENDIX IV

NOTES ON NEUTRALS SENT BY ADMIRAL HORTON TO THE FIRST LORD, MR. CHURCHILL, 29th MARCH 1940

GERMANY'S TOTAL WARFARE

In the war of 1914–18 Germany shocked the world by her declaration of unrestricted submarine warfare, and this was the principal factor which ultimately ranged the United States on the side of the Allies.

But this unrestricted submarine warfare only applied to certain well-defined areas, whereas in the present 'total warfare' no area or nation is immune. In addition, their submarine activity is reinforced by aircraft whose methods are those of deliberate and calculated brutality against defenceless fishermen.

GERMANY'S TOTAL WARFARE IS MORE DEADLY FOR NEUTRALS THAN FOR THE ENGLISH

This total warfare is proving more deadly for the smaller neutrals than for the Allies—for translated into action it appears to mean the deliberate destruction of any vessel irrespective of its nationality, cargo, or destination, completely regardless of the loss of human life.

This ruthless murder on the high seas, by submarine and aircraft, of non-belligerents (men, women, and children) has not its equal in the whole history of warfare, and its complete disregard of every international and moral law should arouse the anger of every nation which pretends to believe in the first principle of justice and human rights.

Far from this—we find that the smaller neutrals, whose very existence depends on the maintenance of these principles of human rights, not only condone the murderers but are, in effect, supporting Germany in numerous ways.

NEUTRALS' ASSISTANCE TO GERMANY

Whilst paying lip-service to International Law by lodging formal and empty protests, these same neutrals, whose sons, brothers, and husbands are daily being shot, drowned and left to die in open boats and rafts, are continuing to help that very power whose submarines and aircraft openly boast of these murders.

In the past, England has been known as a 'nation of shop-keepers,' but it has been left to the neutral powers to earn the distinction of fostering trade and welcoming as customers the murderers of their own people.

APPENDIX IV

Not only do these neutral countries continue to trade with Germany, but they afford every possible facility to German ships using neutral waters—by providing them with every navigational aid including pilots—and in many instances they even go so far as to escort German merchantmen with their warships.

ENGLAND MUST STATE HER OWN CONDITIONS UPON WHICH SHE IS FIGHTING HER SEA WARFARE

We are therefore forced to conclude that the neutrals are not sincere in their protests, as they are not prepared to make sacrifices to uphold them. Although their official utterances may deplore the German methods, by their actions they are actually encouraging them.

The world may well be astonished that these countries should have so little regard for the moral values that they virtually ignore the violations practised on them by Germany.

Consequently, the time has now come when England must herself state afresh the conditions upon which she is fighting her sea warfare, and since the so-called neutral countries are in reality neutrals no longer, England must take over the control of all those waters which are now being used for such un-neutral purposes.

APPENDIX V

ALLIED SUBMARINES OPERATING IN THE NORTH SEA
ON 7th APRIL 1940

2ND SUBMARINE FLOTILLA, *based at Rosyth*

Thistle	Lt.-Commander W. F. Haselfoot
Triad	Lt.-Commander E. R. J. Oddie
Trident	Lt.-Commander A. G. L. Seale
Triton	Lt.-Commander E. F. Pizey
Truant	Lt.-Commander C. H. Hutchinson
Orzel (Polish)	Lt.-Commander J. Grudzinski
Seal	Lt.-Commander R. P. Lonsdale
Porpoise	Commander P. Q. Roberts
Tribune	Lieut. E. F. Balston
Triumph	Lt.-Commander J. W. McCoy, D.S.C.
Wilk (Polish)	
Taku	Lt.-Commander V. J. H. Van der Byl
Tarpon X	Lt.-Commander H. J. Caldwell
Tetrarch	Lt.-Commander R. G. Mills

6TH SUBMARINE FLOTILLA, *based at Blyth*

Unity	Lieut. J. F. Brown (relieved by Lieut. F. J. Brooks)
Spearfish	Lt.-Commander J. H. Forbes
Swordfish	Lieut. J. Cowell
Clyde	Lt.-Commander D. C. Ingram
Narwhal	Lt.-Commander R. K. Burch
Sturgeon	Lt.-Commander G. D. A. Gregory
Ursula	Lt.-Commander W. K. A. N. Cavaye
Severn	Lt.-Commander B. W. Taylor

3RD SUBMARINE FLOTILLA, *based at Harwich*

Sealion	Lt.-Commander B. Bryant
Seawolf	Lt.-Commander J. W. Studholme
Shark	Lt.-Commander P. N. Buckley
Snapper	Lieut. W. D. A. King
Sterlet	Lt.-Commander G. H. S. Haward
Sunfish	Lt.-Commander J. E. Slaughter
Salmon	Lt.-Commander E. O. B. Bickford, D.S.O.

10TH SUBMARINE FLOTILLA (French)

Amazone, Antiope, La Sibylle and *Doris*.

CHARACTERISTICS OF BRITISH SUBMARINES

Class	Tons (Surf. Disp.)	Armament	
River	2206	1–4" 6 Bow T.T.*	Fast ocean patrol S/Ms.
O	1780	1–4" 6 Bow T.T. 2 Stern	Long-range overseas patrol
P	1760	Ditto	Ditto
R	1760	Ditto	Ditto
Porpoise	1770	1–4" 6 Bow T.T. 50 Mines	Minelayers
T	1430	1–4" 9 T.T.	Patrol S/Ms.
S	870	1–4" 7 T.T.	Medium-range patrol
U & V	650	1–3" 4 T.T.	Short-range patrol
L	930	1–4" 4 T.T.	Inter-war type
H	450	4 T.T.	1st-war design (American)

We started the war with 54 S/Ms including 6 minelayers.

We lost a total of 76 S/Ms and built 164. We finished the war with 142 S/Ms.

British S/Ms together with Allied S/Ms under British control sank 1,257 supply ships of 1,800,400 g.r.t. They sank 35 enemy submarines, 6 cruisers and pocket battleships, 17 destroyers and 112 minor war vessels; in addition they damaged more or less severely 2 battleships, 10 cruisers and pocket battleships, 2 destroyers and 35 minor war vessels.

* T.T.=Torpedo Tubes.

APPENDIX VII

GENERAL CHARACTERISTICS OF PRINCIPAL TYPES OF U-BOATS

Type VII C   770 tons surface displacement
Endurance 9,400 miles at 10 kts.
Max. speed 17 kts. (surface) ; 7½ kts. submerged for
  1 hour
2 bow tubes, 1 stern tube, 14 torpedoes

Type IX   1,051 tons.
12,400 miles at 10 kts.
18 kts.; 7½ kts. submerged for 1 hour
4 bow tubes, 2 stern tubes, 22 torpedoes

Type XIV   1,688 tons
(The 'milch   12,300 miles at 10 kts.
cows')   14½ kts.; 6 kts. submerged for 1 hour
No tubes
720 tons of Diesel fuel

NEW TYPES WHICH DID NOT BECOME FULLY OPERATIONAL

Type XXI   1,621 tons
15,500 miles at 10 kts.
15 kts.; 17 *kts. for* 1 *hour*
6 bow tubes, 20 torpedoes (*rapid reloading*)

Type XXIII   232 tons
4,300 miles at 6 kts.
9 kts.; 12 *kts. for* 1 *hour*
2 bow tubes, 2 torpedoes

and

Type XXVI   of which a few were built but never got beyond the
trial stage. Fitted with a special type of engine
which could run submerged off high test peroxide
fuel (known as Ingolin after the daughter of the
inventor, Walther). It was hoped to get a maximum
submerged speed of 20 to 25 knots.

APPENDIX VII

U-BOAT LOSSES [1]

By the end of the war the Germans had built 1,158 U-boats and commissioned 1,131 of them.

637 U-boats were destroyed *at sea*, of which sea and air forces under British control accounted for 505.

Ships destroyed	247
Shore-based aircraft destroyed	247
Ships and shore-based aircraft, in co-operation	32
Ships and carrier-borne aircraft, in co-operation	14
Carrier-borne aircraft destroyed	44
Submarines destroyed	21
Mines destroyed	32

In addition to the above, 63 were sunk by bombing raids, 83 were lost by accident and other causes.

GRAND TOTAL OF LOSSES, 783.

---

[1] Q. v. Cmd. paper 6843 of 1946.

APPENDIX VIII

SEA POWER AND THE R.A.F.

Paper submitted to the Admiralty by Admiral Horton

OFFICE OF ADMIRAL (SUBMARINES),
NORTHWAYS, LONDON, N.W.3
26th February 1942.

The Prime Minister has stated that Hitler hopes to starve us. In other words Hitler's object is and always has been the destruction of our sea power and commerce. He had hoped to hasten the end by invading us, but was baulked in this plan by failure to obtain air superiority in September 1940. He had no reason, however, to abandon his original plan which he believed ultimately would be successful. He used his army and air forces therefore to attack Russia, expecting an early victory which would ensure his supplies of essential raw materials and so provide him with the necessary strength and resources to bring about our final defeat.

2. He has, so far, failed in his course of action against Russia, but to offset this, he has now the Japanese directly attacking our sea power, thus assisting him towards the attainment of his final object. Failure in Russia will not deter Hitler from intensifying his attack upon our sea power. Success by Japan may mean the end of the British Empire.

THE GERMAN THREAT

3. How far has Hitler succeeded in the attainment of his object? He has:

(a) Acquired naval and air bases from the North Cape to the Bay of Biscay, and so provided refuge and air cover for his naval forces operating against our sea communications in the Atlantic.

(b) He has demonstrated that the English Channel can be used for the passage of his warships.

(c) He has, in co-operation with Italy, denied to us the use of the Mediterranean and so compelled us to use the Cape route with its consequent drain on shipping.

(d) He has very nearly rendered ineffective our naval control of the Eastern Mediterranean.

(e) He has sunk 8,719,000 tons of merchant shipping.

(*f*) He has destroyed three aircraft carriers and two capital ships, and. put out of action two more capital ships. He has sunk thirteen cruisers and sixty-two destroyers.

4. This measure of success, coupled with Japanese successes in the East, must encourage Hitler to intensify his efforts against our sea power and commerce in the Atlantic and home waters.

THE JAPANESE THREAT

5. It has been clear from the start that Japanese strategy aims at depriving us of our sea power in the Indian Ocean. As soon as Japan has consolidated herself at Singapore, Penang, and the Dutch East Indies, she may be expected to advance westward. There is little to prevent her establishing herself in Ceylon or even Madagascar, and so be in a position to carry out continuous surface, air, and underwater attack upon the Cape route to the Red Sea and upon our sea communications with India and Australia.

In regard to results Japan, apart from the territory she has gained, has so far sunk, by means of the effective use of air forces highly trained in sea warfare, two of our most important capital ships, not to mention Pearl Harbour and many tons of shipping.

THE FRENCH THREAT

6. Although the French Fleet may not be in a high state of efficiency, the re-entry of France into the war would release a large number of surface craft and submarines for operations against our sea communications in the gap between the German and Japanese zones of operations. French air bases in this area would enable her own and Axis aircraft to operate against our shipping and also against Gibraltar and Freetown without much interference from our own air forces.

AXIS COMBINED PLAN

7. Although the above picture is a black one, it is not overstated, and we have got to face up to it. It is a national characteristic of the British people never to take steps to forestall disaster until the threat of it is actually upon them. We prefer the system of trial and error to foresight. It is not a defeatist attitude to admit that the odds are very strong against us at the present moment, and to suggest measures to meet them before it is too late. It *is* a defeatist attitude to put our heads in the sand and refuse to face the facts.

8. We cannot delay longer the drastic measures necessary to meet the combined Axis attack upon our sea power which in fact is already launched, and in order to deal with it successfully we must be prepared

275

for the worst conditions. The attack may be expected to develop on the following lines:

- (i) Intensification of German attack against our warships and supplies in the Atlantic.
- (ii) Land attack upon Egypt from the North and West.
- (iii) Japanese attack upon our sea communications in the Indian Ocean and approaches to the Red Sea.
- (iv) French attack in a limited but important area.

9. If this plan were to succeed we should lose control not only of the Eastern Mediterranean but also the vital supply routes of the Indian Ocean. All our armies operating in the Middle East would be cut off and would suffer the same fate as that of Napoleon's armies after the Battle of the Nile. All our Middle East oil supplies would be denied to us and become available to the enemy. Neither our prestige nor our latent power could survive such a blow.

10. It is possible that Russia may stop the main land thrust through the Caucasus, and we know the United States will assist us in some measure to maintain control of the Atlantic, but we are still left with the burden of maintaining our sea communications elsewhere, in addition to protecting the United Kingdom against invasion.

RESPONSIBILITY FOR SEA POWER

11. Control of the sea is vital to the British Empire. If we lose it, we lose the war. British sea power is gravely threatened at this moment, and whether we like it or not we have got to concentrate all our resources to hold on to it. It is far beyond the task of our attenuated Fleet with its sorely tried Fleet Air Arm and numerically inadequate Coastal Command.

12. Bombing attacks on Germany, no matter how effective they may be, can do little to counter the existing threat to our sea power. Even Germany has realised that she has little to gain by bombing the United Kingdom until she has dealt with Russia and ensured her oil supply. Germany and Japan know that they can win the war by cutting off our vital supplies at their source and acquiring them for their own use. Japan has made a good start with rubber and tin, and is likely to press on until she can get control of our oil supplies in the Persian Gulf and Dutch East Indies. Bombing attacks on synthetic oil plants in Germany are a mere flea bite in comparison. When these are undertaken we risk losing control of our own supply lines and surrendering our sources of supply to the enemy. Posterity will regard this as an indirect contribution to our defeat. The only way we can ensure final victory is to employ our Air Force where it is most urgently required, i.e. to wear down (in co-operation with the Navy) and defeat the present Axis sea offensive.

APPENDIX VIII

R.A.F. Requirements in Sea Warfare

13. The first step is for the War Cabinet to get the Air Ministry to accept equal responsibility with the Navy for keeping open our sea communications. The next step is to decide the best means of exercising joint command. On the highest plane this is done by the Chiefs of Staff, but as regards the direction of operations, the closest contact between Coastal Command and the Admiralty will be essential and the only practicable arrangement at home would be for Coastal Command Headquarters with representation from other R.A.F. Commands to be established in the Admiralty. As a simple measure of bringing about satisfactory naval and air co-operation in outlying Commands it is suggested that the Air C.-in-C.s should have a naval Chief of Staff and vice versa.

14. Having achieved this, the naval and air staffs must decide how air forces can best contribute to the sea struggle which will be decisive. Broadly speaking the main requirements would seem to be:

   (a) Allocation of more machines and trained observers for naval reconnaissance.
   (b) Destruction of enemy warships and transports in port and at sea.
   (c) Dislocation of enemy dockyard establishments and operational bases.
   (d) Fighter protection for naval surface forces and merchant ships round the British Isles and in focal areas abroad.
   (e) Joint naval and air control of all shore-based aircraft employed on naval operations.
   (f) Training of R.A.F. personnel in tactical co-operation with naval units and identification and destruction of enemy warships.

15. Although requirements (a), (b), (c) and (d) are undertaken to a limited extent by the R.A.F. today, many grave defects have been disclosed by recent operations; e.g. the three branches of the R.A.F. (Reconnaissance, Bomber and Fighter) have not been trained to work together for attacking sea targets, and even if these branches could be co-ordinated within the R.A.F. for this purpose, their co-operation as a whole with Coastal Command is not satisfactory. This is only natural because there is no centralised control of all the branches which could be used for sea operations. Furthermore, Bomber Command at present hold types of aircraft which Coastal Command lack, and which are far better fitted to prosecute sea warfare than many types at present available to Coastal Command.

Although it must be accepted that the R.A.F. as a whole is neither trained nor equipped for operating in sea warfare, we must do the best we can with what we have got during the forthcoming critical months. We have the example, only recently, of Dutch and U.S. aircraft meeting with considerable success against enemy convoys in the Dutch East Indies.

16. The immediate threat is a sea threat, and it is so serious that all our energies and resources must be marshalled to meet it without loss of a moment.

17. The Navy is fighting a losing battle owing to the continually increasing risks it has been compelled to undertake in every theatre of war. The R.A.F. must be induced to realise the seriousness of the situation, and willingly produce that wholehearted major co-operation which should have been part of our general plan from the outset, but which hitherto has been considered of secondary importance.

18. In regard to (f) (Training):

As an immediate measure, this will have to be combined to some extent with operational work. There is in existence in Coastal Command and the Fleet Air Arm a certain proportion of personnel already trained in sea warfare which could be economically distributed in other R.A.F. squadrons for the purpose of giving guidance in actual operations and forming a nucleus to build upon.

After all, we are a maritime nation and the natural will of the R.A.F. flying personnel could be quickly directed to maritime needs, especially when they realise the seriousness of the danger that threatens us.

To assist in this, the principle of interchange should be encouraged, and the Navy can give a lead by offering to the R.A.F. a proportion of naval officers, Fleet Air Arm and others with sea experience for training and operational duties.

STRATEGY

19. The change of policy will also entail switching over strong air forces from their present task of bombing the enemy cities to operations which will assist to maintain our control of sea communications in the Atlantic, Mediterranean, and Indian Oceans.

20. Properly equipped air forces will have to be employed (especially in the Atlantic) either to destroy or to keep enemy submarines submerged for such a length of time that their ultimate operations against our shipping will be seriously curtailed. This, after all, was the principle we applied with so much success in the last war with small surface craft patrols and without the assistance of aircraft. The same principle still applies, only the use of aircraft renders it possible to cope with the greater distances and wider areas involved.

21. Our plan may also require the British occupation of Madagascar to deny it to the Japanese.

APPENDIX VIII

MATERIAL REQUIREMENTS

22. In order to deal effectively with enemy forces, the following material requirements must be rapidly implemented:

(a) More torpedo bombers.

(b) *Some* dive bombers.

(c) More A.S.V. machines [radar-equipped aircraft].

(d) More minelayers.

GENERAL CONCLUSIONS

23. It is clear from the above that the R.A.F. is confronted with a colossal task if it is to bear its full share in securing our sea communications. So great, in fact, that it rules out any possibility of carrying out simultaneously an air offensive against German industrial centres and oil installations. But we have no choice. It is essential that we keep control of our sea communications, prevent the enemy from obtaining his raw material, and procure what we need for ourselves.

24. We are concerned now with a world war in which our existence must depend, as it always has done, on sea communications. It is beyond the task of our much depleted and over-strained Fleet (with its present air auxiliary) alone to provide adequate security to avoid defeat. Recent events have proved that Fleets cannot operate without the close co-operation of air power. If we are to hold our own during this vital year, and wear down the enemy before we are ourselves exhausted, it is essential that the whole of our naval and air strength should be concentrated and employed in the battle for sea power. If we lose our sea power, we lose the war.

(Signed) MAX HORTON.

APPENDIX IX

THREE TYPICAL LETTERS FROM CAPTAINS OF SUBMARINE FLOTILLAS TO ADMIRAL HORTON

THE LOSS OF THE *Medway*

(1) FROM CAPTAIN P. RUCK-KEENE (COMMANDING 1ST SUBMARINE FLOTILLA).

OFFICE OF THE CAPTAIN (S),
FIRST SUBMARINE FLOTILLA.
(BEIRUT)
17th *July* 1942.

Dear Admiral Horton,

I have had no time to write to you about the events of the last fortnight until now.

The situation in the Western Desert had been deteriorating rapidly, and it was extremely difficult to find out what the true picture was.

On the 28th June, speaking from memory, the C.-in-C. had a meeting at which he said we must be prepared to leave at forty-eight hours' notice; he assured us that General Auckinleck had every confidence and that he in fact welcomed Rommel advancing so that he could hit him on his own ground. The C.-in-C. Med. [Admiral Sir H. Harwood] did not himself think Alex. would be overrun, except for a few tanks breaking through and causing panic. However he had been clearing the harbour slowly and quietly of auxiliaries and merchant ships. His task, I should imagine, was made no easier by a personal message from the P.M. protesting against him doing this and possibly causing panic.

I had, some time before this meeting, got the *Medway* fully stored and everything at twenty-four hours' notice; but I made no suggestions or proposals to C.-in-C. either of leaving or staying, as I was naturally very much in the dark as to the true situation.

After the meeting on the 28th I decided to fly to Haifa and Beirut to make a fuller reconnaissance of these two places as a final resting place for *Medway*. Simpson had done a sketchy reconnaissance during his leave which was a great help. But I got no further than Cairo on 29th when Simpson rang me up to return at once as C.-in-C. had ordered *Medway* to sea; I sailed at dusk in order to get at least one night's start before the enemy reconnaissance plane noticed our absence.

280

APPENDIX IX

There were three mines laid the night before, but fortunately well marked; two of these were actually in the swept channel. We were swept out and got safely clear, although one of them went off astern of us and blew a tug (*Pharos*) to pieces and very nearly got *Sikh*,[1] in whom I had sent Simpson and his staff.

Unfortunately when we were twenty miles out of Alexandria enemy planes returning from a raid passed over the *Medway* and one dropped flares which lit up the wing destroyer of our screen, and this probably gave our sailing away to his S/Ms.

When the torpedoes struck I was on the port side outside my cabin which is just under the bridge. I saw what I thought was the swirl of discharge 300 yards on the starboard beam. I heard afterwards from Baker in *Corinthia* that he saw the periscope standards break surface.

I told the Yeoman of Signals to inform the destroyers exactly where the S/M was, and I saw him calling them on the Aldis [lamp], but unfortunately I don't think the signal got through, possibly as all power went when the torpedoes hit and he may not have changed over to battery.

I think three torpedoes hit her [*Medway*] but I am not sure.

We know from a survivor in the Diesel engine room that the starboard side there was completely opened up.

She heeled over very quickly to about seventeen degrees and then stopped, and I thought she might hold. I therefore rang down to go ahead again and gave orders to flood port tanks and take the list off. But Pulvertaft[2] came on the bridge not long afterwards and said that when I rang down "ahead" the water was already well over the manœuvring platform in the Engine Room. She then started heeling steadily to starboard. When she was well over, I told all but repair parties to abandon ship and later when the angle began to get alarming I told them to go too. She continued to heel till she lay almost on her beam ends, then her stern went under, and she rapidly reared up until she was almost vertical, then slid under at an alarming speed. She was about twenty–thirty yards away, and for a moment it looked as if she would come right on top of us.

The losses are much less than I first estimated, being only twenty-one killed and eight wounded; very lucky, as it was only a little over ten minutes from the time she was hit until she had completely gone and there were over 1000 aboard. . . .

. . . I told C.-in-C. I would get a base going in Haifa without further delay, but after a twenty-four-hour reconnaissance I realised we could never make a really good base there. The port is congested with

---

[1] H.M.S. *Sikh*, a destroyer.
[2] Commander (E) W. G. Pulvertaft, R.N., the Chief Engineer.

merchant traffic and it was to be used by cruisers, destroyers and M.T.Bs which would completely fill up the place.

In addition the whole town was packed with military. I therefore came to Beirut and realised at once that of the two places it was infinitely preferable. We were treated with the greatest courtesy by Morse[1], the Senior N.O. Levant Area, who took me to see General Catroux (Free French High Commissioner) and General Wilson of the Ninth Army.

I spun Catroux a number of submarine stories before asking him for what I wanted, and he was so impressed with these yarns (he is a soldier first and Free Frenchman afterwards) that he offered me whatever I wanted. We did not take long to take advantage of this. I got here on 1st July and the nucleus of my staff on the 5th. The main body of survivors were at P. Said and a third at Haifa. Fortunately all my senior officers and nearly all the staff were at Haifa.

I left the survivors where they were, and turned the operational control over to Simpson and his staff at Haifa, which left me free with half my officers to get busy.

The situation up to date is that we have got a complete barracks which is, I think, among the best in the town and is large enough to take the base staff, boats' crews and three spare crews. The barracks are away from the dockyard and bombing area, eight minutes by car from the dock area and S/Ms.

They are on the healthy side of the town away from the area infested by malarial mosquitoes; within five minutes of a lovely fine sandy bathing beach—important for S/M crews. They also face the prevailing wind in summer which should keep them cool.

The officers' mess is just opposite the barracks gate and is a really beautiful place—an old Russian hermitage. It will provide an anteroom, wardroom, cabins; the remainder of the submarine officers will be housed in two separate buildings.

The submarines will be berthed at trots to allow for the scend [swell] in the winter; these I have had laid sixty yards apart so that bombs will only catch one S/M at a time, there is one jetty berth for heavy repairs. Each S/M at the trot is connected to the shore by a floating platform.

Immediately astern of the trots are two magnificent sheds where the old French S/M workshops were situated, one is the Engineers' workshop and the other torpedoes and central stores, alongside these again we are constructing a battery shed, mess room for midday meal and washplaces.

All the Administrative offices are across the street from these sheds in an unused hotel.

The operations offices are within fifty yards of the W/T station, ¾ mile from the barracks and officers' mess and my own house will be

[1] Captain J. A. V. Morse, R.N.

on a hill equidistant between the two six-ten minutes' walk from each.

If our transport is well arranged and ample, the layout should be most satisfactory; we get dispersion, healthy positions and amongst the best accommodation in the town. At Aley, 2,000 feet up in the hills, I have taken an hotel which will accommodate two half-crews for resting, with the Chief and Petty Officers in the annexe. Alongside it a sick bay for about thirty sick. Aley is ideal for S/M crews resting, as besides being high up and refreshingly cool in the summer, there are dance halls, cinemas, a swimming pool and girls and beer plentiful.

Here in Beirut the trouble has, of course, been the getting of fittings and furniture. However we are buying the furniture of the Aley Hotel, which will cover most of the officers' requirements. I am hoping to move in all the crews on 3rd August—just a month after she sank. I already have *Proteus* and *Turbulent* here with their half-crews up in the mountains.

Otus as you know sails for U.K. in a few days calling at Malta en route with supplies for the 10th Flotilla.

Simpson is just about to fly to Malta where he will arrive in plenty of time ahead of his flotilla in case anything is found too bad for their return, but this is unlikely. He is in excellent form and don't worry about him, Sir, he and his party are simply delighted to be going back —as they say "the ground hasn't been shot over for a long time." They will soon be exceeding their original bags.[1]

I must apologise for writing at such length, Sir, but I felt you might like to know fully what has gone on in the last few weeks.

I have sent home four bottles of olive oil for you in *Torbay* and two gallons have gone in *Otus*. My bank is Westminster Bank, Exeter.

Yours sincerely,

P. RUCK-KEENE.

(2) FROM CAPTAIN G. W. G. SIMPSON, R.N. (COMMANDING 10TH SUBMARINE FLOTILLA AT MALTA).

H.M.S. *Talbot.*
22nd October 1942.

Dear Admiral Horton,

King has settled in splendidly, but he is I fear rather frail and his stomach easily upset which is unfortunate because the standard of food is not what it was—for us it is quite adequate, but sometimes a bit unusual in the way of hashed-up economy dishes, which I fear will often upset him. Roxburgh is under-studying, so that I have an immediate standby.

---

[1] The 10th Flotilla returned to Malta on 19th July and operated from there until the end of the war in the Mediterranean.

We have had a busy and successful month, in three weeks so far sixty-two torpedoes have been fired and at least fourteen ships of different sorts sunk.

I am writing to Fawkes[1] to express my gratitude for the fine state of operational efficiency I find on their arrival here from his flotilla [the 8th at Gibraltar].

Stanley,[2] 'P.37,' got five ships in his first patrol—finishing with a close attack from inside a screen of seven destroyers, sinking a 4,500-ton ship and a destroyer with one salvo.

His gunnery earlier in the patrol was of a different order, but nevertheless effective by causing the enemy in schooners to abandon ship which he proceeded to demolish with a can of shale oil and a box of matches!

My chief concern at present is to get torpedoes at all. However, Ruck-Keene will see to that, and I have just had a reassuring signal from him.

I wish the Air Ministry would arrange for the transport of their own eighteen-in. torpedoes, which Ruck-Keene pointed out to me could be done by the temporary diversion of about four Stirling aircraft for a month.

Yours very sincerely,

(Signed) GEORGE SIMPSON.

Newly commissioned submarines on passage to the Mediterranean would spend a few weeks at Gibraltar to be 'worked up' by Fawkes, who had taken over the command of the 8th Flotilla in July 1942. By this arrangement Horton could be kept informed of the state of efficiency of each new submarine before she became fully operational. The following letter from Fawkes to Horton is a good example of reporting technical troubles without tears.

(3) FROM CAPTAIN G. B. H. FAWKES (COMMANDING 8TH FLOTILLA AT GIBRALTAR).

From GIBRALTAR.
24th October 1942.

Dear Admiral Horton,

This should reach you by hand. I have just had a very kind letter from Simpson saying how pleased he is with his latest arrivals from here, they certainly have done well. He said one of the spare periscopes arrived flooded, but we rather foresaw that and purposely left the desiccator caps off so that in case the gland did not hold, the worst damage would be a flooded instead of a stove-in periscope.

---

[1] Captain G. B. H. Fawkes, R.N.
[2] Lieut. E. T. Stanley, R.N.

He very nicely points out that there have been a high percentage of troublesome gyros in torpedoes supplied by *Maidstone* [depot ship] and puts it down to my shortage of E.A.s [Electrical Artificers]. But that is *not* the reason. The reason is this air-blast gyro. The department in this ship are the most efficient, painstaking and hardworking party in the ship and I am certain very few if *any* torpedoes or gyros leave this ship in other than a perfect state. The passage from here to Malta takes ten days and the troubles have occurred after the submarines have left Malta. The fortnightly routine on gyros after leaving *Maidstone* should bowl out any errors, if *Maidstone* has made any. Please don't think I am trying to get at Simpson, or he at me, quite the opposite, the flotillas could not be on friendlier terms. As a matter of fact, I have had considerable troubles with the last lot of six submarines from England, and I thank God I have them for the eight days that I have, otherwise they would not have been fit to be sent out. P.217 had a tin of cooking oil stowed amongst a lot of other gear on top of No. 1 Battery. Unbeknownst to anyone, it had a pin-prick leak and oil escaped and found its way into No. 1 Battery. I honestly don't think this was anyone's fault or could have been avoided, but I will make absolutely certain on that point. As a result the sealings of twenty-eight cells were defective, and on lifting we found that not only was some of the bituros damaged *but* the good portions were only 1/16" thick. So we have got the whole battery out. P.217, P.221 and P.54 *all* had the bitumastic *in their tubes* so bad that we have had to scrape it all off, clean and re-do. P.217's two torpedoes that she did *not* fire had a thick coating of bitumastic all over the range gear, top of gyro, etc., so it wasn't surprising she had two bad runs. Many torpedoes would not have run in several of the submarines, partly due to carelessness, gyro washers left out, one gyro set to 90 R though the indicator outside showed straight, water in gyros, etc., and all together a chronic and *very* serious state of affairs.

You will naturally want full details and you will have them, but you will be the first to appreciate that putting things right and getting the S/Ms fit for their important roles comes first, and the detailed reports and paper work afterwards. We are out to a clinch to get them ready in time and practised in their new roles, and we still have a very depleted staff who are working day and night. I was very sorry to hear that the replace E.A.s don't leave U.K. till the end of this month and the extra repair parties till beginning of next. It is this coming critical week that we most need them. We hope to get down to the paper work in about nine days' time.

The 'reluctant dragon' P.556 gets away today, for which I breathe a sigh of relief. P.51 had a spell of battery trouble too. She had *very* bad weather, and despite having perfectly fitting hatch covers before she left U.K., the violent movement and stresses soon made the flimsy hatch covers no longer tight, so she could not help getting some seas down the conning tower. Full details of this also follow, when we have a moment.

I am very sad about and at a loss to account for *Unique*, no one could give any clue except possibly *Ursula*, and I think that is a bit far-fetched. No U-boat on the N. Atlantic station broke W/T silence anywhere near *Unique*'s track, so I feel fairly happy about that.

We have had a few minor air-raids here, I only hope and pray we shall do no worse for the next ten days or else my plans may go a bit awry, but the full moon doesn't help. Dispersal in this harbour is not easy and is not consistent with doing the work to the S/Ms that has got to be done. However, I have got the eleven of them dispersed amongst five trots or docks and hope for the best. I enclose some uncensored and possibly rather heated remarks by my harassed heads of departments. But they are all doing *magnificently*, and given luck we will make the grade all right. This letter is not meant to be a moan, Sir, but is giving you advance news of important and serious defects.

Forgive this scrawl, but these are exceedingly busy times, as you will guess.

Best of luck to you all, Sir.

Yours very sincerely,

(Signed) G. B. H. FAWKES.

APPENDIX X

FLAG OFFICERS IN CHARGE OF PRINCIPAL PORTS, WESTERN APPROACHES, JULY 1943

Glasgow	Vice-Admiral J. A. Troup, C.B.
Greenock	Rear-Admiral R. Hill, K.B.E., C.B.
Liverpool	Rear-Admiral J. S. M. Ritchie
Belfast	Rear-Admiral R. H. Bevan, D.S.O., M.V.O.
Cardiff	Admiral Sir R. Burmester, K.B.E., C.B.
Milford Haven	Vice-Admiral B. W. Fairbairn, C.B.E.
Tobermory	Vice-Admiral G. O. Stephenson, C.B., C.M.G.

SENIOR OFFICERS OF WESTERN APPROACHES ESCORT FORCES, 14th JULY 1943

COMMODORE (D) WESTERN APPROACHES

Londonderry	Commodore G. W. G. Simpson, C.B.E.

CAPTAINS (D)

Belfast	Captain J. T. Borrett, O.B.E.
Liverpool	Captain T. A. C. Pakenham
Greenock	Acting Captain W. G. Davis, D.S.C.

TRAINING CAPTAIN

Philante	Captain A. J. Baker-Cresswell, D.S.O.

ESCORT GROUP COMMANDERS

Group	Ship	
B.1	*Hurricane*	Commander E. C. Bayldon, D.S.C.
B.2	*Hesperus*	Commander D. G. F. W. McIntyre, D.S.O.
B.3	*Towy*	Commander M. J. Evans, O.B.E.
B.4	*Highlander*	Commander E. C. L. Day
B.5	*Havelock*	Commander R. C. Boyle, D.S.O.
B.6	*Fame*	Commander A. R. Currie
B.7	*Duncan*	Commander P. W. Gretton, D.S.O., O.B.E., D.S.C.
C.1	*Itchen* (Ty)	Lt.-Commander C. E. Bridgeman, D.S.O., R.N.R. (retd.)
C.1	*Assiniboine*	Commander K. F. Adams, R.C.N.
C.2	*Gatineau*	Commander P. W. Burnett
C.3	*Saskatchewan*	Commander R. C. Medley, D.S.O.

C.4	*Hotspur*	Commander A. M. McKillop
C.5	*Ottawa*	Commander H. F. Pullen, R.C.N.
1	*Pelican*	Captain G. N. Brewer
2	*Starling*	Captain F. J. Walker, D.S.O.
3	*Offa**	Captain J. W. McCoy
4	*Milne**	Captain A. G. Scott-Moncrieff
5	*Nene*	Commander J. D. Birch, R.D., R.N.R.
6	*Bogue*	Captain G. E. Short, U.S.N.
7	*Pheasant*	Commander L. F. Durnford-Slater
21	*Shikari*	Commander D. A. Rayner, D.S.C., V.D., R.N.V.R.
37	*Fowey*	Acting Commander L. B. A. Majendie
38	*Enchantress*	Commander A. E. T. Christie, O.B.E., D.S.C.
39	*Rochester*	Commander H. V. King, O.B.E.
40		Commander J. S. Dallison, D.S.O.

* Destroyers lent from Home Fleet, March–May 1943.

PRINCIPAL STAFF OFFICERS
TO ADMIRAL SIR MAX K. HORTON,
COMMANDER-IN-CHIEF WESTERN APPROACHES,
APRIL 1943

Secretary to the Commander-in-Chief
Captain (S) E. Haslehurst.

Chief of Staff
Commodore A. Russell, relieved by Commodore I. A. P. Macintyre
(October 1943 until August 1945).

Deputy Chief of Staff and Chief Staff Officer, Operations
Captain R. W. Ravenhill, later relieved by Captain G. C. Colville.

Chief Staff Officer, Material
Captain A. F. St. G. Orpen.

Chief Staff Officer, Administration
Captain G. H. Brady.

Director of W.A. Tactical Unit
Captain G. H. Roberts.

Duty Captains
Captain H. N. Lake and Captain F. N. Miles.

Training Captain
Captain A. J. Baker-Cresswell, relieved by Captain L. F. Durnford-
Slater, and later Captain M. J. Evans.

Command Engineer Officer
Engineer Rear-Admiral Sir Henry Wildish.

Command Supply Officer
Rear-Admiral (S) H. R. M. Woodhouse, later relieved by Rear-
Admiral (S) N. Wright.

Command Health Officer
Surgeon Commander H. M. Willoughby, R.N.V.R., later relieved
by Surgeon Captain A. W. McRorie, R.N.

Command Superintendent, W.R.N.S.
Miss A. J. Currie.

APPENDIX XII

FINAL REPORT (ABRIDGED) OF ADMIRAL HORTON

From the beginning, Horton felt strongly that the war against the U-boats should be controlled by a single authority. Sir Stafford Cripps agreed with him, but the Prime Minister pointed out that such an appointment could not be fitted in to the existing organisation for High Command which in fact was running smoothly.[1]

At the end of the war, Horton raised the question again with other proposals for the future. In his final report he said:

'*Command.* I am more than ever convinced that my original conception was correct and that there was a pressing need for the appointment of a Chief of Anti-U-boat Warfare with scope analogous to that of Admiral Doenitz.

'With the entry of the U.S. into the war, what is, of course, more desirable is the unified control of all Allied resources with a headquarters in England. It is understood, however, that this is unattainable at present, but this in no way diminishes my conviction that the British resources should be unified under one single control for all theatres of U-boat warfare.

'The following remarks and conclusions are submitted on the termination of my command.

'*Operational Control.* Who is the present authority responsible for anti-U-boat warfare? Presumably the answer is "The Admiralty" and the "Navy Board, Washington." This is thought to be vague and unsatisfactory.

'Authorities who each play a part in the operation of the convoy system are far too numerous. On the British side Commander-in-Chief Western Approaches is responsible for the "safe and timely arrival" of convoys, yet Admiralty approval *must* be sought for the majority of relevant decisions. . . . This procedure is long and cumbrous though at present necessary, as each authority concerned may have information not available to the other.

'On the U.S.A. side there is a formidable list of authorities both American and Canadian, each with a part to play in the operation of the convoy system.

'The switch of operational control in the North Atlantic when the "chop" occurs is obviously undesirable and unsound. With existing communications, however, it is a necessary evil. . . .

[1] *The Second World War*, Vol. IV, Appendix C.

'*Reinforcing Groups.* Owing to the large expansion and comparative lack of training facilities, it is impossible that the average efficiency of all escort groups can reach the desired standard nor can they be of sufficient strength to hunt U-boats, protect the convoy, or look after damaged ships. It is not, however, beyond us to produce highly efficient groups—our 1st XI.

'Without these facilities it appears that the most efficient method of raising the general standard of escorts is to reinforce our convoys in dangerous areas with our reinforcing groups [Support Groups].

'So long as U-boats operate in packs, I am convinced that this is the most effective use of our resources and should be widely adopted.

'*Air.* The most pressing need at the moment is for more long-range shore-based aircraft. The present allocation is totally inadequate. It is considered that this requirement should have a first call on our united resources.

'The air aspect suffers like the remainder of the organisation from the many various authorities on this and on the other side of the Atlantic who have their say in air operations. Close co-operation exists at present between 15 Group R.A.F. and Western Approaches, but this is not general. Proposals to achieve greater co-operation with all British aircraft on the convoy routes have been put forward. But as things are at present this doctrine will not extend to U.S.A. or Canadian aircraft.

'*Personnel.* The frequent change of officers with knowledge based on experience in this specialised form of warfare is to be deplored and has a marked effect on the efficient conduct of operations. When it is necessary to relieve an officer from a sea appointment for rest or any other purposes, then he should be employed on the shore side of the organisation where his special knowledge will be invaluable. The only consideration which should affect appointments should be the building up both afloat and ashore of commanders and staffs with knowledge and experience of the special problems involved.

'*Unified Control.* The arguments put forward in favour of unified control require no further stressing. I am convinced that the only way of achieving most efficient and economical use of all Allied resources is to have a single authority in this country responsible for all problems in connection with trade operations. Authorities for executing the policy ordered by the central control will be required on both sides of the Atlantic and elsewhere in appropriate headquarters.

'When the importance of unified control is so constantly stressed for every theatre of war, it is considered that no effort should be spared to introduce it into the anti-U-boat war, which is fundamental.'

Horton's report was accompanied by detailed proposals for re-organising the naval and air staffs under unified control which, for obvious reasons, cannot be disclosed here.

INDEX

A.1, submarine, 3, 5
Aberdour, submarine H.Q., 69, 71
Abel-Smith, Captain E.M.C., 188
Abortive attack on *Tirpitz*, 135
Abyssinian crisis, 35
Accident, 33
Aconit, 220
Acoustic torpedo, 208
Activity, 215
Acworth, Captain B., 5, 248
Addison, Admiral P., 5
Admiralty, early views on submarines, 4; early opinion of Horton, 19; hint at his retirement, 52; submarine H.Q. close to, 71; procedure, 73; conference on submarine losses, 94; tributes to Horton, 67, 103, 146, 249, 250; control troop convoys, 155; specific requests for V.L.R. aircraft, 176; summarise situation, 205
Adriatic, operations, 110
Aeroplane, Horton's, 152, 225
Affray, loss of, 259
Aircraft, V.L.R., 156, 159, 184, 187, 192, 198, 207
Air co-operation, see R.A.F.
Air defence of Malta, 36, 114, 116
Air power, 184, 198, 110, 115, 274
Air weakness at sea, 61, 66, 126, 156, 274
Ajax, cruiser, 36
Alexander, Rt. Hon. A.V., 100, 215, 223, 250
Alexandria, 36, 104, 115
Alten Fjord, 134
Ambrose, Commander G.W., 128
Anti-submarine, enemy patrols, 69, 75, 82, 95; allied measures, 153, 178, 181; tactics, 157, 171, 190
Anti-U-boat Committee, 144, 177
Archer, 188; sinks U-boat with rocket projectile, 194
Arctic, patrols, 127; convoys, 131
Armed merchant cruisers, 55, 59, 65, 66
Arthur, 135
'Asdic,' 93, 178; skill of operators, 217

Assisi, 253
Athenia, torpedoed, 57
Attack, a record-breaking, 27
Auchinleck, General, 116
Audacity, escort carrier sunk, 157
Australia, cruiser, 36
Australian, Air Force, 216; Navy, 52
Azores, blockade of, 124; air base, 209

B 3 Escort Group, 219
Bacon, Admiral Sir R., 5
Backhouse, Admiral Sir R., 52
Baker, Captain, U.S.N., 177
Baker-Cresswell, Captain A. J., 172
Baltic: navigation difficulties, 13, 18; British Navy in, 19, 23
Banks, Captain W. E., 133
Barcelona, in civil war, 40
Barham, battleship, 33
Barry, Admiral Claud, 134, 145
Bath King of Arms, 256
Battle of Britain, 102
B.B.C., Horton's broadcast, 96; Kimmins's, 106
Beirut, submarine base, 116, 282
Bell, Commander T. I. S., 133
Bequests, App. II
Berwick, cruiser, 36, 125
Bickford, Commander E. O., 74
Birkett, Sir Norman, 178, 189, 204
Biscay, Bay of: Chastity belt, 140; British submarines in, 141; air offensive, 162, 204
Biter, 188
'Black Pit,' 159, 202, 222
Blackett, Professor P. M., 181
Blockade, 57, 90
Blockhouse, Fort, 28, 71
Blucher, German battle cruiser, 14
Bluff, 31, 70
Blyth, 70
Bogue, U.S.A., 188
Bolzano, sunk by 'chariot,' 136
Bomb-proof shelters for submarines, 114
Bone, Commander H. F., 127, 141
Bower, Commander R. T., 73
Bowhill, Air Chief Marshal Sir F., 73
Boyd, Admiral Denis, 107

293

INDEX

INDEX

INDEX

CPSIA information can be obtained
at www.ICGtesting.com
Printed in the USA
LVHW050753130722
723388LV00004B/91